DEBATING THE END OF HISTORY

CRITICAL AMERICAN STUDIES SERIES

George Lipsitz, University of California–Santa Barbara, series editor

DEBATING THE END
OF HISTORY

The Marketplace, Utopia, and the
Fragmentation of Intellectual Life

DAVID W. NOBLE

Foreword by DAVID R. ROEDIGER

Critical American Studies

 University of Minnesota Press
Minneapolis
London

Published by the University of Minnesota Press
111 Third Avenue South, Suite 290
Minneapolis, MN 55401-2520
http://www.upress.umn.edu

LIBRARY OF CONGRESS CATALOGING-IN-PUBLICATION DATA
Noble, David W.
Debating the end of history : the marketplace, utopia, and the fragmentation of intellectual life / David W. Noble ; foreword by David R. Roediger.
(Critical American Studies series)
Includes bibliographical references and index.
ISBN 978-0-8166-8058-0 (hc : acid-free paper)
ISBN 978-0-8166-8059-7 (pbk. : acid-free paper)
1. United States—Historiography. 2. Historiography—Economic aspects.
3. Environmentalism. 4. Globalization. I. Title.
E175.N628 2012
973—dc23   2012019607

Printed in the United States of America on acid-free paper

The University of Minnesota is an equal-opportunity educator and employer.

20 19 18 17 16 15 14 13 12   10 9 8 7 6 5 4 3 2 1

For Gail and the other members
of our four-generation household community:
Tricia and Michael; Ella, Jesse, and Danielle; Jon

CONTENTS

FOREWORD

David R. Roediger

At an American Studies Association session honoring David Noble some years ago, the most arresting tribute came from the Chicana feminist Dr. Edén Torres, a former student of David's. Torres allowed that in her early encounters with him she harbored doubts about what she had to learn from David across differences in race, gender, generation, and class. The process by which she came to treasure David reflected her political sophistication and good judgment. But it also bespoke his ability to listen to, learn from, and care for students rather than to assume that intellectual pyrotechnics could make differences disappear.

Torres's remarks resonated for me because I had my own doubts about what I would make of David Noble on first meeting him. I had come to the University of Minnesota as a historian in the early 1990s. Although David was the most eminent historian on the campus, he had long since left the history department for work "across the river" in American studies. I came to know more of him—his book *Historians against History* was familiar and I knew that he was the most-loved feature of the University of Minnesota for my friend George Lipsitz during George's stay there—through graduate student stories. Those seemed, too, larger-than-life: how he dressed up like Thomas Jefferson or like Norman Mailer to lecture; how the FBI had spied on him; how he would soon supervise his one hundredth dissertation; how he used to, in days of back troubles, lecture lying down, so that stragglers in the back of the room heard a disembodied voice filling the space; how he could seem to sleep through oral examinations—some people swore he was asleep—and then offer summative questions weaving all the strands of the discussion together.

I had only once encountered, decades before, such extravagant word of mouth about a professor, and in that case he seemed not to live up to the hype at all. Then, too, David was an intellectual historian, not exactly a badge of honor in the eyes of my narrowly trained social history generation. I soon learned also that his radicalism was nourished by an active Catholic religious life; I was a lapsed Catholic and a Marxist. Even when I too moved offices across the river to chair the Program in American Studies I was wary. He did not do e-mail!

It was David's presence that made me love him even before I appreciated how critically important his ideas are. This quality was not "presence" in the marketed, overblown sense that star-system academia can foster, but rather a daily, dropping-by presence. An astonishingly productive writer of books, an incredible teacher, an unsurpassed graduate student mentor, and a spectacularly wide reader, he remained unhurried. The Catholic anarchist Dorothy Day once offered the injunction "Sow time" as a magical realist strategy to be of service and still have something left. David made that injunction work in ways not unconnected with his keen observations on time and season in this book.

Again and again, he would end friendly conversation in my office by dropping off a brand-new book he had just read. Offline, usually a no-show at conferences, and past typical retirement age, David was the first to know about new work, especially if it concerned race, sexuality, and gender. Because he mistakenly received free books intended for the "other David Noble," an important historian of technology and work, he often knew about developments in my specialization sooner than I.

David also was present in every important political struggle on campus. On frigid days he was there for campus workers' union rallies. When the faculty began to organize in the face of attacks on tenure, he was for me the most reliable presence. The resort to settling organizing issues by e-mail was not a temptation to David. He came to meetings. He was also a great supporter of ethnic studies, not just institutionally but in his deep commitments to students. His stories of his doctoral work at the University of Wisconsin illuminated the stories of my social history inspirations, Herbert Gutman and George Rawick, roughly contemporary with him as students there. Through conversations I also came to see that David's writing reflected his connections to the leading figures in U.S. history of a generation before (especially Merle Curti) and, through his mentors, to the great Frederick Jackson

Turner. As a colleague he later intersected with the leading figures in the foundations of American studies, especially Leo Marx and Henry Nash Smith.

The book you are about to read is a consistent, careful, and theoretically informed argument focusing on the deep connections of the bourgeois intellectual—by now especially including nominal "conservatives"—to a belief that rationality and markets are forever poised to end history's "timeful" cycles of decay, death, misery, and limits to growth. It argues that post-1948 ecology presents a stern challenge to such views. It further charts the specific ways that "the global" has displaced nationalist visions holding that only a particular nationality was situated to usher in the end of history. Such globalism without concern for the planet itself has permitted evasions that delay confronting limits set by nature, by humanity, and by chance.

As I was about to leave the University of Minnesota a controversy on campus made me reflect on the value of the resistance to progressive consensus that so animates David's work. Over many years and in many books he has made studies of historiography and the philosophy of history speak critically to the biggest questions regarding the self-image and the actions of the United States, which he places in and out of larger Western traditions. The brilliant sections on global warming in this book especially speak to the controversy I have in mind. Campus administrators, who had learned to listen to Native American leaders rather impressively in some contexts, opted for far less dialogue when the issue of Monsanto's cooperation with the university in projects involving the genetic modification of wild rice arose. In many ways, narrow economic calculation—the corporatization of higher learning—explains such a result. But that very turn to the corporation is predicated on a set of desires to overcome nature and to supersede seasons that is not simply foisted on Western intellectual traditions through budgets and backroom deals. Those traditions, this remarkable book shows, seek a life without cycles and risk creating an unlivable world.

ACKNOWLEDGMENTS

My greatest debt is to my wife, Gail. She is a student of American cultures, and we have never-ending conversations about themes in this book. She translates my handwriting into print and in doing so makes important editorial suggestions about particular words, sentences, paragraphs, and chapters.

I thank a group of friends with whom I share an interest in defining the fundamental differences between the modern and traditional worldviews: our conversations have been invaluable to me. The members of this group include Jim Anderson, Dick Nelson, Carter Meland, Joseph Bauerkemper, Bruce Fisher, David Fields, Bill Huntziger, David Miller, Bernie Molitor, and Rick Chase.

I thank Rod Ferguson, chair of the American studies department at the University of Minnesota. He encourages me to transcend my identity as a retired professor and remain continually engaged with the life of the mind and the spirit.

1 TWO-WORLD METAPHORS, FROM PLATO TO ALAN GREENSPAN

WHY DO MODERN PEOPLE BELIEVE that there will be perpetual economic growth? The answer I present in this book is that such a utopian belief is the necessary foundation for bourgeois culture. One can imagine the existence of modern middle classes only as long as the capitalist marketplace is expanding. There must be endless surpluses for capitalists to exchange. The related question, then, is how is it possible for the middle classes to believe that a finite earth is an environment in which infinite expansion is possible? The answer I propose is that the urban middle classes since the time of Plato in classical Greece have explicitly defined an earth that is not a living body. For them it is a timeless space. If the earth were a living body, it, of course, would be finite. All living bodies have a generational cycle leading from birth to death. If one imagines a marketplace of perpetual youth, it will not be interrelated with generational patterns. An eternal marketplace must be an expression of a nature that is immutable.

During the more than two thousand years since Plato and his colleagues created a metaphor of two worlds—an old world of unstable, timeful cultures and a new world of stable, timeless nature—no humans have been able to make the exodus into that new world, but all members of bourgeois cultures have believed they are engaged in such an exodus. Tomorrow we will be free from the limits of generational experience. Tomorrow we will all be independent individuals in the timeless space of the marketplace. Today we are trapped in the meaningless flux of time. Tomorrow we will be free from history.

I am a retired professor of American studies and history. I am near the conclusion of my personal life cycle. As a convert to the belief that the earth is a finite living body, I see the surprising and amusing possibility that the modern belief in an infinite earth that transcends the experience of birth and death also may be at the end of its life span. In this first chapter I will briefly tell the story of how I have moved from modern orthodoxy to unmodern heresy. In subsequent chapters I will talk about my experience with several academic fields where some of my colleagues have come to doubt that universities as modern institutions are in harmony with timeless space. What will academic life be like if the heretical belief in an unstable, timeful earth becomes the new orthodoxy? Will professors stop guarding their boundaries as independent individuals in an academic marketplace free from generational experience? Will they come to imagine themselves as interdependent with timeful cultural and natural environments?

Born in 1925 on a dairy farm near Princeton, New Jersey, I was initiated into a modern metaphor of two worlds. I was told that my German and Irish grandparents had left the "old country" of Europe, a world of scarcity and war. They had come to the "new country" of America, a world of plenty and peace. Forever we, their descendants, would be privileged to dwell in this Promised Land. But early in my childhood I began to doubt this prophecy and the metaphor of two worlds. When I was five I knew that we had a financial crisis. Our farm was not providing an adequate income to meet our expenses. I also was frightened by the behavior of two uncles at family gatherings. I was told they had been "shell-shocked" fighting in World War I. The farm was not foreclosed until 1940. During that decade we experienced increasing poverty. In the fall of 1941, after our removal from the farm, my mother, father, and I were living in a small barn that had electricity and running water. My father was dying of stomach cancer. We did not have the funds to buy morphine to ease his pain.

When I graduated from high school in June 1943, I immediately entered the army. I was now free of poverty but not from war. I was discharged from the army in the fall of 1944 as a disabled veteran with a pension. I now had the opportunity to regain faith in the metaphor of two worlds. I suddenly could leave the troubled old world of my rural childhood. I now had the financial resources to be a student of an elite institution, Princeton University. I could enter a bright new world where poverty did not exist. But, for whatever reason, I knew that in this stimulating and comfortable environment I was not escaping to a world where one no longer experienced crises. And the crises have come. I knew I was an eccentric, but I did not at this point see myself as a heretic. I did not realize that I was challenging a powerful cultural commitment to two worlds.

So during my undergraduate career I hid my eccentricity. I did not engage my professors or fellow students in conversations about my disbelief in progress. I did tell my adviser that I was interested in the Progressive Era, 1890–1920. He suggested I write my senior thesis on *The New Republic,* which was founded in 1914.

I discovered that the founders of the magazine believed that they were participating in a worldwide exodus from a complex and troubled old world to a simple and harmonious new world. Their prophecy was made in secular language. Perhaps I was not surprised by this because in one of my history courses I had read Carl Becker's *The Heavenly City of the Eighteenth-Century Philosophers* (1932). Here Becker argued that these men who saw themselves as rational and secular in contrast to the irrational religious people of medieval Europe were as dependent on faith as their ancestors had been.[1]

Even as my family had faith that they were moving from a troubled European old world to a trouble-free American new world, so did the editors of *The New Republic.* Even as my father had lost his narrative of progress by 1933, the editors had lost their narrative of a revolutionary exodus by 1920. I had taken courses on American literature at Princeton. I knew of the young men like Ernest Hemingway, F. Scott Fitzgerald, and William Faulkner, who went to war in 1917 to help redeem the world. I knew that they were called a "lost generation" because the prophecy they hoped to fulfill had failed. It would take me decades of teaching and writing before I could see a common narrative shared by my father, the editors of *The New Republic,* and the young novelists of the 1920s.

When I went to graduate school at the University of Wisconsin in 1948, I was determined to learn more about the pattern of prophecy that kept predicting an exodus from an imperfect old world to a perfect new world. In 1951, while I was in graduate school, the essence of my senior thesis was published as my first scholarly article, "*The New Republic* and the Idea of Progress 1914–1920." My dissertation widened my analysis to a variety of cultural leaders in the Progressive Era. I looked at philosophers, sociologists, economists, political scientists, and historians. They all believed they were rejecting the authority of an irrational Protestant America. They were bringing the secular and rational authority of the Enlightenment to America. They were leaders of an exodus from a dark old world to a bright new world. And by 1920 they too were aware that their prophecy had failed. The dissertation was published in 1958 as *The Paradox of Progressive Thought*.[2]

Teaching in the Department of History and the American Studies Program at the University of Minnesota in the 1950s, I was not self-conscious that I was participating in a major reconstruction of the modern metaphor of two worlds. I was learning, however, that until the 1940s each modern nation on both sides of the Atlantic had been defined by its citizens as an exceptional state of nature. Each was a new world surrounded by the other nations who were part of old-world cultures. Each particular nation was defined by its citizens as timeless because nature supposedly was timeless. All other nations were defined by their timeful cultures. They were trapped in the flux of history.

Like many historians in bourgeois countries, I had lost my belief in two worlds, the new world of my particular nation and the old world shared by all other nations. Like other members of my international cohort, I was beginning to imagine that the industrialized nations had a common modern experience that set them apart from "undeveloped" nations that remained traditional. My second book, *Historians against History* (1965), expressed my hypothesis that all American historians from the Revolution to World War II had seen the United States as nature's nation. Cultures changed over time, but nature was timeless. My teachers at Princeton and Wisconsin had been taught to see an American identity that did not change. It was, however, a timeless identity threatened by a number of un-American cultural traditions that existed within the political boundaries of the nation. Americans must be taught what was American, what was part of the timeless new world, and what was un-American, part of the old timeful world.

As I began to imagine that the metaphor of two worlds was transnational, I read scholars who looked at how Europeans were arguing about space and time when they rejected the medieval world. For Renaissance intellectuals the medieval was not sacred. It was the ephemeral construction of human imagination. Renaissance philosophers believed they were stepping out of that timeful world. Becoming objective and rational, they were discovering the timeless world of nature. But how could they guarantee that a postmedieval Europe would not step back into the flux of time, back into history?[3]

Now, everywhere I looked in the 1950s and 1960s, I saw modern people from the Renaissance to the present making prophecies that history as complexity and scarcity was about to end. And when each prophecy failed, the next generation would revitalize the prophecy. We must be making progress; we must be participating in an exodus from an old to a new world. As I became certain that the commitment to the metaphor of two worlds was the crucial element of a multinational modern world, I also came to believe that I was not an isolated eccentric. Reading novelists such as Kurt Vonnegut Jr. and Norman Mailer, who were my contemporaries, I identified them as men who were part of another lost generation. They had been persuaded that World War II would bring an exodus from a profane past. Their novels after 1945 expressed their disillusionment with this narrative of redemption.

I had been struck by the contrast between the way historians and novelists had reacted to the failure of millennial expectations in 1918. Historians hid their pain while novelists made their pain public. This pattern, I believed, was being repeated after 1945. And so I asked myself, did some novelists have a different relationship to the exodus narrative than many literary critics had?

My teachers at Princeton and Wisconsin and my colleagues in the Minnesota English department taught that our first major American novelists—James Fenimore Cooper, Nathaniel Hawthorne, and Herman Melville—had shared the vision of the first historians that the United States was nature's nation. But was the imaginative world of literary critics the imaginative world of the novelists they studied?

I had followed William Faulkner's writings from his despair at the failure of World War I to be a millennial experience to his novels in the 1930s, where he powerfully rejected the either/or logic of the metaphor of two worlds. He was now writing that the modern belief in a division of saints from sinners and the belief in an independent individual created a self-destructive culture.

I took Faulkner's second perspective back to Cooper, Hawthorne, and Melville. Rereading them, I realized that they all insisted that individuals coming from Europe did not become independent of European culture. There was, for them, no escape from culture. There was no dichotomy between culture and nature. Humans would always be interdependent within culture. And humans would always be both saints and sinners. The title of my book on major male novelists from Hawthorne to Mailer is *The Eternal Adam and the New World Garden* (1968).[4]

In coming to identify a modern dichotomy between timeful culture and timeless nature, I also became aware that the heretical novelists defined nature as timeful. In addition to arguing that culture flowed across the Atlantic, Hawthorne and Cooper pointed out that so-called independent individuals came from generations of ancestors and their descendants would be part of future generations. Humans, like plants and animals, had life cycles. Nature was not static; it was in motion. So, after all, I was not a solitary eccentric. I was part of a chain of heretics. I was participating in a tradition passed from generation to generation. I was overjoyed.

Because I had converted from a belief in two worlds, an old world of dependence and a new world of independence, to a belief in a single world of interdependence, I was not surprised to see a parallel between the changing American national political identity and the changing understanding by historians of our national identity. National leaders in 1945 insisted that isolation must be replaced by internationalism. Our national economy must be seen as part of the world economy. Indeed, according to the political leaders, the United States was the center of a universal capitalist system that was destined to replace Marxist and traditional economies. Soon all the world would participate in a system of international capitalism that would provide perpetual abundance, harmony, and independence to all individuals.

In 1985 my book *The End of American History* was published. I argued that if the United States is to be understood as part of a system of international capitalism in the past as well as in the present, then historians should stop employing the metaphor of two worlds, Europe and America. I had begun to imagine that all of the various metaphors of two worlds that I had encountered were related to a capitalist ideology. The middle classes identified themselves with a rational civilization and segregated themselves from all irrational "backward" people. My European ancestors coming to America knew that "backward" Indians were not American. All Americans were modern.[5]

In my next book, *Death of a Nation* (2002), I hoped to demonstrate how scholars in a variety of disciplines had rejected the metaphor of two worlds that they had held in the 1930s and replaced it with a new metaphor of two worlds by the 1950s. I wanted to demonstrate how they replaced the nation with the global marketplace as the end of history. Particular nations did not represent the timeless laws of nature; only the global marketplace expressed those universal patterns. I analyzed historians, literary critics, philosophers, architects, composers, and artists to clarify the revolution in spatial attitudes.[6]

At Princeton in 1945 we were required to take a course on the history of Western civilization. It began with the dramatic emergence in ancient Greece of the concept of an independent individual who was rational. Such civilized men had left an uncivilized old world where the individual and rationality were not recognized. In 1945 my concern for the metaphor of two worlds was limited to my family. Then, at Princeton and at the University of Wisconsin, my curiosity about the metaphor widened to include the Progressive Era, 1890–1920. I then learned that the metaphor had been central to the culture of the English colonies and had remained central in the United States down to the present.

As my commitment to an isolated and exceptional United States disintegrated, I began to consider the metaphor of two worlds as the foundation of a transnational modern culture that appeared in the Renaissance. But the men of the Renaissance, as I had been taught in 1945, looked to ancient Greece for inspiration. It was there that the independent rational individual was first created. If I was to pursue the history of the modern metaphor of two worlds, I must travel with the men of the Renaissance back to ancient Greece. Was there, then, a direct relationship between the current prophecy that the global marketplace was a new world in which independent individuals could be rational and the distinction made by Plato's contemporaries between barbarism and civilization?

I discovered that a French sociologist, Bruno Latour, had answered this question with a resounding yes. It was soon after I had completed *Death of a Nation* that I read Latour's books *Politics of Nature* (1999) and *We Have Never Been Modern* (1991). I was excited to find that he shared the hypothesis that to be modern is to believe in two worlds, one timeful and one timeless. We also shared the theory that, for modern people, the timeful world was cultural, a creation of human imagination. And we agreed that modern people saw the timeless natural world as a preexisting entity to be discovered by reason. For Latour, however, humans can never be innocent of cultural creativity. They cannot escape their imaginations. This is why, for him, we have never been modern. There is only one world in which culture and nature are interrelated.[7]

It must have been very painful for Plato (circa 428–347 B.C.E.) and his contemporaries to see the promised land of timeless nature where all individuals would live in harmony and then realize they could not reach it. Perhaps this is why the art form of tragedy and its theme *hubris* became such a powerful expression in this Greek culture. Plato knew the Promised Land could not be reached because of the fragmentation of the Greek middle class. Bourgeois elites in each Greek city were in competition with each other. Businessmen in Athens knew they were rational, but they denied the rationality of their Spartan competitors. One could not escape the chaos of particular culture and enjoy the harmony of universal nature.[8]

I had been surprised at the speed with which bourgeois elites had rejected their 1940 belief that only their particular nations embodied the universal. Perhaps they sensed that now they had the opportunity to escape the Greek tragedy expressed in the bloody bourgeois civil wars—World Wars I and II. At last they could agree on the authentic universal embodied in the global market. Two thousand years of bourgeois civil wars might be at an end. At last the Promised Land was in reach. I, therefore, see the period from the 1940s to the present as one characterized by a resurgence of bourgeois millennialism. For the middle classes the global marketplace expresses the timeless and immutable laws of nature. It provides a politics of nature in which the bourgeoisie can define government intervention in the marketplace as artful and unnatural. Neoliberalism is a current expression of this transnational bourgeois politics of nature. I was now certain that the metaphor of two worlds was created by bourgeois culture and would remain persuasive as long as that culture remains dominant.

Like urban middle-class Greek men of antiquity, current middle-class men see themselves engaged in a negative revolution. They are leaving an old world created by human imagination. Ancient Greeks were leaving an old world of tradition embodied in agricultural communities. Current middle classes are leaving an old world of national governments that tried to regulate the marketplace. This government activism was and is an unnatural politics.[9]

When Plato's urban contemporaries claimed they represented a universal politics of nature, they also saw themselves engaged in a negative revolution. Traditional societies represented positive revolutions in which groups of individuals had used their imaginations to construct artful particular cultural patterns. These complex communities changed over time. Their ephemeral traditions were not sacred. The sacred must be outside the flux of history.[10]

Arguing that all tradition was profane, judged by the politics of a timeless nature, the urban middle-class Greek men had engaged in an amazing magic act. They had made the agricultural communities that fed their cities disappear. Their traditions were not real. Tradition was passed from generation to generation. If one wanted to make tradition disappear, one had to make generations disappear. Middle-class men, therefore, were supposedly not linked to their ancestors or their descendants. Plato's contemporaries were working with state-of-nature anthropology. There was an essential, rational individual trapped within an ephemeral irrational culture. This man must be liberated from timeful, generational culture. Now independent, this objective man was not limited by time. His new world was timeless and limitless.

In this supposedly authentic timeless nature, there were no cycles. There was no daily, no weekly, no monthly, no seasonal, no yearly cycle. To be middle class was to work with surpluses. In the agricultural cycle there was a time of surplus and a time of scarcity. Obviously, for the middle class in the authentic timeless nature that had no cycles, there was only a time of surplus and never a time of scarcity.

The Greek middle-class men who were Plato's contemporaries had used their magic, therefore, to make the cycles of a timeful nature disappear. They imagined they had left an old world of complexity and scarcity behind. They imagined they had entered a new world of simplicity and plenty. By imagining they were in a world with perpetual surpluses, they were able to transcend the crucial economic concern of traditional cultures—sustainable resources. Traditional communities believed their survival depended on the generational continuity of the plants and animals that provided their food. They focused on renewable resources.

But Plato and his contemporaries had mesmerized themselves. They persuaded themselves that they had entered a new world perpetually filled with surpluses. They were the spokesmen for liberty. They had liberated individuals from the prison of profane traditions. They had engaged in a negative revolution. They had not used power to create a new culture that replaced traditional cultures. And so they certainly could not be accused of using power to bring surpluses from the agricultural world into their cities.

From the Renaissance to the present, middle-class men committed to liberty have looked back with admiration at the world of antiquity. They, therefore, repress the knowledge that this world existed only as long as the Roman Empire grew. Roman armies kept expanding the area from which surpluses could be brought back into the major cities of the empire. When the armies no longer could expand the boundaries of the empire, the magical Illusion that urban marketplaces were naturally filled with perpetual surpluses lost its persuasiveness. The enlightenment of the Greek and Roman cities collapsed into the Dark Ages. For the next thousand years, most people in Europe focused on renewable resources produced by the yearly cycle.

Urban middle-class Greek men had engaged in still more magic when they declared that they had left an old traditional world that focused on generational cycles. Traditional cultures sacralized the life cycle from birth to death to rebirth. Segregating themselves from traditional society, middle-class men imagined they had left home and its generations. They had transcended bodies that reproduced and aged. But middle-class men did die. If there was to be a middle class in the future, there had to be middle-class children. The mothers, the wives, the daughters of middle-class men continued to exist in the world of generations. Their only identity came from their bodies. Calling on their magic skills again, middle-class men separated themselves from middle-class women. The men lived in the rational new world of timeless nature. They lived in the marketplace. The women lived in an irrational old world of cyclical nature. They lived at home. As Charles Dickens reminds us in *A Christmas Carol,* it has always been difficult for the middle class to explain the relationship of a nongenerational marketplace to generational families.

Genevieve Lloyd, in her book *The Man of Reason: "Male" and "Female" in Western Philosophy* (1984), and Arlene Saxonhouse, in her book *Fear of Diversity* (1992), have pointed out how Plato and his contemporaries tried to ignore the presence of women and children. The entire story of an exodus from an irrational generational culture to a rational nongenerational nature would make no sense if one saw that self-made men had fathers and fathered children. Who would believe in a new world of independent rational men when they lived in families where they were interdependent with irrational women and children? Who would believe in this new nongenerational world when generation followed generation, as children became elders, died, and were replaced by children who in turn would die? Rational men could believe the exodus story only as long as they pretended that they were not responsible for the children women bore. Women participated in generations, holding past, present, and future together. But men escaped the past and realized the future.[11]

Medieval Europeans, in contrast, believed they were living with renewable resources. They did sacralize the human life cycle and the life cycle of plants and animals. Mary, the mother of Jesus, was the center of their generational world. Each winter, when resources were scarce, she gave birth to Christ. Darkness would give way to light. And his death in the spring symbolized that death is always followed by rebirth. Scarcity will give way to plenty. But, since summer is always followed by winter, Jesus will have to be born again in the darkness of the next December. For most medieval Europeans, then, there was only one world, their home, with its cycles of birth, death, and rebirth. There was only one world with both scarcity and plentitude. There was only one world with both good and evil.[12]

But by the time of what scholars call the late Middle Ages, cities were once again growing. They were home to an increasing number of middle-class men who had fantasies about marketplaces that contradicted the liturgical year of the Catholic Church, with its insistence on the inevitable scarcity and darkness of winter. Next, then, in what scholars call the Renaissance, middle-class urban men throughout Europe rediscovered the world of Plato and his contemporaries. They suddenly saw that the traditions of the church, the aristocracy, and the peasants were not sacred. How wonderful it was to learn that all traditions were irrational and profane. They were born in time; they would die in time. It was almost too good to be true, being told that nature was not characterized by generational cycles in which plenty must give way to scarcity. It made these sober entrepreneurs almost giddy when they came to believe that their marketplaces were part of the timeless space of nature. What joy there was when they saw the link between their marketplace and the rationality and material plenitude of the eternally youthful world of nature. How much they wished that there could be a mass exodus from the limited old world of medieval traditions to the limitless timeless new world, the true world of nature. Carolyn Merchant has described this revolution in her book *The Death of Nature* (1980).[13]

Then these bourgeois men experienced something like a miracle. Renaissance men, eager to reach a new world, found one! They discovered the new world of the Americas. They would bring liberty and rationality to the traditional peoples of the American continents. And so the Renaissance bourgeoisie now repeated the magic trick of Plato's generation. As lovers of liberty they would send their navies and armies to the American new world. They would use their military power to bring material booty back to their European urban markets. Look at us, these magicians said, we are committed to liberty because we, unlike traditional people, inhabit a space with complete rationality and economic plenitude. Here individuals can be free from the tyranny of tradition. But when you, the audience, focus on this message, we hope you will not notice that it takes power to fill our marketplaces. We hope that you do not see that when we middle-class Europeans go to the new world we do so to bring its riches back to our new urban worlds, our markets. We hope you don't notice that we, the apostles of liberty, are going to bring countless Africans to the new world. Here we will make them slaves and discipline them to grow sugar, rice, tobacco, and cotton. These are crops that are in great demand in our European cities. As soon as they reach our urban marketplaces they are purchased. We, therefore, have to seize more lands for planting from the native peoples of the Americas. We must bring more slaves from Africa to work these lands that we liberated from the indigenous savages. We must teach the slaves to be more efficient in growing these cash crops of sugar, rice, tobacco, and cotton. They must be moved rapidly from their old-world heritage of sustainable agriculture to the new world of commercial agriculture. It is not surprising, then, when colonists from England, who had invaded and seized lands of native peoples, also established slavery and commercial agriculture in their new-world colonies. And it is not surprising that when these colonists made a revolution against England in 1776, they said their new nation, unlike England, would be based on the laws of nature. Here, free from traditions, individuals would experience liberty. England, they insisted, was still caught in the false world of artful social patterns. People there did not know liberty. The middle classes of Europe, however, who saw themselves committed to liberty, had no difficulty in accepting George Washington and Thomas Jefferson as fellow apostles of liberty. It did not matter to the European bourgeoisie that these men had created a slaveholding republic. They did not criticize Washington and Jefferson for their plans to expand their republic westward as they foresaw the removal of Indians from lands that were destined to be populated by European Americans. This magic kept the transatlantic middle classes from seeing any contradiction between their commitment to liberty and their exercise of power over slaves from Africa and over American Indians. And most European Americans from 1789 to the present have continued to participate in the magic trick that erases ten thousand years of Native American traditions from the New World.[14]

The bourgeois commitment to state-of-nature anthropology was a crucial aspect of their ability to hide from themselves their use of power. When one traditional culture was replaced by another traditional culture, this, for the men of the Enlightenment, was a positive revolution. One artfully constructed culture was replaced by another artfully constructed culture. These were imagined societies in which individuals were always dependent. But Plato's contemporaries and the middle-class men of the Renaissance saw themselves stepping out of artful culture and going to artless nature. This exodus was a negative revolution. In harmony with nature, bourgeois men had achieved liberty. They had not used power to construct cultural patterns that would entrap an individual.

By 1750, middle-class men throughout Europe and the European colonies in the Americas were creating an imagined age of Enlightenment. They believed that a mass exodus of individuals from artful cultures, from Plato's cave, was about to take place. Soon men would escape timeful culture and find timeless nature. Soon history as constant change would end.

Plato had used this metaphor of two worlds to look forward to the movement from irrational, particular cultures to rational, universal nature. But he reported with sadness that there would be no exodus from the old world of Darkness to the new world of Enlightenment. The supposedly rational middle-class men of the Greek city-states were claiming that their particular city was rational but that other Greek city-states were irrational. If the Greek cities claimed to be in harmony with the universal laws of nature but were, in fact, particular units, then the future foreseen by Plato was endless disharmony. The urban middle classes were creating an environment of irrational particulars no different from that of rural societies.

Now, during the Renaissance, the political philosopher Niccolò Machiavelli (1469–1527) relived Plato's frustration. He too felt he was living between two worlds, the old and irrational world of culture and the new and rational world of nature. One was particular and unstable. The other was universal and stable. One experienced the constant flux of history. The other represented the end of history. He saw medieval Europe as existing in an era of irrationality. He saw Plato and other Greek and Roman philosophers as prophets of a new rational world.[15]

But when Machiavelli looked at the Italian city-states, each dominated by middle-class men, he saw what Plato had seen. Each particular city claimed to be uniquely in harmony with universal natural laws and therefore superior to all the other cities because they were not in harmony with the universal. Both Plato and Machiavelli wanted middle-class men to be modern and universal, but they did not see how the bourgeoisie could transcend their particular political units.

Most of the middle-class men on both sides of the Atlantic, however, continued to keep their eyes focused on Isaac Newton. The modern science that began in the Renaissance killed the living, generational nature embraced by medieval Europeans. Renaissance scientists recovered Plato's belief in a timeless nature from which generational activity was absent. By the eighteenth century, bourgeois men accepted Newton as the most important physicist. Newton was, of course, a prophet of nature as a timeless space. When men reached that environment of universal natural laws, they would be modern. Throughout the eighteenth century urban middle classes continued to become more numerous. As they felt their economic power expanding, they began to anticipate taking political and cultural power away from the aristocracies and their monarchs. Then came the American and the French Revolutions and the creation of republics. The republican revolutionists were replacing subjects with citizens. Subjects, of course, lived in the irrational, artful, timeful world of aristocracy, monarchy, and the Catholic Church. But citizens had escaped this old world. Citizens were rational because they were in harmony with the new world of nature.[16]

Now the middle classes engaged in another powerful magic trick. The most creative magicians who persuaded the middle classes that the modern Promised Land had been reached in the American and the French Revolutions were historians. Physicists such as Newton were successful magicians in arguing that the experience of human life cycles as well as life cycles for animals and plants could be ignored as one embraced the reality of a timeless nature. This nature was universal, and its rationality had to be expressed in the universal language of mathematics. But, of course, as Plato and Machiavelli pointed out, even the middle classes lived in particular political units in which particular languages were spoken. How, then, could a particular American Revolution and a particular French Revolution lead the middle classes into the new rational universal world of nature?

Crucial to the magic used by the bourgeoisie to create the illusion that they had transcended the fears of Plato and Machiavelli—fears that the middle classes could not move from their particular political states to a universal state of nature—was their invention of the category "universal national." By the early nineteenth century, the middle classes were gaining political control of many nations without such bloody revolutions as those in America or France. Everywhere the bourgeoisie imagined that rational citizens were replacing irrational subjects. These subjects were identified with particular localities and particular languages. But beneath these artful and ephemeral cultures was a state of nature. It was a national landscape. Citizens gained their identities as the children of nature from their particular landscape. They escaped irrational particular languages to speak a rational universal national language. Their exodus from humanly constructed particular cultures to a rational universal nation was, therefore, a negative revolution. Local cultures were constructed. They represented positive revolutions that kept people trapped in Plato's cave. In contrast, national landscapes, as states of nature, were discovered, and citizens obeyed the laws of nature.[17]

The bourgeoisie were so mesmerized by their magic that to be a respectable middle-class citizen meant that one must never discuss the irony that the citizens of each particular modern nation claimed that only their particular national landscape was an expression of a universal nature. Any citizen who suggested an ironic or paradoxical aspect of the supposed universal nation was clearly irrational. Since citizens were rational, the eccentric was masquerading as a citizen. Clearly he was un-French or un-English or un-American or un-Danish.

In the nineteenth century dominated by Bourgeois Nationalism, Isaac Newton was superseded by G. W. F. Hegel (1770–1831) as the most influential public intellectual. Hegel was the great philosopher of the universal national. He explained that it was the bourgeois nation that made possible the exodus from the old world of many ephemeral and irrational local cultures to the new world of the eternal and rational nation. In contrast to the complex, diverse local communities of the old world, one found the simple unity of that new world, the nation. Hegel stressed how citizens formed a unified body. In contrast to the meaningless passage of time in the old world of subjects, citizens experienced the meaningful history of the exodus from chaos to order. Only nations populated by citizens had a meaningful history out of darkness into light. Modern nations were not particular. They were participants in a universal pattern of history as progress from diversity and chaos to unity and order. Bourgeois nations, Hegel proclaimed, were the end of history. Clearly it was historians and not physicists who could explain why a group of nations dominated by the middles classes expressed the revolutionary transition from the subjective traditional world of generational complexity to the objective modern world of timeless simplicity.[18]

It was comforting for the middle class in England or France or Germany to be told by Hegel that bourgeois nations were not artful constructions. Their nations were not centers of political and military power necessary to bring distant resources back to national markets. England, France, and, belatedly, Germany and Japan were not forcing Africans and Asians to be parts of their empires. European Americans had not used military power to place the northern half of Mexico within the boundaries of the United States. They had not used military power to destroy the independence of all Native American nations by 1890. It was assumed that citizens participated in a national marketplace while subjects were still dwelling in a decentralized world of many local markets.

The artful mobilization of millions of men and the artful mobilization of national economies to fight World War I and World War II finally undermined the bourgeois illusion that nations were the product of negative revolutions. They were not new worlds. And so in the 1940s and 1950s, many middle-class people from Australia to Germany began to imagine that the exodus from an old world of complexity to a new world of simplicity was about to take place. Artful, particular, timeful national economies were about to be replaced by an artless, universal, timeless global economy. The fears of Plato and Machiavelli were now irrelevant. Now we were reaching the end of history.

As I looked at my fellow historians and at literary critics to find a pattern in which they were abandoning the belief that America was nature's nation, it did not occur to me that my undergraduate students were participating in this revolutionary transition. In the 1950s and 1960s I had not yet defined a distinction between state-of-nature anthropology and cultural anthropology. The academic world into which I had been initiated was committed to state-of-nature anthropology. One studied particular individuals. One did not look for the cultural patterns in which they were participants.

But in the 1950s a steady stream of students were coming to talk to me about the state of the nation. Those who were left of center expressed their fear that artful, powerful corporations were now defining the nation's future. Students on the right told me that they believed the authentic America dedicated to liberty had been displaced by an artful welfare state that destroyed liberty. These conservative students asked me in particular what I thought about *Atlas Shrugged* (1957), by Ayn Rand (1905–1982). She had emigrated from Russia in 1929 and worked as a writer in Hollywood in the 1930s and 1940s. When the success of her novel *The Fountainhead* (1943) made her financially independent, she was able to move to New York. Her many books on philosophy together with her novels have sold more than twenty million copies.[19]

In *Atlas Shrugged* Rand reinvented the politics of nature that Bruno Latour first found expressed in ancient Greece. She, like Plato's contemporaries, advocated state-of-nature anthropology. She was sure that men had a timeless rational identity that was trapped within timeful, irrational culture. But some heroic individuals were capable of rebelling against that culture and of living rational lives. The majority, however, always tried to drag the exceptional heroes back into their dark world, into Plato's cave.

In *Atlas Shrugged* a group of superior individuals in the United States capable of living independent and rational lives have withdrawn from a corrupt establishment. They have engaged in a ritual of purification by climbing up into the clean space of the mountains. They hoped that the people down in old-world America would see how much they need the leadership of the secular saints committed to an exodus into a new-world America. Rand became known in the 1960s as an important philosopher. She advocated objectivism, which became a national movement. Echoing the central figure in Charles Dickens's *A Christmas Carol,* Ebenezer Scrooge, Rand declared that we cannot be objective if we are interdependent. Altruism corrupts both the giver and the receiver of help. She agreed with Dickens's Scrooge that a selfish act is a virtuous act. She also agreed with Scrooge that the marketplace is the only space where rational self-interest can be practiced.

But, although Rand shared the bourgeois hope of an inevitable exodus from unclean old-world cultures to clean new-world nature, she could not in the 1950s and 1960s point to signs that this transition was taking place in the United States. She did, however, write about the superiority of the modern to the traditional. It was fortunate, she declared, that Europeans had come to America and swept the Indians from the landscape. As traditional people, they did not recognize the existence of independent individuals. In *Atlas Shrugged,* however, she presented an America in 1950 that was filled with European Americans who did not practice individualism.[20]

Rand insisted that any modern person who had a religious faith was not truly modern. All faiths were irrational. Only atheists were capable of rational self-interest. Christianity, she declared, is "the best kindergarten of communism possible" because of its emphasis on loving one's neighbor.[21] An independent individual, for Rand, does not recognize the existence of neighbors.

Rand, of course, like the academic economists of her generation, did not inquire about the scientific evidence that supposedly supported the hypothesis that the marketplace was a timeless space. One did not want to know that current physicists saw space and time as always interrelated. If one could not escape time, there was no possibility of a ritual of purification in which a virtuous world would defeat a corrupt world. Current believers in a pure and immortal marketplace certainly will not want to read the recent book by historian of science Steven Shapin entitled *Never Pure: Historical Studies of Science As If It Was Produced by People with Bodies, Situated in Time, Space, Culture, and Society, and Struggling for Credibility and Authority* (2010).[22]

One might read Rand and find her an optimist. She defined a new world, the marketplace, where individuals would make only rational decisions. Here one left timeful irrational, subjective culture behind. Here one transcended the meaningless flux of history. On the other hand, one might read her as a pessimist in the tradition of Plato and Machiavelli. She and a group of disciples could see the Promised Land, but the large majority of her contemporaries did not feel the need to leave their subjective cultures. They were content to exist in Plato's cave, a world without truth. From the 1950s until her death in 1982, she suffered from many episodes of depression. Perhaps her inability to find evidence of a mass exodus to her new world of objectivism played a role in causing these episodes.

In 2010 a group of Americans formed a political movement referred to as the tea party. They believe the authentic American identity is one of independent individuals. And they believe, like the authentic Americans in Rand's *Atlas Shrugged,* that the country is in the hands of un-Americans preaching interdependence. The tea party is committed to the use of force, if necessary, to restore the virtuous national heritage of rational self-interest. One of the leaders of the tea party is Rand Paul. An ardent admirer of Ayn Rand, he gave up his original first name to acknowledge his intellectual debt to her.

Most of the undergraduate students who talked with me about Ayn Rand in the 1950s focused on her optimistic side. She showed them that the simple, virtuous world of the marketplace provided an alternative to the complex, corrupt world of the welfare state. They could reject dependence and choose independence. These students were found on campuses across the country. In the 1950s Alan Greenspan began making pilgrimages to Rand's apartment. Born in 1926, he studied economics in college and graduate school in New York. And he also participated in the imagined replacement of the nation as a timeless space with the marketplace as the timeless space. He became one of a group of disciples who joined Rand in looking forward to the purging of the subjective welfare state and the liberation of the objective marketplace. He was excited in 1964 to discover that Barry Goldwater, the Republican presidential candidate, was crusading against a corrupt big government. He was delighted to be a public supporter of this spokesman for a pure and free marketplace.[23]

At last there was a political leader who was critical of the welfare state created by President Roosevelt in the 1930s. Richard Nixon, the Republican president elected in 1968, had recruited Greenspan to help his campaign. He rewarded Greenspan's political activities by appointing him director of domestic policy research. Nixon's Republican successor, Gerald Ford, appointed Greenspan chairman of the Council of Economic Advisers. Given his high visibility as an economic adviser in the Republican Party, he was appointed a director on the boards of several large corporations, such as J. P. Morgan.

A number of objectivists criticized Greenspan for his participation in the corrupt establishment. He was not making it clear that the laws of the marketplace were true while the laws passed by the government were false. He answered his fellow objectivists by saying that one must compromise with the complex status quo even as one pursues the long-term goal of liberating the marketplace from big government. See, he said, how our Republican president, Ronald Reagan, is moving toward free-market capitalism by reducing taxes on the rich and working to reduce the power of labor unions. President Reagan, in turn, named Greenspan the chairman of the Federal Reserve Board. He continued to hold this important position under Presidents George H. W. Bush,

Bill Clinton, and George W. Bush. He strongly supported the efforts of George W. Bush to privatize Social Security, and he approved a second round of tax cuts for the rich. He also joined in the successful effort in the 1990s to do away with the Glass-Steagall Act, which had been passed in 1933. President Roosevelt had found that after the economic collapse in 1929 the private banking system was disintegrating. He used the government to stabilize the banks. The Glass-Steagall Act was designed to restrain banks from making irresponsible loans in the future. Now in the real estate boom in the early twenty-first century, bankers were able to make irresponsible loans. Greenspan also used his authority on the Federal Reserve Board to fuel that boom by lowering interest rates. He resigned from the Federal Reserve Board in 2006 at the age of eighty, a year before the real estate boom crashed. Elected in 2008, President Barack Obama again had to use the government to bail out bankers who had not made the rational choices predicted by Greenspan and most academic economists.[24]

By the 1990s Greenspan had become the best-known spokesperson in the United States for the segregation of a timeless market from a timeful government. His national popularity and influence are evidence of how dominant the exodus narrative was and is in American culture. Many citizens were and are waiting for the moment when they will leave the old timeful, artful world and enter the new timeless, artless world. Greenspan, as a major prophet of that miraculous future, received an exceptional number of honors. These included, in 2005, the Presidential Medal of Freedom, the highest civilian award in the United States. He also received the Dwight D. Eisenhower Medal for Leadership, the Harry S Truman Medal for Economic Policy, and the Thomas Jefferson Foundation Medal for Citizen Leadership. Because leaders in all bourgeois nations looked to the global marketplace after 1945 and because they were increasingly critical of the welfare state by the 1980s, Greenspan was also honored by England, which made him a Knight Commander of the British Empire, and by France, which made him a Commander of the Legion of Honor.

Then in 2007 the United States and the rest of the world experienced a severe recession. Alan Greenspan and countless millions of modern people believed that the market as a timeless space has a natural equilibrium. There would be no economic crises in the future. Called to testify before Congress in October 2008, Greenspan admitted that he had overestimated the natural stability of the marketplace. Perhaps he had been wrong when he insisted that the market never benefited from government regulation. But his vision of two worlds was part of an international modern culture. Political leaders on all continents are committed to the exodus narrative. Imagining they are leaving home for a better future, these leaders can ignore the issue of sustainable resources. They are moving to a new world that has endless plenitude. In April 2010 Greenspan reaffirmed his admiration for Ayn Rand. We must, he said, continue to be inspired by her ability to identify our irrational status quo. We must continue to be guided by her ability to identify a rational future. Alan Greenspan, therefore, minimized the significance of the drastic economic downturn that began in 2007. He wants us to focus on that supposedly rational and objective world that has permanent stability. If only we could all discipline ourselves and repress our subjective impulses, we would dwell in this Promised Land. Since the time of Plato, middle-class men have been waiting for that moment when we would leave our irrational identity behind. For more than 2,500 years, middle-class men who fear imagination have portrayed a divided world in which virtuous rational people have been locked in combat with corrupt irrational people. Within the circle of the earth there are two worlds. There is the old world created by imagination that must disappear. There is the new world discovered by reason that must displace culture. This is the timeless world of nature that is always threatened by the timeful world of culture.[25]

I have been a participant in this melodrama all my life. Since 1945 I have been a participant in this never-ending melodrama as it has played out in history and English departments. For this book I have written a chapter on how historians have struggled with the dualism of old-world culture and new-world nature. When they lost their belief in a universal national after 1945, historians could finally write about the variety of American cultures. They could also relate these cultures to cultures in other countries. They were shifting from state-of-nature anthropology to cultural anthropology. This paradigm revolution made it possible for them to begin to interpret nature as dynamic and timeful. Some historians began to see the world in ways similar to ecologists. They began to see that power had been used to conscript resources for the market. They began to see imperialism as a necessary part of economic growth.

Then, in a chapter on literary critics, I point to parallels between their changing worldview and that of historians. Literary critics also moved from state-of-nature anthropology to cultural anthropology. They, too, moved from a universal national literature to a pluralism of literatures. Now defining all literature as timeful, they erased the distinction between supposedly timeless high literature and timeful popular literature. Both literary critics and historians were forced to confront the euphoria of the 1990s that believed a new world of plenty and harmony had been reached. Those who accepted the good news were forced to reconsider after 2000.

In my chapter on economists there is no debate about a utopian future. From the 1940s to the beginning of the new century, almost every economist was certain that the global marketplace was the end of history. When economists participated in the rejection of the universal national, they, more than any other academic group, were able to replace it with a vision of a universal universal. Beyond all national political boundaries, there was an artless, timeless marketplace. From 1940 to the present, academic economists have chosen to ignore that the physics of Newton, which assumed space to be timeless, had been replaced by 1900 with a physics that assumed space to be timeful. Since 2000, however, a growing number of economists have begun to reject the metaphor of two worlds—timeful, irrational cultures and a timeless, rational marketplace. It is difficult in the second decade of the twenty-first century to see how the complexity of the many nations is giving way to a harmonious and simple unity. A few economists are even beginning to ask where the resources come from that are exchanged in the marketplace.

A chapter on ecologists will show that the question of resources has been central to their perspective since the 1940s. If economists have represented modern orthodoxy, ecologists have been the most important heretics. They see a complex and timeful world characterized by limits. They recommend that we focus on sustainable resources. They see time expressed in a variety of cycles. At the moment their focus is on the cycle of global warming. Orthodox modern people sometimes accuse ecologists of regressing back into a traditional worldview. Ecologists, like these "backward" people, are romantics who can see only one world.

In the final chapter I discuss how scientific doubts about the global marketplace as the end history have found expression in popular and political culture. There are signs that as hope in a global paradise wanes some groups of Americans are trying to revitalize the pre-1940 faith in the United States as nature's nation. They have faith in an isolated American paradise. Such revitalization leads toward the supposed isolation of a pure and perfect United States from a corrupt and imperfect world. And if these isolationists see the welfare state as socialism coming from an alien Europe, then it becomes an even greater threat to nature's nation today than it was to Ayn Rand in the 1950s.

Unlike the Bourgeois Nationalists of the 1930s, however, these isolationists define themselves as capitalists. They forget how World War II exposed the contradiction between national political boundaries and the capitalist need to transcend all boundaries. Can capitalism survive in a world of revitalized political boundaries? Ecologists as antimodern heretics proclaim that capitalism cannot survive within a living earth that expresses itself in myriad boundaries within which we are all interdependent. But most Americans continue to believe in an unlimited future where independence is the norm. This is the fantasy discussed by Robert Collins in his *More: The Politics of Economic Growth in Postwar America* (2000).[26]

2 HISTORIANS AGAINST HISTORY

THE AMERICAN FOUNDING FATHERS had defined their revolution in negative terms. They had made an exodus from an old world of artful culture to a new world of artless nature. They had escaped timeful societies to achieve harmony with timeless space. They also recognized the gift given them by classical Greece and Rome—the gift of knowing that two worlds existed. They acknowledged this gift by using the architecture of classical antiquity to define their public buildings. They saw the gothic architecture of the Dark Ages as symbolizing an irrational feminine spirit. In contrast, classical architecture was rational and masculine. And they had left an old world of irrational power to find a new world of rational liberty. Their public architecture announced that they were at the end of history.

But when the Founding Fathers looked at their fellow citizens, they had to qualify their vision of a successful exodus from an old to a new world. Most of these citizens seemed incapable of rationality. The Founding Fathers, therefore, saw themselves as an embattled minority. They were a natural aristocracy surrounded by an unnatural majority. It was imperative, then, that they design the constitution of their new nation to avoid majority rule. The president was to be elected by an electoral college whose members were chosen by the legislatures of the states. Members of the Senate also were chosen by the legislatures of the states they represented. Popular voting elected only members of the House of Representatives, and the president and the Senate could block the voters' decisions. The Supreme Court could also rule their decisions unconstitutional.

The Founding Fathers were dismayed, therefore, by the development of political parties. These artful creations might be capable of mobilizing irrational majorities, first in the states and then at the national level. The Fathers saw the republic as the most virtuous form of government, the one most capable of rationality, the one best to protect the individual from the irrational actions of the group. Democracies represented a decline from the virtuous republic. Imagination, not reason, was in control of majorities, and power replaced liberty.

Recent scholarship has reminded us that the Founding Fathers became more and more pessimistic as they saw signs of timeful change. Even at the personal level, their sons refused to wear wigs and remain clean shaven. They replaced their fathers' pants that ended at the knee with pants that came down to their shoes. Everywhere the Founding Fathers saw signs that their republic was losing its foundation in the timeless laws of nature. Their beloved republic was slipping back into Plato's cave, a space of meaningless flux.

This was the cultural crisis that George Bancroft (1800–1891) apparently solved when he began to write history in the 1830s. During the 1820s Democratic parties in many of the states were working to bring about a major unwritten change in the U.S. Constitution. They wanted to separate the electors in each state from the state legislatures. They wanted the electors to give their votes to the presidential candidate who won the majority of votes in each particular state. By 1828 this revolutionary unwritten change in the Constitution had taken place, and the presidential candidate of the new national Democratic Party, Andrew Jackson, was the first president to be elected by popular vote. Once again sons had broken from generational continuity. From 1828 to the present we have defined the United States as a democracy. Our foreign policy since World War I speaks of spreading democracy to the rest of the world.

Bancroft's historical writing became immensely popular because he created still another persuasive narrative that Jackson's election symbolized the completion of the exodus from the old world of artful culture to the new world of artless nature. It celebrated the completion of the exodus from the old world of power to the new world of liberty. Democracy, Bancroft proclaimed, was not, as the Founding Fathers feared, a declension from republicanism. Instead, democracy was the highest form of politics. It was the end of history.[1]

Young men from the Northeast who, like Bancroft, were attracted to the exciting new field of history writing looked for guidance from the historians in a variety of German states, especially Prussia. Throughout the nineteenth century many young Americans went to study in the Germanies. By the 1870s and the 1880s they were bringing the new Ph.D. degree home from Germany and establishing graduate education at a number of eastern universities. Soon this pattern of graduate education would spread across the country. This admiration for intellectual life in Germany would erode dramatically after 1900, however. Bancroft, the son of a Protestant minister, saw himself in dialogue with Hegel. He agreed with the Prussian philosopher that the major exodus from medieval darkness to the light of modernity was caused by the Reformation. Downplaying the Renaissance and the Enlightenment because of their commitment to the transnational universalism of the physical sciences, Bancroft celebrated the born-again outlook of Protestantism. Independent Protestant individuals had stepped out of Plato's cave in the form of the Roman Catholic Church. Protestants, for Hegel and Bancroft, were creating the modern nation because, in contrast to Catholics, they rejected the pattern of complex overlapping loyalties characterizing the medieval past. Only Protestants were capable of complete loyalty to the universal national. Only Protestants could fuse into a uniform national people. Only Protestants could speak with a single national voice. Only Protestants could transcend the power of traditional cultures to impose false, transitory identities on the individual. Only Protestants could provide liberty to the authentic individual.[2]

For Bancroft, then, as for Hegel, Protestants were destined to be participants in particular nations, but a universal national characterized those nations. Bancroft also agreed with Hegel that a particular Protestant nation always provided more leadership than other Protestant nations in the exodus out of the irrational and timeful traditional world. But, unlike Hegel, Bancroft saw the United States as that leader. Engaging in the tradition of bourgeois magic that obscured the use of power by the middle classes, Bancroft argued that only the United States, in contrast to Protestant Prussia and Protestant England, had escaped the use of power in its exodus from the oppressive traditional world. The national peoples of Prussia and England had engaged in many wars to free themselves from a past of ephemeral local communities and the oppressive Catholic Church. They had to use armies to complete this ritual of purification. But now Bancroft, waving his magic bourgeois wand, wrote about how the United States did not need to use power to fulfill its national destiny. Bancroft celebrated American liberty, although slavery was a crucial national institution. He waved his magic wand and obliterated all memories of the constant wars of European settlers against the Native Americans ever since the invasion of America by Europe had begun in the early seventeenth century. He celebrated Andrew Jackson as a symbol of liberty, although Jackson was a slaveholder and a renowned warrior against American Indians. Instead he celebrated Jackson as the first president who came from west of the Appalachian Mountains.

When the War of Independence began in 1776, Bancroft wrote that the revolutionists were not an America people. They were rooted in the cultures of their particular colonies. And when these colonies became independent states, they still retained their particular cultures. They continued to be part of a traditional world. Jackson, then, symbolized the birth of the American nation. When individuals moved from an east coast still rooted in particular traditions, they became universal Americans in the Mississippi Valley. They had left the fragmented past to find a unified future in this virgin land. Bancroft, of course, in imagining the America west of the Appalachians as a virgin land, was cleansing the minds of his European American readers of all recognition of the ten thousand years of Native American history in his supposed new world. If there were no American Indians, then no power had been used or was now being used against them. White Americans had not and were not now engaged in the brutality of ethnic cleansing.[3]

Here, then, in the Mississippi Valley, for Bancroft, was that space, the national landscape, where the Promised Land was reached and history ended. Here was the fulfillment of the prophecy that there would be a nation whose citizens shared the same outlook. Here from this national landscape was born a national people who participated in a national will.

It is my long experience as a historian from the late 1940s to the present that most American history textbooks have not emphasized the ironic relationship of Bancroft's prophecy to the Civil War. Only a generation after Bancroft began to construct his vision of the Mississippi Valley as the authentic American national landscape from which a unified national people was emerging, the people divided North and South and fought the bloody Civil War. And certainly the Northern

American people used great military power to force the Southern American people to return to the nation that supposedly had transcended the dramatic conflicts characteristic of traditional cultures. This willingness of Northerners to marginalize the Civil War indicates why Bancroft's histories were so popular. His books spoke to an audience that shared his faith in a mythic geographical space. And that faith flowed into the twentieth century.

When a group of American colleges in the Northeast redefined themselves as universities in the late nineteenth century, central to this revolutionary change had been the bringing of the Ph.D. degree from Germany. Universities, in contrast to colleges, had graduate as well as undergraduate students. Professors who now had graduate degrees and instructed graduate students were professionals. As graduate education spread to the rest of the country, national professional organizations were created for the various disciplines in the humanities, the social sciences, and the physical sciences. There is powerful evidence of how Bancroft's thesis identifying the Mississippi Valley as the authentic national landscape and source of American national identity had become an essential myth for most Northerners. The new professional historians who specialized in American history named their national professional organization the Mississippi Valley Historical Association. And the professional journal for American historians was titled the *Mississippi Valley Historical Review*. When I began graduate school in 1948, I joined the Mississippi Valley Historical Association, and my first article was published in 1951 in the *Mississippi Valley Historical Review*. In retrospect, I believe my undergraduate professors at Princeton and my graduate professors and fellow graduate students at Wisconsin had no sense that we were participating in a revolutionary desacralization of a major myth when we helped change the name of the Mississippi Valley Historical Association to the Organization of American Historians. We also changed the name of the *Mississippi Valley Historical Review* to the *Journal of American History*. I believe that we were motivated to make these changes because by the 1950s a new generation of historians wanted a definition of the nation that was more inclusive than that proposed by Bancroft. His democracy symbolized by Andrew Jackson was only for white male Protestants.[4]

The next historian to become a public intellectual was Frederick Jackson Turner (1861–1929). Still a young man, he gave an address at the Chicago Exposition. This world's fair had been organized to celebrate in 1892 the discovery of an American new world by Columbus in 1492.

It was poetically appropriate that this young historian from Wisconsin should present an elegy titled "The Significance of the Frontier in American History" for Bancroft's belief that history had ended in the Mississippi Valley around 1830. Turner in 1890 was at a point of cultural crisis comparable to that of Bancroft in 1830. Bancroft was aware of the failure of the prophecy made by the Founding Fathers that 1789 marked the end of history. And Turner was aware of the failure of Bancroft's prophecy. But Turner could not make a prophecy that history was to end in the 1890s. For Turner the new world discovered by Columbus no longer existed.[5]

The census of 1890 indicated, Turner declared, that there no longer existed "an area of free land." Continuing the tradition of the urban middle-class Greek men of antiquity, Turner could not imagine that the middle classes ever used power to bring resources into their markets. But, of course, his statement about the final disappearance of free land coincided with the final military defeat of the Native American nations, the transfer of their land to whites, and the imprisonment of the few survivors on reservations.

For Turner, however, the crisis of the modern narrative of an exodus from an old world of tradition to a new world of nature meant that young men (implicitly middle-class young men) would no longer become independent of their fathers. How could they leave home if there was no alternative space? In his writings about the American past, he, like Bancroft, assumed an exceptional American relation to nature. Only the United States was America, the state of nature so different from European culture. The other American nations were like Europe because they buried their national landscapes under the pattern of European culture that they had brought across the Atlantic. This was especially true of the power of the Roman Catholic Church in all the other American nations. Only in the English colonies were there Protestants who were ready to leave European culture behind.

Turner's writing became poetic when he preached the orthodox myth of an American new world. "European men, institutions and ideas were lodged in the American wilderness and the Great American West took them to her bosom, taught them a new way of looking upon the destiny of the common man, trained them in adaptation to the conditions of the New World." But the tragic flaw of this faith, for Turner, was that young women as well as young men had participated in the exodus. The Greek middle-class men of antiquity had tried to protect their vision of a nongenerational world by segregating women from their anticipated utopia. And Turner, like Bancroft and the Founding Fathers, always spoke only of young men leaving an artful home to reach an artless nature. But somehow in this timeless space young self-made men met young women who brought them back into the generational world of the family. These young men became fathers from whom their sons must flee.[6]

Turner sadly reported, therefore, that from 1600 to 1800 there had been a series of moments when self-made men had reached harmony with a timeless nongenerational nature only to fall back into an artful, generational world of families. But his overall narrative stressed that each of these moments of exodus brought European settlers closer to an American nation that expressed the laws of nature.

Like Bancroft, Turner did not believe the Founding Fathers had escaped hierarchical European culture. Like Bancroft, then, he believed that an exodus into a democratic American nation did not occur until the election of Jackson in 1828. "Jefferson was the first prophet of American democracy," Turner wrote, but "he was the John the Baptist of democracy not its Moses." It was a generation after Jefferson that the people "were rallying around the man who personified their passion for democracy and nationalism—the fiery Jackson."[7]

But Turner, in contrast to Bancroft, did not believe that the exodus into the Mississippi Valley marked the end of history. Even in a state of nature humans could not escape generational experience. Self-made young men married and had children. They became interdependent with their wives and children. Now that the American West was no longer a state of nature, the sons of these fathers would not repeat the exhilarating experience of leaving home and, for a fleeting moment, becoming independent. It is important to notice that coinciding with Turner's loss of faith in an exodus from generational culture to nongenerational nature, male writers from the Northeast, such as Owen Wister, began to write novels in which women from the East traveled to the West and threatened to seduce cowboys out of their relationship with timeless nature. In the 1930s I attended many movies that evoked this tension. Then from the 1940s to the 1960s there were many television series set in the West that continued to explore this tension between timeful women and timeless cowboys. In the series *Bonanza,* which centered on a father with three adult sons living on a ranch, the scriptwriters had many opportunities to create dramatic episodes in which there was the possibility that one of the members of this all-male family would develop a relationship with a woman. But the timeless ranch, as a state of nature, was always saved when the relationships with women were aborted.[8]

Perhaps it was Turner's sense that the Mississippi Valley had failed to be the space where history ended that led him to accept an invitation to teach at Harvard. Perhaps the East now seemed more vital than his native Wisconsin. At Harvard, then, in the 1920s, Turner directed the dissertation of Merle Curti. After I received my bachelor's degree from Princeton, I became a graduate student at Wisconsin in 1948, and Merle Curti became my dissertation adviser. I remember vividly sitting in his office while he told me about his relationship with Turner and Charles Beard. I, of course, in 1948 was not aware of such a concept as the "end of history." I had not considered that historians might be participants in cultures that gained their meanings from sets of mythic narratives. I did know, however, that when I was discharged from the army in the fall of 1944 I did not believe in progress. And when I became an under-graduate at Princeton in 1945 I knew I wanted to learn about the idea of progress. I also discovered that my professors thought that Charles Beard was the most important American historian.[9]

I was surprised, therefore, when Curti told me that although Turner was his official adviser, Beard was his actual adviser. He recounted how he "sneaked" out of Cambridge to travel down to Beard's home in Connecticut. He talked about his fear that Turner would become aware of these trips. In retrospect, I think my professors at Princeton and Wisconsin felt that Beard was more important than Turner be-cause Beard, unlike Turner, continued to have faith in an exodus that would end history.

At Princeton I did my senior thesis on an aspect of the Progressive Movement in the United States, 1890–1920. For my dissertation at Wisconsin I analyzed the idea of progress expressed by a number of academics during this Progressive Era. One of these academics was Charles Beard. My dissertation, *The Paradox of Progressive Thought,* was published in 1958. Given the segregated way national history was written, I had not considered the possibility that the idea of progress was a transnational myth and that patterns of thought in the United States, 1890–1920, had parallels in other modern countries.

The paradox of progressive thought that I saw in the 1950s was that academics like Beard saw progress as an escape from current complexities and a return to a time of origins. I was implicitly analyzing a contrast between timeful culture and timeless nature. It would take another forty years before I would make this contrast explicit.

In contrast to history as meaningless flux, Turner had seen a meaningful history, the exodus from the timeful flux of culture to the timeless stability of nature. He identified the exodus, meaningful history, with a westward movement. Western Europe was more natural than Eastern Europe. America was more natural than Western Europe. The American West was more natural than the American East. But Turner's vision was collapsing by the 1890s. The past, the East, kept catching up with the future, the West.

But Charles Beard (1874–1948) as a young man had traveled to England, where the Industrial Revolution had begun in the eighteenth century. This revolution, for Beard, had brought unprecedented prosperity to England. Beard never asked about the patterns of economic and political power related to the Industrial Revolution. It was for him a magical force. Rising standards of living made it possible for the common people of England to imagine ending their deference to elites. They began in the nineteenth century to imagine that England could become a democracy.

The young Beard published his first book, *The Industrial Revolution*, in 1901. Look, he asked his readers, look at this Industrial Revolution. Look at how it contradicts the pessimism of historians such as Turner. Nature is not a static world. It is not an unchanging given whose vitality is being overrun by this force, the Industrial Revolution, which is coming from the East and conquering the West. We young men know the law of nature is that of evolution. The Industrial Revolution is not something unnatural destroying what is natural. The Industrial Revolution is the most recent expression of a dynamic nature that is carrying us away from an unstable past and into a stable future.[10]

Implicitly Beard was urging his fellow historians to give up their commitment to a universal national. We must, he argued, return to the Enlightenment and its vision of a universal universal. We historians must end our segregation from the physical sciences. We must write about how our national histories are interdependent with the universal laws of evolution. We must see that our democracy did not emerge from a national landscape. We must see that it will emerge from our participation in the transnational Industrial Revolution embodying the universal laws of nature.[11]

In the early twentieth century Beard published books at a furious pace. More explicitly than Bancroft and Turner, he wanted to demonstrate how antidemocratic the Founding Fathers were. He wanted to demonstrate that Andrew Jackson did not symbolize the triumph of democracy in the 1830s. Look, Beard continued, look at how undemocratic the United States is in 1900. He wanted his readers to recognize that there was not a declension from a democratic America. From 1789 to the present, he insisted, elites have been in control. It is now in our Progressive Movement that we will make the United States a democracy.

Implicitly rejecting Hegel when he rejected national history, Beard, however, was not returning to Isaac Newton. Instead it was Charles Darwin (1809–1882) who became Beard's authority for the inevitable victory of rational nature over irrational culture. It was Beard's thesis that people build cultures that fit the natural environment in which they find themselves. But then nature changes, and the existing culture becomes unnatural. We are, Beard insisted, in such a moment of culture lag. We are now, however, recognizing how irrational our culture lag is, and we are creating a new rational culture in harmony with the current laws of nature. But this energizing universal industrial democracy is the final stage of evolution. When it becomes the status quo, we will be at the end of history. Beard and many other academics, therefore, had expectations of a millennial experience as they approached 1914 and the beginning of World War I.

Certain that they were standing only moments away from a utopia of permanent peace and prosperity, Beard and other academic leaders such as the philosopher John Dewey and the economist Thorstein Veblen called for the immediate entry of the United States into the war. They had rejected the interpretation of the Industrial Revolution put forward by Karl Marx. He argued that the forces of industrial production were rational and caused workers to be rational. The bourgeoisie, however, were irrational because they dwelled in an environment of irrational profit making rather than rational production. Reaching the rational world of the end of history, Marx argued, depended on a violent revolution that destroyed the irrational bourgeoisie and brought the rational proletariat to political power.

For men like Beard, Dewey, and Veblen, however, the rationality of industrial production could make both the middle classes and the factory workers rational. Class revolution was unnecessary. But Germany in 1914 was controlled by a medieval aristocracy. Germany had become industrialized, but the rationality of the middle classes and workers involved in production was suppressed by an irrational feudal aristocracy. If the United States used violence to destroy that unnatural aristocracy and liberate the natural middle classes and workers, the inevitable transition to the coming universal utopia would be speeded up.[12]

Finally in 1917 the hopes of Beard, Dewey, Veblen, and many of their colleagues were fulfilled when the United States entered the war as an ally of England and France in their war against Germany. And then their prophecy failed. The surrender of Germany and the ending of monarchy in that nation did not bring the millennium. There was no new world of perpetual peace and prosperity. In the United States several young novelists became known as members of a "lost generation." Ernest Hemingway, F. Scott Fitzgerald, and William Faulkner were in their teens when the war began. They had learned that the Progressive Movement marked an exodus from a corrupt old world to a virtuous new world. They rushed to join the military and be crusaders who would help bring about a miraculous transformation of societies everywhere. When the prophecy failed, they lost the narrative that had given meaning to their lives.[13]

Hemingway explained in his novel *A Farewell to Arms* how his hero, Frederic Henry, became aware that he lived in a world that would never be transformed into a utopia. He focused on the woman with whom Henry lived. She has his child, and then she dies. She symbolized, for Hemingway, the traditional world of generational continuity—the constant cycle of birth and death. Henry, and Hemingway, would never experience timeless stability. Fitzgerald in his novel *The Great Gatsby* also focused on a child to demonstrate the impossible dream of timeless stability. Jay Gatsby had fallen in love just before he went to fight in Europe. While he was away, Daisy, the woman he loves, married another man and had a child. When Gatsby returns he hopes to win Daisy away from her husband. He wants to erase the period of time that they were separated. But Daisy cannot forget that during those years she had a child. She cannot deny her participation in the life cycle.[14]

William Faulkner, like Hemingway and Fitzgerald, wrote in the 1920s about young men for whom life had lost all meaning. In the 1930s, however, he wrote a novel, *Light in August,* in which some of the characters find meaning by embracing life cycles. A young woman arrives in a town pregnant with an illegitimate child. An older and a younger man decide they will help her and her unborn child. They can believe that this child is worthwhile. They can believe there is meaning in an unstable world where birth and death are natural. I read *Light in August* in the 1950s, and it played a major role in the development of my understanding of how modern and traditional people understand the passage of time. Faulkner taught me to look back to James Fenimore Cooper, Nathaniel Hawthorne, and Herman Melville and to see their critiques of the metaphor of two worlds.[15]

My professors at Princeton and Merle Curti at Wisconsin would not in the 1940s have admired Charles Beard if he had become a member of a lost generation. But several of his colleagues had. Carl Becker had joined Beard during the first decade of the twentieth century in looking back to the Enlightenment as an alternative to the false vision of nations as autonomous and segregated states of nature. Rationality was, as the eighteenth-century philosophers insisted, universal. The exodus from the traditional to the modern must include all of humanity in a universal universal. By 1919 Becker, like Beard, had lost faith in this narrative. He self-consciously expressed his loss of faith in his book written in the 1920s, *The Heavenly City of the Eighteenth-Century Philosophers.* In this book, which I read for a course at Princeton, Becker attacked the belief of modern people that they were rational in contrast to the imaginative world of the medieval past. This modern belief in two worlds, rational and irrational, Becker insisted, was untrue. The eighteenth-century vision of a rational utopia was created by imagination. It was an act of faith.[16]

In contrast to the way Becker responded to his crisis of faith in 1919, Beard was able to revitalize his faith in the modern metaphor of two worlds. He did this by returning to Bancroft's faith that history had ended with the exodus from the east coast and its colonial heritage into the valley of democracy, into the national landscape, into a timeless state of nature.

This isolationist message by Charles Beard, now writing with his wife, Mary Beard (1876–1958), was immensely popular in the 1920s and 1930s. Many Americans had shared Beard's internationalism between the 1890s and 1919. But many intellectuals and artists throughout Europe also shared it. Architects in several Western European countries had begun to criticize the isolationist message of Bourgeois Nationalism that buildings should grow organically out of particular national landscapes. But, for architectural rebels, reality was the universal urban-industrial environment, and architecture must express this authentic universal universal rather than the false universal national. Many painters also by 1900 were in rebellion against representing national landscapes and an authentic timeless individual. Varieties of abstract painting challenged the faith that nations and their rational citizens were the end of history. In philosophy, academics, again in a variety of nations, denied the possibility that a universal national could be rational. They said it was a scandal that philosophers had segregated themselves from the physical sciences. When philosophers recognized the absurdity of this segregation, they would recognize that one could be rational only when one spoke the universal language of science—mathematics.[17]

Beard, unlike Becker, was a participant in a transnational revitalization of Bourgeois Nationalism that rejected this return to the Enlightenment. Between 1919 and World War II many artists, intellectuals, and politicians argued that only segregated nations were real. In the United States, the philosopher John Dewey abandoned his internationalism after 1919 and insisted that American philosophy was an analysis of traditions unique to the United States. The painter Thomas Hart Benton had studied in Europe, but in the 1920s he insisted that American painters must use a representational style to evoke the American landscape and its people. Benton and his colleagues in the American scene school of painting were celebrated by most art critics in the 1930s.[18]

Frank Lloyd Wright was the most influential American architect between the wars. Echoing the Beards, Dewey, and Benton, he declared that American architecture should organically grow out of the American landscape. Cultural critics also celebrated him. At the end of the 1920s Charles and Mary Beard had begun to publish their multivolume *The Rise of American Civilization*. During the 1930s this series helped motivate a large number of scholars in the Ivy League universities to create programs in American civilization. Men from

English, history, art history, music, architecture, and philosophy departments would work together in these programs to demonstrate how different the American new world was from the European old world. And, of course, American civilization existed only in one American nation, the United States. Only the United States was in harmony with the American state of nature. All the other American nations were still part of the European old world because they participated in the unnatural traditions of Catholicism.[19]

The Beards, then, recounted in *The Rise of American Civilization* how English colonists lost their English traditions and were reborn as the children of nature. In telling this story of the movement from European power to American liberty, the Beards, like Bancroft and Turner, wrote history that purged Native Americans from the landscape. The English colonists did not meet and interact with thousands of years of Native American traditions. All they saw was a redemptive state of nature. Like Bancroft and Turner, the Beards told the story of the transition from English tradition to American nature as not having been completed until the final exodus from the colonial east into the state of nature that existed west of the Appalachians.

In describing this moment of earthly salvation, the writing of the Beards, like that of Bancroft and Turner, became filled with religious imagery. "It was a marvelous empire of virgin country," the Beards intoned, "that awaited the next great wave of migration. The valley of the Mississippi now summoned the peoples of the earth to make a new experiment in social economy in the full light of modern times." They continued: "In the vanguard was the man with the rifle. He loved the pathless forest, dense and solitary, carpeted by the fallen leaves of a thousand years and fretted by the sunlight that poured through the Gothic arches of the trees, and where the camp fire at night flared into the darkness of knitted boughs as flaming candles of the altar of a cathedral cast their rays high into the traceries of the vaulted roof." The relationship between the national landscape and the international Industrial Revolution as seen by the Beards between the wars, therefore, was the absolute opposite of the relationship Charles Beard had seen between 1890 and 1918. Then he had denied that the national landscape was the end of history. Instead, he had proclaimed that a universal industrial revolution was bringing the end of history. But now in the 1920s and 1930s Charles and Mary Beard insisted that industrialism was not universal. It came to particular nations and was fitted into the unique tradition of each nation. The United States, they argued, was the only nation whose national landscape had given birth to a democracy. Industrialism, therefore, was fitted into the American democratic tradition. Industrialism did not supersede the national landscape as Charles Beard had argued from 1890 through 1918. Instead, it was absorbed by the national landscape.[20]

The Beards, in *The Rise of American Civilization,* painted the national landscape, then, as an eternal entity that provided timeless plenty and harmony for its children. But if this was true, how did they explain away the bitter political conflict that began in the 1790s? How did they explain the Civil War and World War I? Their explanation came from their creation of a division between good American sons and bad un-American sons. The good sons wanted to guard the unique purity of their mother, the national landscape. They would keep corrupt foreign influences from infiltrating the nation's borders.

The first bad son was Alexander Hamilton. He was not content with the modest plenitude provided by the national landscape. We can become rich, Hamilton declared, by engaging in international trade. We must not segregate ourselves from the rest of the world. Material gain is more important than guarding our exceptional national spirit. Americans, for the Beards, were committed to private property. But loyal Americans wanted that private property to work always in the national interest. A good citizen was committed to public interest rather than private interest.

In contrast to this system of spiritual private property, the Beards pointed to the selfishness of international capitalism. International capitalists had no loyalty to their nations. They were concerned only for their private fortunes. They celebrated self-interest rather than public interest. The Beards now argued that the Civil War had so undermined the vision of public interest that international capitalists were able for a generation to seize control of the national economy. To make themselves rich they opened the national borders to workers whose heritage was alien to the democracy created by the national landscape. "Roads from four continents now ran to the new Apian Way—Wall Street," they lamented, "and the pro-consuls of distant provinces paid homage to a new sovereign. The land of Washington, Franklin, Jefferson, and John Adams had become a land of millionaires, and the supreme direction of its economy had passed from the owners of farms and isolated factories and back to a few men and

institutions." The Beards continued their angry denunciation of international capitalists by pointing out how these bad sons were willing
to disrupt a unified national people with immigrants who had no understanding of democracy. "Not since the patricians and capitalists
of Rome scoured the known world for slaves," they scornfully wrote,
"had the world witnessed such a deliberate overturn of a social order
by Masters of Ceremonies."[21]

But the Beards reassured their readers that the middle class had
begun to organize a progressive political movement by the 1890s that
was well on its way to restoring the democracy of the 1830s when
World War I came. Once again international capitalists momentarily
regained control and replaced public interest with self-interest. By the
1930s, however, the Beards could report that the good sons committed
to a spiritual and isolated democratic nation were defeating the bad
internationalist capitalist sons. President Franklin Delano Roosevelt
was the leader of this democratic renaissance in the 1930s.

And then at the end of the 1930s the Beards had to report that FDR
was a bad son masquerading as a good son. The president wanted to
take the nation into World War II, which had begun in Europe in 1939.
In their fourth and final volume of *The Rise of American Civilization*
the Beards at the beginning of the 1940s insisted once again that the
democratic America born of the national landscape was immortal.
Even if American entry into World War II again gave new power to
the selfish materialism of international capitalists, this victory, they
reassured their readers, would be temporary. International capitalism,
they continued, was an ephemeral human creation. This artful, timeful
world could not compete with the artless, timeless world of the national
landscape. The American people would always find their way back to
their national landscape that had given them their eternal identity as
Americans.[22]

But this prophecy made by Charles and Mary Beard about what
would happen in the United States after World War II collapsed almost as quickly as the prophecy Charles Beard had made about the
new world that would follow World War I. President Roosevelt had
seen World War II as providing a revolutionary opportunity to move
the United States, the Western European nations, and Japan from
isolation to internationalism. He and his successor, President Harry
Truman, had great success in reaching this goal at home and abroad.
What was most devastating for the Beards and the many Americans

who shared their thesis—that a mortal conflict existed between the democratic national tradition and an antidemocratic international capitalism—was that by the end of the 1950s most American political, economic, and cultural leaders argued that international capitalism was an integral part of American national identity.

By 1960, therefore, the many critics who in the 1930s and 1940s had joined the Beards in denouncing international capitalism were themselves denounced as un-American. It was no longer legitimate to contrast private property that was linked to the national interest against private property linked to international capitalism. The intensity with which the Beards' position was attacked as un-American was multiplied by the way the United States in the 1950s became a competitor with the Soviet Union for world leadership. Washington, D.C., proclaimed the capital of virtuous international capitalism, was locked in a life-and-death struggle with Moscow as the capital of international communism. I remember going to a meeting of professional historians in 1955 at which a professor presented a paper in which he supposedly proved that Charles Beard had been a communist. There was a significant minority of Marxists in the United States who in the 1930s and 1940s considered themselves patriotic Americans. Many of these individuals were purged from their jobs in Hollywood, in labor unions, and in the academic world. The politicians leading this purge insisted that any critic of international capitalism was helping an enemy, the Soviet Union, in what was named "the Cold War." I was aware that two of my new friends at Wisconsin were purged from graduate school because they were members of the Communist Party.

We can comprehend the power of this revolution from isolation to internationalism and from private property that blended with national interest to private property that blended with international capitalism by observing the career of Richard Hofstadter (1916–1970). Hofstadter began graduate school at Columbia University in 1938. His adviser was Merle Curti, who had not yet moved to the University of Wisconsin. Hofstadter in 1938 was an admirer of the Beards' *The Rise of American Civilization,* and his dissertation, published in 1944 as *Social Darwinism in American Thought,* followed closely the patterns that the Beards had outlined for the years between the Civil War and World War I. For Hofstadter, as for the Beards, a democratic America was in existence before the Civil War. Then, like the Beards, he wrote that the chaos caused by the Civil War made it possible for bad sons, international capitalists, momentarily to gain control of the national government. Most of his book, however, focused on the conflict in the academic world in the 1880s between good and bad sons. He focused on William Graham Sumner as a representative bad son. Sumner borrowed the idea of the Englishman Herbert Spencer to justify an international capitalism whose only value was self-interest. Sumner wanted Americans to give up their commitment to a unified people who had a strong sense of public interest. They must learn that the only reality was self-interest.[23]

In contrast to Sumner, who wanted to destroy the American democratic traditions, Hofstadter pointed to another academic figure, Frank Lester Ward. Ward, for Hofstadter, was a good son who wanted to preserve the tradition of national interest. Sumner had argued that evolution proceeded through the competition of independent individuals. Ward argued that evolution proceeded through the cooperation of groups of individuals. Again following the Beards, Hofstadter argued that by the 1890s more and more academics were rejecting Sumner's use of European ideas and returning to American ideas. And the public, participating in the politics of the Progressive Movement, was removing international capitalists from their position of political power. Then, like the Beards, Hofstadter asserted that the entry of the United States into World War I had destroyed the Progressive Movement and allowed the international capitalists to regain political power.

The Beards at the end of their lives could ignore President Roosevelt's successful revolution that was destroying the legitimacy of isolation and establishing legitimacy for internationalism. But would Hofstadter and other young historians continue to share the Beards' faith that an America given birth by the national landscape was immortal? Hofstadter's second book, *The American Political Tradition and the Men Who Made It,* published in 1948, made clear that he had lost all faith in the national landscape. It also made clear how angry he was at the Beards and other teachers who had given him a totally false picture of American history. This second book, then, constituted a savage attack on the pattern he had presented in his first book. There is no conflict between good democratic sons and bad international-capitalist sons. We must, he declared, tear the democratic masks off Jefferson, Jackson, Lincoln, Theodore Roosevelt, Wilson, and Franklin Delano Roosevelt. When we do that we will see that all of these men were capitalists. There has never been a democratic America. There has only been a capitalist America.[24]

Hofstadter in this second book was on the verge of saying that only Karl Marx's thesis of industrialism and the proletariat could defeat capitalism and complete the exodus into a new world of permanent harmony and plentitude. But if he wrote such a book he would never have an academic career. He was aware that Marxism by 1950 was defined as dangerously un-American.

His third book, *The Age of Reform,* published in 1955, made him a public intellectual. Many of our generation of young postwar historians were enthusiastic about Hofstadter's criticism of the Populist and Progressive reform movements. He helped us understand how Populists and Progressives defined the American people as white Anglo-Saxon Protestants. Many of us were trying to free ourselves from an exclusive definition of the American people and embrace an inclusive definition. When I joined the history department at the University of Minnesota in 1952, all of the faculty and graduate students were descendants of Northern European Protestants. As an undergraduate at Princeton, I had Eric Goldman for an adviser. He made me aware that coming into the 1940s there was a gentleman's agreement in higher education that no profane Jew would be allowed to teach the sacred history of the United States. By the mid-1940s Princeton, Yale, and Harvard had broken the taboo in order to disassociate themselves from the Holocaust in Nazi Germany. This had been the context for Goldman's coming to Princeton. At the University of Minnesota the first Jew to teach American history, Hyman Berman, was hired in 1961.

In *The Age of Reform* Hofstadter disassociated Franklin D. Roosevelt's New Deal in the 1930s from Populism and Progressivism. Roosevelt for the first time in American history was leading a reform movement that was self-consciously pluralistic. Roosevelt had worked to make Jews and Catholics feel they were valued members of the Democratic Party. Hofstadter also echoed the influential Protestant theologian Reinhold Niebuhr when he celebrated the pragmatism of the New Deal.[25]

Niebuhr as a young man had participated in the millennial expectations for World War I. After the failure of his dream he then directed his theology toward a critique of several utopian traditions in America. His book *The Irony of American History,* published in 1952, was a synthesis of these criticisms.[26] Like Niebuhr, Hofstadter now declared that there would be no end of history as the Populists and Progressives had believed. Because Populists and Progressives believed that a timeless agrarian utopia had been achieved in the early nineteenth century, these reformers saw change as unnatural. They developed a paranoid style of politics in which they saw change caused by the conspiracy of evil men.

Hofstadter quickly followed *The Age of Reform* with two books, *Anti-intellectualism in American Life* (1963) and *The Progressive Historians* (1966), that continued his attack on Anglo-Protestant culture for its futile but destructive attempts to escape time. And he explicitly linked Turner and Beard to this utopian dream that time had stopped in early nineteenth-century America. These men had denied conflict and insisted that reality was a single state of nature.[27]

Hofstadter's position in *The Age of Reform, Anti-intellectualism in American Life,* and *The Progressive Historians,* therefore, was that there was no usable American past before the New Deal. But in his last two books before his death from leukemia, he dramatically reversed this position. His new thesis in *The Idea of a Party System* (1970) and *America in 1750* (1970) again was similar to that proposed in Niebuhr's *The Irony of American History.* Niebuhr had argued that although Americans imagined the possibility of reaching utopia, their political life was, nevertheless, realistic. They acted as if the world was complex and that politics, therefore, must be based on compromise.

Now Hofstadter in *The Idea of a Party System* declared that the United States was the first nation to accept the legitimacy of two parties. It was the first nation where one party could peacefully replace the other party. The old world, Europe, produced utopian visions. But the new world, America, produced the realistic practice of compromise. Europeans dreamed of a single homogeneous people. America recognized that the world was always pluralistic. In his *America in 1750,* he celebrated the pluralism of the English colonies. The variety of Protestant denominations, he wrote, encouraged the colonists to accept pluralism as normal. The colonists also accepted the reality of pluralism because they were capitalists. The dynamism of capitalism undermined every status quo. All of American history since the landing of the first English settlers, therefore, was a usable past.[28]

Hofstadter, therefore, saw no ideology at work when the English settlers divided their new white civilized world from the old barbaric world of red savages. He, like Bancroft, Turner, and the Beards, saw no power used by the English settlers to bring kidnapped Africans to the new world and to establish a system of slavery that denied the humanity of these Africans. Like these historians, he saw no ideology involved in the Anglo-American definition of someone who looked white as someone who was really black because that person supposedly was stained by one invisible drop of black blood. Growing up near Princeton, New Jersey, I was initiated into this pattern of white racism. It seemed natural that the town had both a white and a black public elementary school and that the high school was characterized by informal but strict patterns of segregation. Nevertheless, when I went from high school to the army at the beginning of July 1943, I was surprised by the racial patterns of my first army camp near Tyler, Texas. A high fence separated white and black soldiers, and we white soldiers were told that when we went into town we should not fraternize with the black soldiers. But there were German prisoners of war in our white camp, and we were encouraged to fraternize with our white enemies. The restaurants in Tyler refused to serve blacks. Our white officers, however, took German officers into town on weekends to dine in these segregated restaurants. It was not until the 1950s, however, that I began to see the relationship between white racism and the economic exploitation of the slaves and then, after emancipation, the continued exploitation of the former slaves.

In 1977 a younger colleague, Peter Carroll, and I published an overview of American history, *The Free and the Unfree*. It implicitly denied that European American history was the story of liberty. When one looked at the relationship of white Americans to red, black, brown, and yellow Americans, one saw the stark use of power by white Americans against these Americans of color.[29]

My intellectual journey led me, therefore, to see that history as the story of liberty depended on the constant use of magical rhetoric and writing that obscured the use of power. In this journey I learned much from William Appleman Williams (1921–1990), my fellow graduate student at Wisconsin. In his dissertation, published as *American-Russian Relations* (1952), and in *The Tragedy of American Diplomacy* (1959), Williams was on a mission to convert his colleagues from their false belief that America had been an isolated nation until World War II. He had implicitly lost faith in the national landscape and in the pattern of Bourgeois Nationalism that insisted that each bourgeois nation was autonomous. He appealed to his generation of young historians to see what Bancroft, Turner, Charles and Mary Beard, and Hofstadter had not seen. They must see the overwhelming evidence that the United States had constant economic, intellectual, and political interrelationships with the rest of the world. Diplomatic history, ignored by the most influential historians of the past, must no longer be ignored. Williams, therefore, helped me imagine that I could and should write about America in a transnational context.[30]

In also moving away from the Bourgeois Nationalist commitment to the modern dichotomy between a rational universal and irrational particulars, Williams was imagining a pluralistic world in which particulars were neither rational nor irrational. Particulars, for him, were what humans experienced. In *The Tragedy of American Diplomacy* he argued that Americans had the false hope that their particular form of democracy was destined to be the universal model for everyone in the world. And so they tried but failed to make the world in 1917 safe for their democracy. When they continued after 1918 to export their democracy, they continued to fail. In losing faith in the national landscape and the democracy to which it supposedly gave birth, Williams, as had Hofstadter in his *The American Political Tradition*, suddenly saw an America in which capitalism brought from Europe was always the dominant culture. Williams's next book, *The Contours of American History* (1961), agreed with Hofstadter's book of the late 1940s that all our presidents had been capitalists. In *The Tragedy of American Diplomacy* he had seen the political choice in the 1890s to expand overseas as a novel experience. But now he saw expansion as the nature of capitalism. It was capitalist expansion that brought Europeans to America. It was capitalism that had driven the expansion of European Americans from the Atlantic to the Pacific. And Williams, unlike Hofstadter, saw the power involved in the conquest of the homes of the Native Americans and now also saw the power used to develop the institution of slavery. He could no longer see the 1890s as an unprecedented decade of expansion. He no longer could ignore how white Americans had gone to war against brown Mexicans in 1846 with the explicit purpose of making the northwestern half of Mexico part of the United States. President Polk wanted the Mexican port cities of San Diego and San Francisco to give us windows on the Pacific.[31]

Hofstadter in *The Progressive Historians* had attacked Turner and Beard for their belief in a nineteenth-century agrarian utopia. Now Williams criticized the commitment of Turner and Beard to a metaphor of two worlds. For Williams in 1960 there was a modern capitalist world spreading out from Europe since the Renaissance. Progressives, like Beard and Dewey, Williams wrote, had underestimated the power of capitalism because they believed in an exceptional America. There was no usable American anticapitalist critique, Williams continued, because of this false tradition of American uniqueness. Those of us who were critics of capitalism in the 1960s must, therefore, look to the writings of Karl Marx. Beard and Dewey had said that Marx's belief in a universal capitalist history was wrong. But if we want to understand the United States in the 1960s, Williams warned, we must take Marx seriously.

This was the message of his book *The Great Evasion* (1964). Marx was correct that all capitalist nations practiced imperialistic foreign policies. He was correct that capitalism promised prosperity but created misery. We must look beyond our national prosperity, Williams declared, to see increasing poverty throughout the world. Marx was correct that capitalism created alienation. Look at the statistics, William said, that indicate that only half of eligible Americans vote. Look, he continued, at the many expressions of alienation in the culture of young Americans.[32]

In *The Great Evasion* he had seen Marx's commitment to community and critique of selfish individualism as comparable to that of the first Christian congregations. But Williams soon changed his mind about Marxism as a usable alternative to capitalism. Capitalists said that a community of interdependent individuals cannot create an economy of perpetually increasing prosperity. But to control the resources necessary for perpetual growth, capitalists have to create larger and larger private and government bureaucracies. The competition of these national bureaucracies with other national bureaucracies has led to ever more destructive wars, such as World War I and World War II. If modern people continue this competition, they will engage in a self-destructive nuclear war.

But Marx does not offer a usable alternative to capitalism, Williams now declared, because he believed that one can have both community and economic growth. The result, according to Williams, was a Soviet Union of vast political and military bureaucracy. If modern people, capitalists and communists, are to avoid a suicidal nuclear war, Williams preached, they must give up their dream of perpetual growth. They must accept limits. In accepting limits they will be able to re-create the bonds of community that existed before the emergence of a modern world, capitalist and communist, that refuses to accept limits.

In his next two books, *Some Presidents: Wilson to Nixon* (1972) and *America Confronts a Revolutionary World* (1976), Williams hoped to persuade his readers that limits and particulars are the reality of the planet they inhabit. In his book on the presidents he pointed out that the United States was too large and too diverse to be governed effectively by a single political leader. Since, for Williams, the bourgeois nation was no longer immortal, he could imagine a movement to create a number of smaller political communities within what had been the political boundaries of the United States. Only in a decentralized world, Williams declared, could modern people escape their alienation and achieve fulfillment as interdependent members of small communities. In *America Confronts a Revolutionary World* he repeated his message that diversity is the nature of the world. The American foreign policy that tries to force this diversity into the American model is, therefore, unrealistic and will always fail.[33]

When Hofstadter and Williams lost their faith in the national landscape as a timeless space, they both moved away from the state-of-nature anthropology that informed the writings of Bancroft, Turner, and Beard. They both moved toward cultural anthropology. Hofstadter, however, by the end of his life in 1970, insisted that American culture minimized the role of imagination. For him, a timeful American culture had a realistic relation to a pluralistic world. But Williams went into the 1970s certain that capitalists and communists were participants in a modern culture committed to the unrealistic and self-destructive expectation of endless economic growth. If modern people throughout the world were initiated into such a powerful cultural imagination, how could a single historian such as Williams persuade them that the illusions of their culture were carrying them toward a catastrophe? How could he persuade Americans that their lifestyle as consumers would lead their children and grandchildren to death and destruction? Who could persuade consumers that they should give up dreams of ever-greater affluence to follow the more spiritual way of life expressed in the first Christian congregations and also in the Native American communities? This was Williams's lament in his final two books, *Americans in a Changing World* (1970) and *Empire as a Way of Life* (1980). But he continued to tell his students until his death in 1990 that democracy could exist only in small communities. Hierarchy, bureaucracy, and alienation, he insisted, characterize all larger societies.[34]

All across the modern world in the early nineteenth century, historians had played a major role in creating the vision of a universal national. Now in the 1940s and 1950s my generation began to write obituaries for our national landscape. My book *Historians against History* was published in 1965, and my *The Eternal Adam and the New World Garden* appeared in 1968. Hofstadter and Williams were merely particularly strong voices, therefore, as many of us moved from state-of-nature anthropology to cultural anthropology. During the twenty years from the 1940s to the 1960s most historians had rejected the possibility of individuals living outside culture.

From the perspective of cultural anthropology, the Northern male Anglo-Protestant culture that dominated the writing of history from 1789 into the 1950s was as artful as the American cultures that it had refused to recognize—those of women, Native Americans, African Americans, Mexican Americans, Asian Americans, Catholics, and Jews, as well as those of gay, lesbian, and transgender Americans. Much of the energy of professional historians from the 1960s to the present has gone into the recovery of those repressed histories. With this strong commitment to pluralism, it has been difficult for many historians to take seriously the way in which economists since the 1940s have replaced the universal national of the natural landscape with the universal universal of a global marketplace. This vision of a utopian future leading to another prophecy that history is about to end is the subject of the next chapter.

Those historians who have observed the prophecy have been critical of it. Some, like Christopher Lasch in *The Culture of Narcissism* (1979), have built on Williams's jeremiad against the consumer culture. In this jeremiad the insatiable demands of individuals create an imperial foreign policy. Power has to be used to guarantee that resources from around the world will flow into the American marketplace. The warning of these historians is that if Americans do not accept limits, they will drive the nation into bankruptcy and into resource wars. From the 1980s to the present one historian after another has warned against our imperial foreign policy and the militarization of our society. The most recent historian continuing the Williams tradition is Andrew Bacevich. Since receiving his Ph.D. after retiring from the U.S. Army as a colonel, he has published, at a furious pace, several books that echo Williams's jeremiad. These are *American Empire: The Reality and Consequences of U.S. Diplomacy* (2002), *The New American Militarism: How Americans Are Seduced by War* (2005), *The Limits of Power: The End of American Exceptionalism* (2008), and *Washington Rules: America's Path to Permanent War* (2010), in addition to his edited volumes *The Imperial Tense: Prospects and Problems of American Empire* (2003), and *The Long War: A New History of U.S. National Security Policy since World War II* (2007).[35]

In *Washington Rules,* Bacevich uses the writings of Reinhold Niebuhr as the foundation for his jeremiad. Niebuhr insisted that while divinity is unlimited, humanity is limited. Williams also participated in this theological tradition. Bacevich presents a United States that from 1945 to 1965 produced more goods than most of the world's other nations combined. We were an economic powerhouse. We exported much more than we imported. The United States was a creditor nation loaning more money abroad than we borrowed. But, as Bacevich points out, by 2008 this position had been reversed. We are today deeply in debt to the Chinese government. We import much more, especially from China, than we export. China is about to replace us as the leading manufacturing country. We have become a debtor nation. Bacevich's discussion of the end of the United States' position as a superpower is similar to that of several of his contemporaries. The most recent of these analyses is *The End of the American Century* (2009), by David Mason. Younger historians also continue to preach that pride goeth before a fall. This is the message of Peter Beinart's *The Icarus Syndrome: A History of American Hubris* (2010).[36]

Why this rapid reversal? For Bacevich, as for Niebuhr, the answer is pride. We have refused to recognize that there are limits to our power as we also refuse to recognize that there are limits on individual consumption. We have acted as if we were given limitless power to reshape the world in our image. We have acted as if individuals can perpetually increase their consumption of goods. But in building a military strong enough to dominate the world, we as a nation are living beyond our means, as are individuals within our nation. Writing before the economic collapse of 2007 and 2008, Bacevich warned against the willingness of individual consumers to go into debt to sustain the illusion that they had no limits. He warned against the willingness of the government, especially the administrations of Ronald Reagan and George W. Bush, to go into debt to sustain the illusion that the power of the United States is limitless.

For Bacevich the subtitle of his book *The Limits of Power: The End of American Exceptionalism* means that economically we are now one nation among other nations. We can be compared to other nations. We are not extrahuman. We are not a semidivine nation. His subtitle is also something like a prayer. Bacevich desperately hopes his book will help persuade Americans that they are limited human beings. He hopes that they will swallow their pride. And, like Niebuhr and Williams, he warns that unchecked pride will lead to national self-destruction. Perhaps because as an undergraduate I did not believe in an exodus from a limited old world to an unlimited new world, I discovered Niebuhr in the late 1940s. In this sequence of prophecies of a limited future—Niebuhr, Williams, and Bacevich—I am able to relate to both Williams and Bacevich.

But unlike Niebuhr, Williams, and Bacevich, I have come to inter-relate human and cultural limits with limits in nature. A small number of historians have become aware that current scientists do not accept Newton's vision of the universe as a timeless space. Nature is time-ful as culture is timeful. Over the past several decades this minority of historians has been creating a new field of research, writing, and teaching in history departments in environmental history. Courses in this new field explain how timeful cultures interrelate with their time-ful environments.

One of the most influential leaders in the creation of this new field is Donald Worster, author of *Nature's Economy: A History of Ecological Ideas* (1977) and *The Wealth of Nature: Environmental History and the Ecological Imagination* (1993). Following Worster's lead, Ted Steinberg has written *Down to Earth: Nature's Role in American History* (2002).[37]

My emphasis in this book on the antigenerational outlook of the modern middle classes owes much to the scholarship of Carolyn Merchant, another leader in the development of this new field. She is a past president of the American Society for Environmental History and the editor of *Major Problems in American Environmental History* (1993) and *Key Concepts in Critical Theory: Ecology* (1994).

Merchant's graduate training was in the history of science. More than most historians, therefore, she is aware that current scientists have replaced Newton's vision of a timeless universe with a vision of a timeful universe. Her book *The Death of Nature: Women, Ecology, and the Scientific Revolution* (1980) focused on the way in which the new science of the Renaissance leading toward Newton's synthesis at-tacked the belief of medieval Europeans that nature was a living body. Although scientists in the late twentieth century had come to agree with medieval Europeans on that point, her book was nevertheless heretical. Most Americans continue to see the Renaissance as a mo-ment when medieval superstitions were replaced by modern rationality, but here was Merchant lamenting the victory of the modern middle classes. The shocking implication of her book was that medieval Europeans understood nature while modern Europeans did not. She was also critical of the modern worldview as one that implicitly denied the existence of women. In the metaphor of leaving a limited cultural home for an unlimited natural frontier, self-made men left women behind in their irrelevant homes. Merchant continued to contradict the orthodox narrative of how modern Europeans brought rationality to the entire world in *Ecological Revolutions: Nature, Gender, and Science in New England* (1989). As the attempted murder of a living feminine nature by Renaissance men was a tragedy, so the bringing of that modern belief in a lifeless nature to the new world also was a tragedy. Merchant, the heretic, supported the Native American belief in a living nature as she had supported the medieval view.[38]

She continued to define herself as a heretic in her book *Radical Ecology: The Search for a Livable World* (1992). The modern world constructed and dominated by males was, for her, not livable. As one of the first generation of women to have a leadership role in the academic world, Merchant was aware of how this part of the modern world also had repressed the existence of women. Niebuhr, Williams, and Bacevich all wrote as if women do not matter. Initiated as I was into the male-dominated academic culture, it is not surprising that my first three books also assumed an all-male world. Merchant made her feminist position very clear in her book *Earthcare: Women and the Environment* (1996).[39]

In her book *Reinventing Eden: The Fate of Nature in Western Culture* (2003), she continued her analysis of how we moderns have denied the timefulness of a living nature. She especially focused on how European Americans created the myth that America was a new Eden. Here they had supposedly escaped the cycle of birth, death, and rebirth. In this new Eden, as in Newton's imagined rational universe, they would have no responsibility to care for their environment because it was timeless. They had no responsibility to be conservationists for their utopian space. Merchant, a believer in limits, is also writing jeremiads, but she is reminding her readers that the preservation of the earth as a home for humans must depend on women as well as on men. In a future economy based on sustainability rather than perpetual growth, it will be essential that men and women cooperate.[40]

In *Radical Ecology* Merchant was bitterly critical of the academic economists who are the subject of my next chapter. They, in her analysis, continued to celebrate the death of nature. For the economists of her generation, a lifeless nature presented a timeless foundation for a marketplace that enjoyed perpetual equilibrium. In the next chapter I will discuss how economists after the 1940s have, therefore, taken on the intellectual burden shouldered by historians in 1830, when they defined an American national landscape as a timeless space. That burden was to explain away their experience with timeful change. For economists after World War II, the global marketplace had replaced the national landscape as the authentic timeless space. Now economists have the burden of explaining away their experience with timeful change.

When I try to understand why it was possible for political, cultural, and economic leaders in many countries to move so quickly from the orthodoxy of Bourgeois Nationalism in the 1930s to the orthodoxy of Bourgeois Internationalism after 1945, I remember how Bourgeois Nationalism was created simultaneously in a number of modern nations. Paradoxically, Bourgeois Nationalism was an expression of an international bourgeois culture. From the 1800s to the 1930s this culture defined hair and clothing styles for the middle classes. It defined furniture and architecture styles as well as styles in painting and music. Symphony orchestras and modern universities were constructed about the same time in many nations. The patterns of dealing with sewage, trash, water, heat, transportation, and public safety were similar in the rapidly growing cities of nineteenth-century Europe and North America. This transnational middle-class culture also created professions. Doctors and lawyers no longer would be trained as apprentices. Now, in the late nineteenth century, they would have two levels of formal education and pass standardized examinations. There, of course, has always been the exchange of raw material and manufactured goods among the modern nations from the 1830s to the 1930s. Bourgeois Nationalism obscured this transnational complexity. Since 1945, however, Bourgeois Internationalism has obscured the continued importance of national boundaries and national politics. Bourgeois Internationalists, like Bourgeois Nationalists, have tried to transcend complexity. Both groups have hoped to find a simple, uniform world. Both have failed.

3 ECONOMISTS DISCOVER A NEW NEW WORLD

SACVAN BERCOVITCH, in his *The American Jeremiad* (1978), argued that the first English settlers coming to North America believed they had received a promise from the Divinity. They were promised that they were entering a land of timeless harmony. When they quickly experienced timeful change, they lamented that this was a sinful declension from the perfect world given them by the Divinity. They searched for scapegoats on whom they could blame the declension. Bercovitch declared that this pattern became secularized and was used by successive generations of European Americans to define America as a nation blessed by timeless harmony. Then always experiencing declension into timeful disharmony, they made prophecies that if scapegoats were purged the promise of an earthly heaven would be restored. I have described how Charles and Mary Beard used such a pattern in their *The Rise of American Civilization*. Good American sons, for the Beards, wanted to conserve their exceptional, timeless nation. Bad un-American sons committed to international capitalism wanted to end America's isolation from the timeful chaos of other nations. But the Beards could prophesy that when the evil men creating a declension into time were defeated, then the American promise would be restored.[1]

In this chapter, where I discuss academic economists, I will argue that most American economists from the 1880s to the 1940s defined their nation in terms very similar to those used by the Beards. They too assumed that the American nation was a timeless space with perpetual equilibrium. They too assumed this equilibrium was not shared by other nations, which continued to experience timeful instability. They too saw a few Americans becoming un-American when they gave their loyalty to international capitalism. These bad sons were prepared to lead their country out of the promise of endless harmony into the declension of timeful disharmony. Until the 1940s, most economists saw themselves fighting to defeat bad sons who had become international capitalists and to restore the promise of a uniquely stable America.[2]

Then in the 1940s economists were caught up in a revolution. National leaders managed to redefine the supposed isolation of the United States as un-American and internationalism as American. Indeed, the United States had suddenly become the political and economic center of international capitalism locked in mortal combat with international communism. In this revolution the promise of a timeless space where humans could live in perpetual harmony shifted from the nation to the global marketplace. And the members of the dominant nationalist school of economics abruptly found they had lost their status as good American sons. Overnight they had become bad un-American fathers. A younger generation of economists in the 1940s who embraced the global marketplace declared that their teachers, their academic fathers, in the 1930s were attacking the promise of a universal and timeless economic space. Their bad fathers were causing a declension into time because they seduced people into accepting the artful, timeful role of national politics in the artless, timeless global marketplace. But the good international sons would end the declension and restore the promise by purging the bad nationalist fathers.[3]

This is the story I will tell in this chapter. But, of course, the story of the jeremiad described by Bercovitch seems to be a never-ending one. The revolutionary sons of the 1940s became academic fathers. Today are we seeing, therefore, another generation of rebellious academic sons who reject the free-market capitalism of their teachers? Are they saying something similar to what their grandfathers had said? Are they saying that a laissez-faire policy leads to instability and a declension into timeful chaos? Are they contradicting their academic fathers by making a prophecy that action by the national government can end the declension and restore the promise of perpetual prosperity?

First, however, I will discuss how difficult it was for me and other historians of my generation to comprehend this revolutionary conflict in departments of economics. When we historians accepted that humans are always within culture, it was difficult for us to know whether our colleagues in other departments were experiencing similar conversions. In the late nineteenth century academics redefined themselves as professionals, and they created powerful boundaries between the disciplines. For example, if one were a political scientist, one was judged by other political scientists. A political scientist could lose his professional identity if his colleagues identified him as really a sociologist, an anthropologist, or a historian. Dwelling intellectually within these closely guarded departmental borders, most of us in my generation of historians, therefore, did not know if colleagues in other departments shared our new understanding of the world.

Along with most of my fellow historians at Minnesota as well as colleagues in the English department with whom I worked in the American Studies Program, I had no idea then that a dramatically different paradigm revolution was taking place within the discipline of economics. It was not until I was writing my book *Death of a Nation* in the 1990s that I was able to make comparisons among varieties of academic disciplines. It was then that I became aware of how differently academic economists and historians had reacted to the death of the national landscape.

When modern universities began to be created in several German states in the early nineteenth century, it was necessary for these academics to establish a profound separation between the physical sciences and the humanities and social sciences. These universities were becoming the intellectual and spiritual centers of each new bourgeois nation. It was the responsibility of the humanists and social scientists to demonstrate how their particular nation was an autonomous and uniform cultural unit. French, German, English, Swedish, or American scholars were committed to the celebration of their universal national. These scholars, therefore, tried not to think about the physical sciences. It would be scandalous if it were brought to public attention that the physical scientists remained committed to the Enlightenment belief in a universal universal. It was best, then, if the closet door were kept shut so that one did not see the profound philosophical division within the university. Academic humanists and social scientists would pretend that the physical sciences were not part of the university. How could one be proud to be a participant in a superior modern civilization if it were based on two incompatible truths—the universal national and the universal universal?[4]

This is the context, then, that helps explain why most economists, in contrast to historians, had a positive response to the death of the national landscape. Historians had played a crucial role in establishing the vision of a universal national for their particular nations. Most of us historians, therefore, shared the confusion of Hofstadter and Williams as we lost our faith in an American universal national and saw no clear alternative. The overwhelming majority of economists in all the modern nations, like historians, had focused on their particular nations. They rejected Marx's claim that there was a transnational economy. Most assumed that private property should work within the national interest. This is why most economists in the bourgeois nations rejected international capitalism as well as international communism. But now in the 1940s economists were told that Americans should embrace a new sacred—the international marketplace. They should produce scholarship that would demonstrate how their nation's economy had transcended national political boundaries. They should recognize that the international marketplace is the only universal.

Academic economists in the 1940s, therefore, were in a position to become leaders in moving public economic analysis away from a dying universal national to a supposedly perpetually youthful universal universal. Academic economists were experiencing a momentous conversion. The public face of national universities had been the social sciences and humanities. The physical sciences had been the hidden face. But if the economy was now to represent a universal universal, the public face of universities should be the physical sciences. And economics as an academic discipline should be considered a physical science. Dramatically, then, in the 1940s many economists began to imagine that their discipline was very similar to physics. They wanted to be segregated from the other social sciences.[5]

But because most economists, like other social scientists and humanists, had ignored the physical sciences since the 1840s, they were not aware that a paradigm revolution had occurred in physics by the late nineteenth century. The physics of Newton had defined space as timeless. Atoms, the essential building blocks of the universe, were, for Newton, immutable. This was the new world that, for the Enlightenment, offered an alternative to timeful and ephemeral cultural patterns. What young economists sensed in the 1940s, therefore, was that national economies were not the end of history. The modern nation did not represent a particular state of nature. Alone among all the academic disciplines, whether they were social or physical sciences, economists saw themselves in a position to lead the exodus out of an old timeful, ephemeral world of national economies to the new timeless, eternal world of the international marketplace. Economists would be the most important prophets of this impending end of history. How wonderful it was to know that the fears of Plato and Machiavelli finally had become irrelevant. The economists of the 1940s knew a universal universal existed beyond particular nations. Humankind had not been able to reach that Promised Land because of continuing political divisions. Irrational political particulars had blocked the exodus into the harmony of the rational universal. But now the exodus from national economies into the global marketplace was bringing humanity to a space filled with perpetual harmony and prosperity, a space free from artful politics.

With this new responsibility to be prophets of the authentic end of history, young economists between 1940 and 1960 moved the focus of economic discourse from particular national languages to the universal language of mathematics. When Bourgeois Nationalists around 1800 claimed that their nations were the end of history, they crafted a revolution in the understanding of languages. In each country there were many local languages. Now Bourgeois Nationalists claimed that these local languages were artful, irrational particulars and must be replaced by a single, uniform national language. Such a language was rational because it had grown out of the national landscape, the national state of nature.[6]

But the revolutionary economists of the 1940s and 1950s now claimed that these national languages were themselves local, artful, irrational. There was no universal national. There was only a universal universal, and mathematics was its language. As Robert Lucas remarked, "Like so many others of my cohort I internalized the view that if I couldn't formulate a problem in economic theory mathematically I didn't know what I was doing. Economic theory is mathematical analysis. Everything else is just pictures and talk." The revolutionists, however, were not able to force complete compliance to the language of mathematics until the 1960s. For example, at the end of the 1950s an internationally recognized economic historian at Minnesota, Herbert Heaton, retired. From the 1930s to the early 1950s a steady stream of graduate students from the economics department had been sent to work with him. When he retired he asked me to replace him as a nonreader on the dissertation defense of an economics graduate student. This young man was still concerned in the early 1950s with the historical context of economics, but then he had converted to the vision that the global marketplace, a timeless space, had no historical context. He wrote his dissertation, a five-foot-long mathematical formula, on the blackboard. For him and the economists on his committee, history no longer existed. I felt I was in an alien world.

I, of course, was and was not in an alien world. I was in another modern world with another metaphor of two worlds—one rational, one irrational. But in 1960 I was not able to relate my critique of the metaphor of two worlds in the writing of the American historians Bancroft, Turner, and the Beards to a transnational bourgeois culture. In 1960 I was not even able to see how a variety of academic disciplines shared definitions of time and space. It was not until the 1980s, then, that I began to see our dominant national metaphors of two worlds as part of a transnational bourgeois culture. And it was only then that I could imagine how this metaphor of two worlds was present in a variety of academic departments as it was present in a variety of middle-class nations.

I am still bemused that for so long I was unable to find a narrative that could link my experience with paradigm crises in several departments during the 1950s. Thomas Kuhn, in his *The Structure of Scientific Revolutions* (1962), wrote about the pain experienced by those who do not convert when an established paradigm is displaced by a new dominant paradigm. As a participant in the destruction of the paradigm used by the Beards in *The Rise of American Civilization,* I had little empathy for my older colleagues who continued to share the Beards' paradigm. In the early 1960s several graduate students told me that one of these older colleagues had shown them a holster and pistol on his belt. He then informed them that one day he intended to shoot David Noble. I was shocked, but at that moment I was unable to understand why he was so angry with me.[7]

In retrospect I am shocked by my insensitivity toward my elders, because I did feel empathy for colleagues my age in the philosophy and English departments who felt defeated by revolutions that replaced a focus on the national with a focus on the international. I felt I understood why they looked for positions at other universities. From this perspective one can see that the collapse of the cultural authority of the national landscape that influenced economists had profound impacts on many departments. And this crisis of belief was experienced in universities in all the modern nations.

At Wisconsin I had a double minor in American philosophy and

American literature. Then at Minnesota in the 1950s I became friends with young members of the philosophy department and the English department. Between 1950 and 1960 the authority of John Dewey in the philosophy department was replaced by the authority of logical positivism. For logical positivists, who had begun to teach in several European countries before World War I, philosophy must be concerned with the universal universal, not the universal national. And philosophy must express the universal in the language of mathematics.[8]

Postwar economists shared much with the logical positivists. They also shared much with the exponents of the international style of architecture, which used the language of mathematics. During the political revolution from isolation to internationalism in the 1940s, the nationalist architecture of Frank Lloyd Wright lost its aesthetic authority. Suddenly American architectural critics endowed the international architectural style brought to the United States by exiled European architects with aesthetic authority. This style also emphasized that the rational cannot be expressed within the boundaries of particular nations.[9]

The philosophy I had studied at Wisconsin focused on Dewey and how he related to earlier American philosophers. The professors who taught American literature at Wisconsin also emphasized its exceptionalism. And the men in the Minnesota English department who had created the American Studies Program in 1943 shared the commitment to national uniqueness expressed in the American civilization programs formed in the Ivy League universities in the 1930s. Now in the 1950s leadership in the English department at Minnesota was passing to New Literary Critics. These were professors of literature who insisted that the nationalistic form of literary criticism should be replaced with an international form. American literature, for them, was part of the literature of Western civilization and should be studied within that transnational context. Teaching in the American Studies Program as well as in the history department helped me become aware that the political and cultural revolution from our supposed isolation to internationalism was also expressed in painting. In the 1930s art critics had celebrated the paintings of Thomas Hart Benton and other American scene artists. Before World War I Benton had gone to study in Europe, but after the war he, like his friend Charles Beard, renounced his internationalism. Like the Beards in *The Rise of America Civilization,* he too would use his art to celebrate the American people and the American landscape. He took in a student, Jackson Pollock, who, for him, was like a son.

But, as Hofstadter had identified himself as a son symbolically killing his intellectual father, Charles Beard, Pollock by 1940 also saw himself engaged in patricide. The good, true, and beautiful, Pollock wrote in the 1940s, are universal. We doom ourselves to the evil, the false, and the ugly if we accept artificial national boundaries. And in order to express the universal we must transcend the boundaries of representational art and paint in an abstract style. Art critics across the country moved quickly to participate in this ideological shift from supposed isolation to internationalism. Abruptly they ended their admiration of Benton and all American scene artists and began a love affair with Pollock and other abstract expressionist artists.[10]

Perhaps it is because modern people define themselves as outside history, outside patterns of cultural change, that scholars have had great difficulty in defining the 1940s as a decade of revolutionary change. But in one department after another there is evidence of academic sons killing their intellectual fathers. If we were to focus on a major cultural change taking place in the modern world, then the modern would no longer be modern. The modern could no longer claim that it is superior to traditional societies because it, unlike them, is in harmony with a timeless universal. We would have to accept the claim of Bruno Latour that we have never been modern. But, of course, for the young economists, who in the 1940s and 1950s were killing their intellectual fathers, they were not changing culture. They were modern because they were leaving culture and moving to nature. They were not making history; they were ending history. They were engaging in the final negative revolution. It is poetic, then, that in this supposed negative revolution they were killing the historical school of economics that had been dominant among academic economists in all the modern nations until the global marketplace became a more sacred space than bourgeois national economies.[11]

German historians had provided instruction to historians in a variety of the new bourgeois nations on how they could substitute the universal national for the Enlightenment's universal universal. And this was true also in the area of economics. For scholars such as Wilhelm Roscher, Friedrich List, Karl Knies, and Albert Schäffle, the Enlightenment vision of a universal world community contradicted the reality that humans live in particular nations. These particular nations were liberating themselves from the false and evil universalism of Roman Catholicism. Uniform bodies of citizens, in contrast to the irrational fragmentation of the world of subjects, were rational. Rationality was found, therefore, not in autonomous individuals but in the will of the homogeneous people. And the laws of nature were those embodied in a particular nation. Classical economists, such as Adam Smith, believed that independent individuals deduced the abstract and universal laws of nature. In contrast, historical economists believed that individuals, as interdependent members of their nation, induced its lawful pattern from their direct experience with the nation's body.

For the economists of the German historical school, but also for historically minded economists in France, England, and the United States, competition was not between individuals. Rather, competition was between nations. Classical economists, primarily British, had demanded that artful national governments should be segregated from the transnational laws of the marketplace. Historically minded economists, however, demanded that their national governments play a critical role in helping their national economies grow. The government of a particular national people should work to increase the wealth of its citizens. Liah Greenfeld, in her book *The Spirit of Capitalism: Nationalism and Economic Growth* (2001), has argued that competition among the modern nations played a major role in causing economic expansionism.[12]

Industrialism had developed first in England. If countries like the United States or Germany were to develop industrialism, factories in those nations needed protection from the advanced English economy. Under the leadership of the first American president, George Washington, it became conventional wisdom until the 1940s that the national government would protect American manufacturers from foreign competition by establishing tariffs. If American steel cost forty dollars a ton to produce, then a tariff placed on English steel would increase its price in the United States to forty dollars a ton. This was the pattern of conventional wisdom that shattered in the 1940s when American leaders redefined the United States as the center of international capitalism. Again we should notice that this new commitment to free trade also became the established economic orthodoxy in most bourgeois nations after World War II.

Throughout the nineteenth century, German economists, like those in the United States, advised their government to subsidize the building of railroads. All historical economists saw railroads as essential to national economic growth. And all national political leaders wanted their nations to have dynamic economies. But economists in the various national historical schools also saw the need for governmental action in the economy to preserve the Bourgeois Nationalist ideal of a homogeneous people. By 1890 it was obvious that Karl Marx was correct in arguing that industrial capitalism was creating a class of dependent and impoverished factory workers. If Bourgeois Nationalists were to avoid the class warfare predicted by Marx, then they must persuade these workers that they were part of the nation, that they were part of a national people. By 1890 many German economists were urging the government to put a floor under the industrial workforce. They advocated unemployment insurance, old-age pensions, health insurance, and safety measures for factories. All of the measures made sense to the many young Americans who were going to Germany to get doctorates in economics. Programs to confer this postgraduate degree were established for many disciplines in the United States by the 1890s. In American physical sciences as well as the humanities and social sciences, German was the essential international academic language. In many of these new programs graduate students were required to become fluent in German.[13]

The American Economic Association (AEA) was created in the 1880s by young American professors who had studied in Germany. From the late nineteenth century until the 1940s most members of the AEA were concerned with the stability of the American national economy. Leaders of the AEA such as Richard Ely shared the concern of their German teachers that growing class divisions would destroy the unity of the national people. This transnational pattern of Bourgeois Nationalism shared by German and American economists assumed that each bourgeois nation as the end of history had a natural equilibrium. It was international capitalism, with its false doctrine of self-interest, that was causing national instability. Ely, then, represented a large group of American economists who hoped that the commitment of the German government to old-age pensions and unemployment insurance could be transferred to the United States. And government regulations, for them, must teach corporate leaders that national interest represented virtue while self-interest represented vice. Mona Harrington, in her book *The Dream of Deliverance in American*

Politics (1986), focuses on this powerful commitment to a natural and eternal equilibrium that, for her, characterizes the American political imagination.[14]

Ely and the other economists who shared his concern for restoring virtue and stability to the national economy vigorously advocated the development of non-Marxist labor unions. A strong labor movement would give workers a sense that they were members of the national people because they had agency. They were participating in making meaningful decisions as citizens of their country. Ely, like his contemporaries the historian Charles Beard and the philosopher John Dewey, felt he was part of a Progressive Movement that was ending the chaos caused by the self-interest of international capitalism and restoring a national unity in which private property always expressed national interest. President Theodore Roosevelt's demand for a "New Nationalism" that would restore unity to the people especially gave hope to these academic intellectuals.

Most of these economists who were participants in the Progressive Movement also shared the belief of Charles Beard, John Dewey, Thorstein Veblen, and many other academic leaders that an industrialism characterized by an ethic of rational production was not only restoring democracy in the United States but also bringing democracy to the rest of the world. Like Beard, Dewey, and Veblen, they had millennial expectations that World War I would end an old world of chaos and bring a new world of harmony. Their expectations crushed by 1919, they, like Charles Beard, turned away from internationalism. The international was not the stable space of rational production. It was the unstable space of international capitalism and its ethic of self-interest. Nevertheless, Ely and his colleagues continued to believe that this alien source of disharmony could and would be defeated in the United States. Until the intellectual revolution of the 1940s, most professional economists remained committed, therefore, to the restoration of a homogeneous national people and an economy that expressed the natural equilibrium of the nation. Ely's textbook *Outlines of Economics,* first published in 1893, retained its popularity until 1940, selling more than three hundred thousand copies.[15]

Ely's student, John R. Commons, who headed the economics department at Wisconsin in the 1920s, and Wesley Mitchell, who was influential at Columbia, no longer expected after 1920 that the unnatural influences of international capitalism would soon be purged from their beloved nation. World War I had brought a wave of anti-German hysteria into higher education. In 1918 Mitchell suggested to some of his colleagues that they disassociate themselves from the German historical school and rename themselves as the institutional school of economics. Through new organizations such as the National Bureau of Economic Research, headed by Mitchell from 1920 to 1945, economists would scientifically study their nation's institutions. Their scientific method was that of induction. They would determine which institutions worked to stabilize and which worked to destabilize the natural equilibrium of their country. They expected that their analyses would lead them to make recommendations to the national government. Representing the American people, the government would then intervene in the economy to curb the disruptive self-interest of international capitalism that led to business cycles.

When the American economy collapsed in 1929 as part of an international economic crisis, institutional economists responded by suggesting a variety of plans to the new administration of Franklin D. Roosevelt, who took office in March 1933. FDR had no personal vision of how to cope with the Great Depression and was bewildered by the often-conflicting advice given him by different institutional economists. The major accomplishments of his first administration were to save the private banking system from collapse and help large corporations regain stability. Little of this pleased institutional economists, who hoped that the dramatic economic downturn would hasten the recovery of an egalitarian democracy that they imagined had existed before the hierarchical patterns of corporations had been brought from Europe by international capitalism.

Institutionalists took heart, however, after Roosevelt's reelection in 1936. The leaders of the American Federation of Labor (AFL) had concluded by 1900 that industrial workers could not be unionized because of their cultural diversity. Recent immigrants from a variety of European countries who worked in factories and mines spoke many different languages. The AFL leaders believed that these workers could not develop the sense of solidarity necessary to confront and defeat corporate leaders. Unions were possible, therefore, only among skilled workers who did have a sense of solidarity. But by the 1930s some labor leaders believed that such solidarity was now possible among unskilled workers. They began the Congress of Industrial Organizations

(CIO) and were increasingly successful in helping factory and mine workers form unions. These new unions were becoming an important part of the Democratic Party in 1936. They, then, pushed Roosevelt to advocate old-age pensions, unemployment insurance, and the right of workers to unionize. And Congress made these recommendations into law. Most institutional economists who had urged such measures since the 1890s were, of course, delighted. From their perspective the national government was forcing private property away from the self-interest of international capitalism and returning it to the discipline of national interest. The national government was working to reconstruct a homogeneous national people that enjoyed the natural equilibrium of their national landscape.

Institutional economists became still more hopeful when the United States entered World War II in 1941. They had been disappointed with the cultural legacy of World War I. They had expected that the widespread use of national economic planning in 1917 and 1918 would remind Americans that private property should be used for national interest, but war failed to teach that lesson. Now, however, in World War II there would be much more national planning of the economy. Rationing of food and fuel, price controls and wage controls, allocation of materials for war industry, and the massive conscription of men for the military—all of these would remind citizens that private property must work for the national interest. Another major success in the subordination of self-interest to national interest was expressed in the pattern of taxes. In 1929 taxes on the rich were low, and there was a huge gap between the wealthy and the poor. But starting in the 1930s and accelerating during World War II, taxes on the rich reached unprecedented levels, and the gap between the rich and the poor narrowed dramatically.

Looking out at their America in 1945, most of the institutional economists must have been very pleased. There was a large and rapidly growing non-Marxist labor movement promising that the American people would not be divided into warring classes. High taxes had reduced the economic and political power of the rich. Social Security and unemployment insurance had put a safety net under the poor. The people had learned how effective government economic planning could be as the country experienced a miracle of production between 1941 and 1945 that made military victory over both imperial Japan and Nazi Germany possible in the short span of four years.

The nostalgic vision of Ely and other founders of the AEA in the 1890s—that the chaos caused by international capitalism could be purged from the United States and the inherent equilibrium of the nation restored—appeared from the perspective of the institutional school to have become reality. They had reached the gates of the Promised Land. But when they opened those gates, the Promised Land as they had defined it was revealed as a nightmare come to life. They saw an America in which they were aliens. They saw an America captured and controlled by international capitalists. And their bad academic sons were working to destroy the nation's borders. They were blending the sacred nation into a profane world. The bad sons insisted that the future of the United States was to spread international capitalism to the entire world. So when the institutionalists opened the gates to the Promised Land, they found that the graduate students they trained had created a grotesque new world. And these former students were prepared to use any available weapon to symbolically slay their institutional fathers.[16]

These patricidal sons shouted at their institutional fathers, You are not scientists. Scientists do not induce reality from concrete particulars. Scientists deduce reality from abstract universals. You are not rational because the particular nation to which you are loyal is an irrational particular. We modern sons must become free from you traditional fathers. As artful unmodern people you may not enter and pollute the Promised Land of the pure and rational global marketplace. The most influential of the young revolutionists was Milton Friedman. He was committed to making the Department of Economics at the University of Chicago the most important leader in the purification of the marketplace.

We must, Friedman declared, teach all economists and the American public that the marketplace is a space of perfect equilibrium. In this timeless space production and consumption are always in balance. Wages and profits also are in perpetual balance. Why, then, did we experience an economic crisis in 1929? For Friedman the answer suggested the wages of sin. American politicians had brought the government into the marketplace. The marketplace, of course, was artless, the equivalent of being heaven on earth. The market was not created by humans. It was a gift to them. But government was artful. It was a human creation. It was frightening to think of human beings so prideful that they imagined they could improve on the marketplace that they had inherited.

So for Friedman human pridefulness had caused politicians to bring their ephemeral artfulness into the eternal marketplace. This had disturbed its natural equilibrium. Human modification of what had been given them was the cause of all economic crises. Institutional economists, therefore, were false prophets. If people followed these secular sinners, they would be led out of their secular Eden into a fallen world of chaos. But it was not too late for people to turn back and recover that perpetual order with which they had been endowed. First, according to Friedman, the false prophets, the institutional economists, must be discredited. When these preachers of economic untruths were silenced, then the economists who were truth givers could begin to lead the public back to the timeless orthodoxy of free-market capitalism.[17]

When Friedman and many of his cohort came to doubt the teachings of their institutional fathers, they discovered that the truths of Adam Smith and the Enlightenment had been kept alive in the nineteenth century. A few men who had been marginalized by the dominant historical school had preached the truth that there were no autonomous national economies that could be kept in equilibrium by government actions. William Jevons (1835–82), Carl Menger (1840–1921), and Léon Walras (1834–1911) were three martyrs who had guarded the light during this second Dark Age. Now when it was revealed to Friedman's generation that nations were not the end of history, they could go to these classical economists to find a usable past. To dramatize the yawning chasm between themselves and their institutional school fathers, the young economists became known as the neoclassical school.

The most powerful false prophet whose reputation they had to destroy was the English economist John Maynard Keynes. In the 1930s, Keynes had declared that laissez-faire as an economic philosophy was dead. A philosophical position that denied a constructive role for the government in the economy could not survive the worldwide Great Depression that began in 1929. For Keynes a perfect equilibrium did not exist in the capitalist marketplace. Periodically there was more production than consumption. Periodically, therefore, government funds must be used to increase consumption. The debt governments acquired through this necessary moment of deficit spending would be eliminated in the future because the restoration of economic growth would enlarge the tax base.[18]

Friedman declared Keynes to be a dangerous heretic. According to Friedman, there is no structural disequilibrium in the capitalist marketplace as Keynes claimed. The crisis of 1929 and all other crises have been caused by the long destructive history of artful government intervention in the marketplace. Purge all of these threats to the purity of the marketplace, Friedman declared, and we will have a future of perpetual stability and prosperity. If we all become market fundamentalists, we can reach the end of history. Throughout the 1960s and 1970s most economists agreed with Friedman that the blending of national economies into a universal international marketplace would bring endless prosperity. The brief, abnormal winter of the Great Depression was giving way to that perpetual spring anticipated by the middle classes since they had escaped Plato's cave.

The dramatic weakening of the aesthetic authority of Bourgeois Nationalism in the 1940s and 1950s had made it possible for social scientists in many academic fields to escape an either/or choice—either study the autonomous nation or use the teachings of Karl Marx to study an international industrial space in which the proletariat would defeat the bourgeoisie. Now middle-class social scientists could study a universal urban-industrial space in which the bourgeoisie would be victorious over their communist enemies. They could shift their academic focus from national middle-class patterns to modern international middle-class patterns.

The context of a cold war between an international communism and an international capitalism was one, therefore, in which modernization theory became important to American sociologists, political scientists, anthropologists, and economists. The U.S. government provided funding for a group of social scientists at the Massachusetts Institute of Technology (MIT) to create scholarly predictions about an inevitable American victory. This was the Center for International Studies (CIS).[19]

Transcending the American Bourgeois Nationalist dualism between an American new world and a European old world, Daniel Lerner, an anthropologist in the MIT group, published his *The Passing of Traditional Society* in 1958. For Lerner all the nations of Western Europe and the United States were modern. The rest of the world was still traditional but destined to become modern. Walt Rostow, an economist in the group, agreed with Lerner in his book *The Stages of Economic Growth* (1960). But he went beyond Lerner when he explained how traditional societies were destined to become modern. He argued that all humans are part of an inevitable evolutionary process taking them from the cultural instability and economic scarcity of primitive agricultural societies to the cultural stability and economic plenty of current urban-industrial societies. Rostow theorized that there are five stages in this evolutionary process, culminating in the final stage of high consumption. So far, as of the 1950s, only the United States had reached this end of history. But the Western European countries were close to this final stage of high consumption, and slowly all countries in the world would converge on this universal and ultimate human experience.[20]

Rostow and his colleagues saw no irony in defining a world of high consumption as evidence of the successful exodus of humans from an irrational traditional world to a rational modern one. After all, they were repeating the magic used by Plato and his cohort of urban middle-class Greek men when they persuaded their audience and themselves that their new world combined the plenitude of abstract philosophy with the plenitude of the concrete marketplace. The endless spring envisioned by the urban middle-class Greek men of antiquity continued to make common sense to the social scientists of the 1960s. Rostow explained that modern people had endless economic plenty because they exploited nature in a rational fashion, in contrast to traditional people, who lived in economic scarcity because their approach to nature was irrational.[21]

Rostow worried, however, that in the evolutionary passage from lower stages to higher ones it was possible for "adolescent" primitive peoples to lose their way. Communism, he declared, was the most dangerous "disease" that might tempt "adolescent" peoples to try a shortcut from the traditional to the modern. But he warned that peoples who became "infected" with Marxism were doomed to live forever at a lower stage of evolution. In order to save traditional peoples from such a future of perpetual darkness, we must, Rostow insisted, be prepared to use military power everywhere in the world to "quarantine" the communist disease. In the 1960s Rostow became a national security adviser to President Johnson and always voted to increase the level of troops in Vietnam in order to minimize the danger of the communist "virus" in that developing country.[22]

Rostow's belief that evolution guaranteed the inevitable victory of international capitalism over international communism was a variation on the narrative used by the academic intellectuals of the Progressive Era. In 1890 Turner had proclaimed the death of the national landscape. The United States was no longer a timeless space segregated from a timeful world. The nation had fallen back into the flux of history. But men like Charles Beard, John Dewey, and Thorstein Veblen had contradicted Turner. The United States and the rest of the world were within a universal evolutionary nature that was taking humanity to the end of history, a worldwide industrial democracy. They wanted the United States to participate in World War I because the defeat of a reactionary Germany would speed the exodus into this Promised Land.

With the failure of that prophecy in 1918, Charles Beard and many other Progressives returned to the belief in an exceptional American state of nature. This timeless space was unique in a world of timeful cultures. Evolution disappeared from the histories written by Charles and Mary Beard between World War I and World War II. In 1941 international capitalism, for the Beards and other artists and intellectuals, represented timeful culture and threatened to corrupt a timeless American space. Now Rostow and the group of social scientists committed to modernization theory had rejected Turner in the 1890s. A timeless United States was not threatened by timeful international capitalism because capitalism represented the natural laws of evolution. A dynamic nature was taking humanity from a timeful, irrational national economy to a timeless, rational international economy.[23]

Arturo Escobar, in his *Encountering Development: The Making and Unmaking of the Third World* (1994), has demystified the bourgeois magic that creates the illusion of negative revolution. Supposedly international capitalism is liberating people in "underdeveloped" countries from bondage to irrational economic patterns. But Escobar sees development theory as a positive revolution. Modern people will use cultural, political, economic, and military power to force "backward" people to become modern and participate in the freedom of market economics. Traditional people cannot choose to remain traditional. Modern cultural power insists that the immutable laws of nature move people away from dependence on renewable resources. As always, the middle classes believe they represent liberty and not power.[24]

It is an indication of how middle-class magic continues to be persuasive that most scholars who are critical of the current attack on traditional economies do not compare it to the European American attack on Native American subsistence economies in the nineteenth century. Toward the end of that century, the U.S. government took children away from their parents and sent them to boarding schools far from their homes. There they had to have haircuts and clothing that transported them out of their dark traditional past and lifted them into a bright modern future! There they would lose their parents' language and learn English. Again this was seen as a negative revolution leading to liberty. One did not notice the power used in this attempt to break generational continuity in American Indian communities.

The prophecy of these social scientists that humanity was experiencing the final exodus from an old world of unstable cultures whose people lived in poverty to a new world of rational stability whose people lived in plenty was put on hold by the failure of the United States to achieve military victory in Vietnam. The "disease" of communism had not been successfully "quarantined." And at home, while the neoclassical economists continued to consolidate their leadership in academic departments, they had not been able to persuade political leaders to renounce publicly the usefulness of Keynesian policies or to declare that the existence of the welfare state was a source of constant corruption of the marketplace.

But all of the U.S. presidents, Democrats and Republicans, from the 1940s to the 1970s had been in favor of expanding international trade by lowering or eliminating tariffs. They were implicitly attempting to remove artful, timeful human creations so that the intrinsic harmony of a universal marketplace could be achieved. In 1944 European leaders had come to Bretton Woods, New Hampshire, to help create the World Bank and the International Monetary Fund (IMF). They agreed with American leaders that the economic chaos brought by the Great Depression was a major cause of World War II. If another major economic crisis were to occur in the future, the World Bank and IMF would intervene to attempt to minimize any economic collapse.[25]

By the end of the 1950s, however, American officials in the World Bank and the IMF were using these agencies to force the poor countries of Africa and Latin America to open their borders to foreign investors. The pattern imagined by these officials was that the so-called developing countries were on a path toward that final evolutionary stage of high consumption predicted by Walt Rostow. This "natural" history could take place, however, only if the marketplace was free to work its magic. Officials of the World Bank and the IMF worked, therefore, to persuade governments in Africa and Latin America that they must step back from intervention in their nations' economies. They must not engage in planning. They must not have the government own and direct parts of the economy, such as transportation. They must not waste funds necessary to finance development by using taxes from the well-to-do to provide welfare for the poor. And they must be open to foreign investors.

Milton Friedman had bitterly criticized the creation of the World Bank and the IMF because he saw them expressing the position of John Maynard Keynes that governments must provide equilibrium to the marketplace. How relieved he must have been in the 1960s, therefore, to see that the experts in control of those agencies were committed to reducing government intervention in the economy. How wonderful it must have been for Friedman and other neoclassical scholars that these economists assumed that the artless, natural marketplace must be purged of corruption by artful, human interference. In the United States the collapse of the Bourgeois Nationalist belief in the autonomy of the nation and the rationality of a uniform people meant that it was difficult if not impossible to criticize the self-interested individual. One no longer could demand that private property work in the national interest.

The policy of protecting American manufacturers from foreign competition with tariffs that had lasted from 1789 to 1940, therefore, was now officially dead. In the new ethics of the global marketplace, American corporations felt free to move the manufacturing of items such as clothing, shoes, furniture, and electronics overseas. Corporate leaders had the responsibility of providing maximum returns to stockholders. They could succeed by finding overseas workers who accepted lower wages than American workers did. This meant that the pattern of increasing union membership from the 1930s to the 1950s had ended. Union membership now started a long decline that has continued to the present day. Unions, then, are no longer a major factor in the Democratic Party. The prosperity that exploded from the 1940s to the 1960s lifted many Americans from the working class to the middle class. But from the 1970s to the present the income of the average American has not increased. During the 2008 presidential campaign both candidates promised to save the middle class, which, according to them, was in danger of shrinking.[26]

Institutional economists had advocated government intervention in the economy to restore the nation's natural equilibrium. They also believed that the government expressed the will of a unified and rational people. But by the 1950s and 1960s it was difficult to imagine a national equilibrium because any equilibrium must now be found in the global marketplace. And the will of a national people had been replaced by the self-interest of an individual consumer whose meaningful environment was this global marketplace. How, then, could politicians continue to celebrate the small welfare state created in the 1930s and 1940s? How could politicians continue to advocate taxes on the rich to prevent the development of antagonistic classes? In our America of self-interested consumers there was no such thing as class.[27]

Leaders of the Republican Party had, from the 1940s to the 1960s, accepted the limited welfare created in the 1930s. But by the 1960s new leaders were emerging in the Republican Party who felt that the economic patterns of the nation should be those affirmed by neoclassical economists. The activism of the national government had been justified as an expression of the will of a national people. But if that people was an illusion and the only reality was the self-interested consumer, then an activist government was the enemy of that individual. This individual should not be taxed to provide welfare for those who had not taken advantage of opportunities in the marketplace. Corporations should not be regulated in the name of national interest because the economy was now international. Unions should not be encouraged, because they interfered with the working of the laws of the global marketplace. This was also true of government ownership of parts of the economy. Those policies must end. Privatization of previously public corporations would free the laws of the marketplace. Some Republicans even began to urge the privatization of Social Security.

In 1980 the Republican presidential candidate, Ronald Reagan, won easily on a platform that rejected the welfare state. "Government," Reagan declared, "is not the solution. Government is the problem." In office he was critical of unions and government regulations, and he persuaded Congress to cut taxes on the rich. Simultaneously Margaret Thatcher was becoming prime minister in Great Britain on a platform very similar to that of Reagan. And so from New Zealand and Australia to countries in Western Europe, strong political voices emerged that, in the name of internationalism, were critical of government activism and the welfare state. This transnational political movement has been labeled "neoliberalism." These neoliberal political leaders all had faith that the instability of a world of timeful nations could be replaced by the equilibrium of the natural laws of a universal marketplace. Neoliberalism echoed the political outlook of the

Founding Fathers. These men in 1789 had seen themselves as a rational minority surrounded by an irrational majority. They had designed the Constitution so that the irrational majority was politically marginalized. Neoliberal leaders saw corporate leaders as a rational minority who worked within the natural laws of the global marketplace. The majority of people in the United States and in all other nations did not work within the rational space of the marketplace. These irrational people and their irrational politics must be kept from corrupting the rationality of the marketplace. They must not be allowed to use irrational politics to impede the rational actions of corporate leaders. Neoliberals did not explicitly state that they did not believe in democracy, but they certainly feared that democracy could impose artful, unnatural patterns on the marketplace. Their politics of nature demanded that majorities in every country be excluded from making decisions about the economy. Nonelected officials in the World Bank and the IMF should make the economic decisions for countries in Africa and South America. Nonelected corporate leaders freed from government regulation should make the economic decisions in the United States. This is the message of Bryan Caplan's book *The Myth of the Rational Voter: Why Democracies Choose Bad Policies* (2007).[28]

Although neoliberal political leaders proclaimed their desire to shrink government, they were willing to enlarge the military. President Reagan was committed both to a balanced budget and to the use of threat of military force to defeat the Soviet Union in the Cold War. The result of tax cuts for the rich and increased military spending was a rapidly growing national debt. The national government also funded the Central Intelligence Agency to destabilize Marxist governments in Africa and Latin America. Throughout the long history of the middle classes, they have seen a profound difference between power used supposedly to advance liberty and power used by those who supposedly oppose liberty. Then in 1989, with the disintegration of the Soviet Union into a number of independent nations, neoclassical economists and neoliberal politicians felt that they were close to that happy conclusion of human evolution predicted by Walt Rostow. But what was the evidence that the world's population was accepting free-market capitalism?[29]

Ironically, then, it is possible for me, a historian, to suggest that today one can see a cycle of the rise and decline of neoclassical economics and neoliberal politics. Their prophecy has failed, and in the second decade of the twenty-first century one can see the emergence of economists who offer alternative theories to the orthodoxy of neo-classical economists. By the 1890s the United States had surpassed England and Germany as a center of manufacturing. At the end of World War II in 1945 the American lead in manufacturing was gigantic. No wonder American neoclassical economists imagined that the United States would be the industrial leader of the world until the end of history. But Western European nations recovered from the devastation of the war and became important manufacturing centers. Japan, South Korea, and Taiwan also rapidly expanded their manufacturing bases. These were small countries, however, compared to the United States. In this new millennium it became clear that the economies of large countries—Brazil, Russia, India, and, above all, China—were growing more rapidly than that of the United States. It was also clear that these nations were operating within the framework of national competition described by Liah Greenfeld. In the nineteenth century the governments of the United States and Western Europe had intervened in their nations' economies to speed economic growth. That was a matter of national pride.

Now the governments of Brazil, Russia, India, and China are directing the expansion of those nations' economies. They are acting out of national pride. American neoclassical economists, like American neoliberal political leaders, had announced that the national marketplace had, after 1945, been left behind in the dustbin of history. They had announced that national competition had vanished from the global marketplace. Only individuals were competitors there. After all, had not the United States allowed Japanese automobile manufacturers such as Toyota and Honda to start producing their cars in America? Had not American companies been allowed to close factories in the United States and reestablish them abroad?

In such a world economy we would not worry that China was close to surpassing the United States in manufactures. We were not competing with China, India, Russia, or Brazil. But they were competing with each other and with us. Not surprisingly, then, there is now a group of economists who deny the existence of a universal marketplace and a universal form of capitalism. They are saying that they no longer believe the illusions created by neoclassical magicians that obscured our experience with both national and international pluralism. Instead they see a variety of capitalisms and do not believe this variety is going away. Implicitly this group is saying we are not at the end of history. Some major books that express the point of view of what appears to be a new school of institutional economists are Michel Albert's *Capitalism against Capitalism* (1993); *National Diversity and Global Capitalism* (1996), edited by Suzanne Berger and Ronald Dore; and *Varieties of Capitalism: The Institutional Foundations of Comparative Advantage* (2001), edited by Peter A. Hall and David Soskice. Implicitly they seem to be saying that Plato and Machiavelli were correct that political divisions would keep the bourgeoisie from reaching the Promised Land, where everyone would be in harmony with a universal universal.[30]

Another significant indicator that the authority of neoclassical economics is waning is the emergence of a group of economists who see themselves as members of a behavioral school. Rejecting the neoclassical school, they also find their usable past in the writings of John Maynard Keynes. Milton Friedman and other neoclassical economists had worked to destroy Keynes's reputation as a legitimate economist. Now, a half century later in the midst of another major economic crisis, behavioral economists are working to reestablish Keynes and to define Friedman and neoclassical economics as illegitimate. In 2009 Robert Skidelsky published his book *Keynes: The Return of the Master*.[31]

Behavioral economists have been looking at the research done by neuroscientists. One of these scientists, Antonio Damasio, in his book *Descartes' Error* (1994), sums up their aggressive attack on the Enlightenment. For him the division between mind and body imagined by Descartes and other modern thinkers does not exist. Neuroscientists are now able to observe the activity of the brain and its constantly changing chemical balance. The mind is an integral part of the body. So it makes no sense to talk about a rational mind. This complex part of the body inevitably makes both constructive and destructive decisions, and the brain's biological heritage also makes it part of a culture.[32]

Thomas Metzinger, in his book *The Ego Tunnel: The Science of the Mind and the Myth of the Self* (2009), declares, "Neuroscience has demonstrated that the content of our conscious experience is not only an internal construct but also an extremely selective way of representing information. This is why it is a tunnel: What we see and hear, or what we feel and smell and taste, is only a small fraction of what actually exists out there."[33] In other words, neuroscientists believe we have lived and will always live in a world of particular patterns. Plato and current neoclassical economists see most individuals dwelling within an environment of artful particulars. But they believe individuals can leave that artificial world for the real world of an artless universal. For current neuroscientists, however, the belief in the possibility of achieving timeless harmony with a universal is a grand illusion.

At the moment, then, neuroscientists seem to be saying that traditional peoples, with their sense of limits and their rejection of an either/or world, are more in harmony with their environments than are the modern people who believe they can leave an old world of complexity and find a new world of simplicity. The politics of nature affirmed by neuroscientists tells us that we cannot abolish mystery.

One can imagine the anguish experienced by neoclassical economists when they witness the emergence of the new institutional school and the behavioral school as they challenge the premise of a timeless, rational marketplace. Here was the return of the old timeful, irrational world Plato had described in his parable of the cave. How could these current institutional and behavioral economists continue to prophesy perpetual economic growth in this old world in which irrational people live with irrational particular institutions?

In his recent book *The Romantic Economist* (2009), Richard Bronk discusses at length the romantic writers of the early nineteenth century. Those poets, novelists, and historians, like current neuroscientists, wanted to replace the mechanical metaphors of the Enlightenment with organic metaphors. They wanted to replace an individual motivated by rational self-interest with an individual motivated by a variety of emotions—love and hate, joy and despair, altruism and greed, confidence and anxiety. They wanted to replace the Enlightenment vision of a universal world community with the vision of a world of particular nations. Bronk sees the institutional economists, unaware of neuroscience, moving away from the Enlightenment vision currently expressed by neoclassical economists and toward the romanticism that had been so powerful during the first half of the nineteenth century.[34]

It is my guess that Bronk would also identify the economists George A. Akerlof and Robert J. Shiller with romanticism. Akerlof, who won the Nobel Prize in Economics in 2001, currently teaches at the University of California, Berkeley, and Shiller teaches at Yale. In their book *Animal Spirits: How Human Psychology Drives the Economy and Why It Matters for Global Capitalism* (2009), they explicitly reject the Enlightenment view of humans as rational. The state-of-nature anthropology first constructed by middle-class men in the Greek cities of antiquity declared that an inherently rational individual was trapped within an irrational culture. As a participant in that culture, he acted in irrational ways. But when the individual could leave his irrational community and reach a space that embodied rationality, then that individual could express his authentic rational identity.[35]

I see neoclassical economists implicitly working with state-of-nature anthropology. When, for them, an individual steps out of the old world of his family, friends, and neighbors—a world of emotions, of generations, of time—and steps into the new world of the marketplace, he becomes a secular saint in a timeless heaven on earth. He is free of emotions; he is free from complex human relationships; he is free from generations. He is free, as Ebenezer Scrooge in Charles Dickens's *A Christmas Carol* wanted to be free, to pursue only his economic self-interest. Now more than a century after Dickens wrote his cautionary tale, Akerlof and Shiller agree with him that we are never really free from our emotions. But Akerlof and Shiller also implicitly challenge the more than two thousand years of the bourgeois cultural imagination that proclaims our freedom from generational continuity. They argue that we receive a complex inheritance from our parents and pass it on to our children. Dickens's contemporary Robert Louis Stevenson also had challenged the bourgeois hope that nineteenth-century middle-class men were completely rational in his *Dr. Jekyll and Mr. Hyde.* He would have agreed with these twenty-first-century economists that we are motivated by animal spirits.

This position also challenges our current postmodern cultural anthropology, which sees human identity as completely shaped by culture. This viewpoint is modern in the sense that it also represses the experience of generational continuity. It is committed to what Steven Pinker calls "the blank slate" in his 2002 book *The Blank Slate: The Modern Denial of Human Nature.*[36] Now, however, neuroscientists focus on our inherited characteristics. The fact that neuroscientists see all humans as both rational and irrational illustrates how the modern middle-class metaphor of two worlds has no scientific authority today. The hope of liberating a rational individual from an irrational culture that has characterized the urban middle-class imagination since Plato cannot be fulfilled. And this neuroscience builds upon the work of almost two hundred years of scientists in a variety of areas who have denied that there is a timeless, rational state of nature that can provide an alternative space to timeful, irrational cultures.

In spite of this widespread deconstruction of the modern bourgeois faith in two worlds, the majority of academic economists still cling to the belief that a rational timeless market embodying the laws of nature will tell them and their fellow citizens what economic decisions they should make. But a growing group of heretical economists is telling the orthodox majority that there is no escape from history, from timeful complexity. One of these lectures is found in *This Time Is Different: Eight Centuries of Financial Folly,* published in 2010. The authors, Carmen Reinhart and Kenneth Rogoff, are senior professors at major universities. They point to how in the long history of financial crises political and economic leaders have always declared that each crisis reveals that the history of economic instability is over. Now we have experienced an exodus into a new economic space of timeless stability. Reinhart and Rogoff hope that their fellow economists will look at the crisis of 2008 and understand that it is not the final crisis that will be succeeded by endless stability. They want to teach their colleagues that there is no escape from the complexities of unstable history.[37]

That so many economists continue to ignore the evidence that our environment, including the marketplace, is timeful and unpredictable is the inspiration for another recent book, *Zombie Economics: How Dead Ideas Still Walk among Us* (2010). The author, John Quiggin, an economist, is outraged that so many of his colleagues continue to make pilgrimages to the marketplace expecting that truth will be revealed to them. They know this faith is bankrupt, but they seem to be afraid to look to alternative sources of truth.[38]

As the magic of the marketplace loses its persuasiveness among economists, scholars in other academic fields also are becoming critical of the metaphor of two worlds. For a generation a growing number of sociologists have been saying that a timeless marketplace is not an alternative to timeful culture. Instead, these sociologists are saying that culture creates and defines the marketplace. Viviana Zelizer is one of the leaders of this school of sociologists. Her 2011 book *Economic Lives: How Culture Shapes the Economy* is another major challenge to the modern metaphor of two worlds.[39]

From the 1970s to the present, ecologists have been expressing their disappointment that their colleagues in other academic fields have not joined them in warning that the commitment to infinite growth in a finite world will lead to a catastrophe. Ecologists should be pleased, therefore, with the 2010 book *Unearthed: The Economic Roots of Our Environmental Crisis* because its author, Kenneth Sayre, is a professor of philosophy. He borrows data from the ecologists to point out how our increasing use of nonrenewable energy is causing global warming, ozone depletion, loss of species diversity, and unmanageable amounts of nonbiodegradable waste. His contribution as a philosopher is to ask how our social values are related to this impending catastrophe. It is our modern desire for limitless wealth, Sayre declares, that is our major problem. To survive we must create values that will inspire us to be content with limited amounts of material goods. He is repeating the declaration made forty years ago by E. F. Schumacher in *Small Is Beautiful*. But, as in 1970, most U.S. voters are committed to their American Dream. Most continue to expect that their children will be richer than their parents. And they see no connecting relationship between their insatiable lust for more consumer goods and the mounting evidence of environmental degradation. Perhaps, however, Sayre does represent a growing number of university teachers in a variety of fields who are challenging the students in their classes to make the connection between their economic values and their changing physical environment. Will these students find an alternative to their current commitment to the modern metaphor of two worlds?[40]

Akerlof and Shiller present a brief history of the victory of the neoclassical economists over Keynes and his followers. But, for them, Keynes was right when he insisted that the capitalist marketplace does not have a natural equilibrium. He was correct in predicting inevitable cycles of boom and bust caused by human overconfidence and then underconfidence. To escape an underproductive economy caused by the rush of fear when the bubble of expansion breaks, governments should engage in deficit spending to stimulate economic expansion. Akerlof and Shiller again point to Keynes's advice that to escape or limit these cycles, governments should create regulations that restrain the human tendency to be overconfident.

But, as Akerlof and Shiller see it, somehow neoclassical economists gained control of the academic world. They persuaded most economists that Keynes was mistaken and that the market does have a natural equilibrium. They also somehow persuaded neoliberal politicians to reduce the financial regulations created in the 1930s that were designed to restrain moments of wild optimism. Well, then, Akerlof and Shiller are saying to their readers, who do you think is correct—Keynes or the neoclassical economists? Of course, for them writing in 2008, this was a no-brainer. Many Americans, swept away by overconfidence, decided that the boom in housing prices would go on forever. Unrestrained by government regulations, overconfident banks and other financial institutions made irresponsible loans to borrowers giddy with expectations about the increasing value of their assets. And, as Keynes had predicted during the Great Depression of the 1930s, another bubble caused by overconfidence collapsed. As the economy sank in 2007 and 2008, President Bush recommended large-scale deficit spending, and then his successor, President Obama, recommended even greater deficit spending. They implicitly recognized that with the collapse of the boom overconfidence had been replaced by underconfidence. They shared Keynes's belief that government must engage in deficit spending to restore confidence and encourage the return of private investment.

This did not mean, however, that Bush and Obama or Keynes had rejected the bourgeois utopian belief that we dwell within the miracle of a perpetual spring. In the 1960s and 1970s a few economists, such as Nicholas Georgescu-Roegen and Herman Daly, had converted to the concept that the earth as a living body has limits. They hoped to create a revolutionary economics focused on sustainability rather than growth. But most economists down to the present have assumed that it is common sense that economic growth will continue forever.

Akerlof and Shiller, like Paul Krugman, were engaged, therefore, only in a debate about how best to guarantee endless economic expansion. The ecological position that there are limits to growth had no place within the debates between neoclassical and Keynesian economists. Krugman, in his book of 2009, *The Return of Depression Economics and the Crisis of 2008,* had no doubts that the replacement of neoclassical by Keynesian economics would guarantee endless prosperity. He, like Akerlof and Shiller, saw ecological issues as peripheral to the concerns of economists and political leaders.[41]

This was also true of Robert Samuelson's position in his book *The Great Inflation and Its Aftermath: The Past and Future of American Affluence* (2008). For Samuelson, as the population grew older, more economic resources would go to Social Security, Medicare, and Medicaid. There would be fewer financial resources, then, to invest in the technological innovations necessary for future economic growth.

The lingering debt burden of the average American and the national government also would restrict economic growth. But Samuelson expressed confidence that economic expansion would continue, although at a slower pace than in the past.[42]

When Samuelson discussed the issues of greenhouse gases and global warming, he placed them within the timeless world of the marketplace. Continuing the Platonic tradition of seeing two worlds—one of timeless simplicity, the other of timeful complexity—Samuelson could not imagine that the environment, the old world of timeful complexity, was more powerful than the new world of timeless simplicity, the marketplace. He argued, therefore, that it would not be cost-effective for corporations to spend their economic resources on lowering emissions from factories and autos. Instead it would be more cost-effective to invest in long-term innovations in technology that in the future would provide less expensive ways of limiting emissions into the atmosphere. Clearly Samuelson could not imagine that climate change might destabilize the marketplace. In 2009 his position represented that held by the majority of academic economists. For example, William Nordhaus, a member of the Department of Economics at Yale, had also marginalized the issue of climate change. In the United States, he pointed out, only 3 percent of the people were engaged in agriculture. They might be affected by global warming. But it was obvious, for him, that the vast majority involved in the urban-industrial world had nothing to fear from changes in the environment.

But, again, one can hear the warnings of the neoclassical economists. If we are really trapped in Keynes's old world of cycles, there is no immutable environment in which the economy can experience a permanent spring. If we depend on artful government regulations, we are also segregated from the artless laws of nature on which perpetual growth depends. Thomas Kuhn, in his first book, *The Copernican Revolution,* argued that aesthetic factors played a major role in the dramatic shift during the Renaissance from the view that the earth is the center of the solar system to the view that the sun is the center. As defenders of the earth-centered paradigm were confronted by contradictory evidence, they found ways of marginalizing these anomalies. By the time of the challenge of Copernicus, the defenders of the Ptolemaic system had constructed a very complex and sometimes contradictory apology. In contrast, Copernicus offered an aesthetically appealing outlook characterized by clarity and simplicity. Might the neoclassical economists have reason to fear that the behavioral economists and the new institutional economists were creating a complex and sometimes contradictory defense of the marketplace as a space where there was endless economic growth?[43]

Perhaps the recipient of the 2009 Nobel Prize in Economics, Elinor Ostrom, symbolizes an ongoing weakening of the imagined boundaries between this supposed new world and the supposed old world. A seventy-six-year-old heretic, she is the first woman to win the award. During her long career she has been critical of neoclassical economics. She was the founding director of the Center for the Study of Institutional Diversity at Arizona State University. In her book *Governing the Commons: The Evolution of Institutions for Collective Action* (1990), she argued that common resources—forests, fisheries, oil fields, grazing lands—can be better managed by the people who use them than by the government or private companies. This, of course, is a direct rejection of the neoclassical commitment to a marketplace of independent, rational individuals. It is a direct rejection of the neoclassical demand that irrational particulars be replaced by rational universals. It is a direct rejection of the neoclassical claim that the universal language of mathematics is superior to the particular languages of local communities. Implicitly Ostrom is denying that there are two worlds—modern and traditional.[44]

Further evidence that the economists who are the defenders of the metaphor of two worlds are struggling with contradictory evidence such as that presented by Ostrom can be found in Benjamin Friedman's *The Moral Consequences of Economic Growth* (2006). Friedman argues that we must preserve the marketplace because it does good moral work. In his book it is implicit that the crucial issue is not the truth of the marketplace; rather, the crucial issue is that economic growth has created a modern civilization that is moral. Our virtues are superior to those of traditional societies. If we do not sustain economic growth, we will slide back into the moral evils of the Dark Ages. Clearly Friedman is not writing with the confidence that Francis Fukuyama expressed in 1992. For Fukuyama all backward cultures were being pulled inexorably into the modern enlightenment. We were at the end of history. But in 2006 enlightenment for Friedman seemed precarious. Lacking the sense of triumph characteristic of the 1990s, we must guard against regression.[45] And then in 2010 Kenneth Sayre had denounced growth economics as immoral.

In 2011 Robert Frank, an economist at Cornell University and the author of five previous books, published *The Darwin Economy: Liberty, Competition, and the Common Good.* He informs his readers that he began teaching behavioral economics in the 1980s, and after learning from thirty years of experience that individuals do not always make the rational choices predicted by neoclassical economists, he believes it is time to sweep away the whole structure of those followers of Adam Smith. Frank believes that economists and the general public will soon replace the authority of Adam Smith with the authority of Charles Darwin.[46]

Implicitly Frank is trying to replace Smith's mechanical universe, where everything is supposedly predictable, with Darwin's organic universe, where complexity and change lead to unpredictability. Implicitly Frank is replacing Smith's metaphor of two worlds, a lower one that is timeful, complex, and artificial and that keeps the individual from being rational and a higher world of the artless, simple, natural, and timeless marketplace, where individuals can be rational and independent. For Frank, however, Darwin demonstrated that we are always interdependent with past and future generations. When an individual forgets this interdependence, that individual puts the community in danger. The marketplace is part of this single world where self-interest and competition can harm the community.

It is Frank's hope, therefore, that economists and the general public will reject the widespread belief that the government and the marketplace represent two incompatible worlds. They must learn that the government and the market are interrelated and interdependent. When they do so, they will see what John Maynard Keynes understood. They will see that he accepted Darwin's complex, timeful, and unstable world. Frank, however, does not define himself as a heretic. He does not seem to be aware that the orthodox science of Newton and Smith was challenged by geological physics as well as by Darwin's biology in the nineteenth. He does not acknowledge that this heretical science challenges the faith that he shares with Keynes. Although they both see reality as timeful and unstable, they believe that government activity can make capitalism immortal. However, if Frank believes that species appear and disappear in time, why does he not imagine that capitalism appeared in time and will disappear in time?

In the next chapter we will see how literary critics reacted to the collapse of the aesthetic authority of national landscapes in the 1940s.

Losing faith in bourgeois nations as the end of history, they did not join economists in defining the global marketplace as the new end of history. Instead, literary critics and cultural critics rejected the modern concept of two worlds. They rejected the modern idea of progress from an old to a new world. They replaced this modern world with a post-modern one. They insisted that no major narratives were to be found in this postmodern world, where we had no choice but to exist within the boundaries of a single culture. From the 1970s to the 1990s, most of these literary and cultural critics were stoic about their entrapment by the status quo. But by 2000 a number of them saw that they had been mistaken about being in a postmodern world where major narratives did not exist.

These dropouts from the modern were becoming dropouts from the postmodern world. They were beginning to see what the economists had seen. They now saw the persuasive power of the meta-narrative of global capitalism. But where the economists saw global capitalism bringing about heaven on earth, many literary and cultural critics by 2000 saw global capitalism creating hell on earth. These academic humanists at the beginning of the new century were now seeing the pattern that the ecologists William Vogt and Fairfield Osborn had presented in their books *Road to Survival* and *Our Plundered Planet,* both published in 1948. Literary critics who had come to fear the modern now remembered that the art form of tragedy had appeared for the first time among urban middle-class Greeks of antiquity. Only when one could imagine a man so prideful that he believed he transcended all human limits could one create a literary tragedy. This art form had disappeared during the Middle Ages, but it was reborn in the Renaissance, and tragedies have continued to be written down to the present. How could modern literary critics believe that the history of the modern world might itself be a tragedy? How could they believe that a group of people was so prideful that they would engage in self-destruction? Slowly over the many decades from the 1940s to the present, some literary and cultural critics have seemed to be moving toward the antimodern critique put forward by some members of the scientific community. Ecologists tell us that we can escape collective suicide only by rejecting the dream of perpetual growth. We can replace tragedy with a comedy of survival. We can choose humility and work with an economy whose aim is sustaining life.

4 LITERARY CRITICS BECOME CULTURAL CRITICS

WHEN I STARTED my graduate work at Wisconsin I planned to focus on American intellectual history. My adviser, Merle Curti, encouraged me to substitute courses in American literature and in America philosophy for the usual requirement of a cluster of courses in European history. Earlier, when my professors at Princeton had learned of my interest in intellectual history, they recommended that I read Vernon Louis Parrington's *Main Currents in American Thought,* published at the end of the 1920s. Parrington was a professor of American literature, and his narrative was very similar to that presented by the Beards in *The Rise of American Civilization.* Working from the fundamental assumptions of Bourgeois Nationalism, both books told the story of the conflict between European culture and American nature. Both books ended the conflict with the victory of American nature in the 1830s. Parrington and the Beards agreed that now an American culture segregated from the artful European past could grow out of the national landscape. Now American novels and poems could express the identity of the American people.[1]

Echoing the pattern of Bourgeois Nationalism that informed the histories of George Bancroft in the 1830s, Parrington defined the new people as a uniform body. Local cultures in the United States were artful, particular, irrational. The new national culture of 1830 was artless, universal, rational. A true believer in an autonomous American national culture, Parrington, in his survey of American literature from the 1830s to the 1920s, did not include the writing of women because they were irrational and focused on particulars rather than the universal national. Like the Beards, Parrington would not include African Americans, Native Americans, Mexican Americans, or Asian

Americans in his American people. They, like women, dealt with the irrational and the particular. This also was true of the writings of Jews and Catholics.

Implicit in Parrington's selection of the authors of American novels and poems was that they must be male Northern Anglo-Protestants. Male Southern Anglo-Protestants had chosen to leave the American nation. They had chosen to become irrational and particular. Their literature was timeful in content compared to the timeless literature produced by their Northern cousins. There was a series of texts, then, beginning with the novels of James Fenimore Cooper, Nathaniel Hawthorne, and Herman Melville, that formed a sacred canon. This canon must be segregated, and its purity protected from the variety of non-American literatures being written within the political boundaries of the United States.[2]

The professors who taught me American literature at Princeton and then at Wisconsin uncritically accepted the boundaries of this canon in the late 1940s. The professors of American literature with whom I worked in the Minnesota American Studies Program during the 1950s also accepted this canon as a timeless truth. It was in the 1960s, then, that this supposedly immutable canon began to be challenged.[3]

But when Parrington built his book on the American variation of Bourgeois Nationalism, he, of course, faced the same crises of change that caused so much anxiety among historians. Just when the supposedly eternal and immutable natural landscape had purged timeful old-world culture from the new world, industrialism coming from Europe was creating a new urban-industrial landscape. Henry Nash Smith and Leo Marx were two of my colleagues in the American Studies Program. They were in the English department and had recently completed their graduate work in the Harvard Program in American Civilization. There they had worked with F. O. Matthiessen, one of the major architects of that program in the 1930s. His book *American Renaissance*, published in 1941, had many parallels to that of Parrington.[4]

Matthiessen also was a guardian of the canon. He too defined an exclusive American people and an exclusive American literature. His pattern of inclusion and exclusion was the same as Parrington's. And the historical change he most feared was the same as that seen by Parrington. Henry Nash Smith's dissertation became the book *Virgin Land* (1950). Leo Marx's dissertation became the book *The Machine in the Garden* (1964). They both shared the belief of Parrington and

Matthiessen that the American national landscape had defeated European culture in the 1830s. But they also shared their elders' belief that a new landscape, urban-industrial, was coming from Europe by the 1830s. A European culture was raping the national landscape, and an illegitimate culture was the consequence.[5]

Parrington had become increasingly angry in his book because he felt that many American writers were not focusing on the threat to their utopian democracy that supposedly existed in the 1830s. For him, as for the Beards and Matthiessen, the great enemy of our national garden, our virgin land, was international capitalism. If the America of the 1830s represented timeless harmony, international capitalism represented timeful chaos. Parrington, like the Beards, affirmed the virtue of private property that worked within the national interest. Why, Parrington kept asking, why aren't most novelists dramatizing the crucial difference between the good, true, and beautiful America of 1830 and the evil, false, and ugly America created by international capitalism after the Civil War? Why aren't our novelists calling us to resist the materialistic temptations of international capitalism? Why aren't they calling us to return to the spiritual landscape of the 1830s? Like the Beards, Parrington saw an ugly popular culture in the growing cities created by non-American African Americans, Jews, and Catholics. This false culture threatened to obscure the true American popular culture of that golden era between the 1830s and the Civil War.

Parrington was dead by 1930 and did not live to see the revolution of the 1940s, when international capitalism became a legitimate part of American national identity. But Matthiessen did live into the 1940s, long enough to see his authentic America be redefined as un-American. He shared the fate of the institutional economists: he too was symbolically slain by a younger generation. Unable to cope with the awful pain of falling out of an American Eden into an international hell, he committed suicide. Another creator of the Harvard Program in American Civilization, Perry Miller, also chose suicide rather than live in an America that had fallen back into its European past. My colleagues Henry Nash Smith and Leo Marx were the center of the thriving American Studies Program at Minnesota in the 1950s. I was surprised, therefore, when they walked away from Minnesota and took academic positions in which they would no longer teach graduate students. When this occurred in the early 1960s, I was not yet working with the concept of the national landscape and its crucial role in

Bourgeois Nationalism. I had no appreciation, then, of the tension Smith and Marx must have felt when they were confronted by numbers of incoming graduate students who wanted to study African American music or the creative roles played by Jews and Catholics in the urban entertainments of vaudeville and the movies.[6]

But later in the 1960s I became self-conscious that I was on a collision course with the Beards, Parrington, Matthiessen, Smith, and Marx. I was on a collision course with Bourgeois Nationalism. I was beginning to see the distinction between state-of-nature anthropology and cultural anthropology. I was beginning to see the antigenerational assumption expressed in the distinction between timeful European culture and timeless American nature. I was beginning to see that Bourgeois Nationalists defined supposedly national works of art as creations of artists who had transcended timeful culture to express the truths of timeless nature. Works of art associated with Bourgeois Nationalism were supposedly not born in time and would not die in time. For my colleagues the popular art created by African Americans, Jews, and Catholics was timeful. Its popularity would wane and die. Canonical art, in contrast, was eternal.

As I became aware of the antigenerational outlook of the historians and literary critics whom I had been encouraged to imitate, I suddenly saw a dramatic distinction between the historian George Bancroft and his contemporaries, the novelists Cooper, Hawthorne, and Melville. I now believed that these authors were committed to a generational outlook. They had not participated in the celebration of the exodus of Europeans from their old-world cultures to an American state of nature. I now believed that Parrington, Matthiessen, and my professors of American literature had imposed their Bourgeois Nationalist paradigm on these writers. I now believed that these novelists were writing to refute Bancroft and the metaphor of two worlds. How relieved I was to find myself part of a tradition of antimodern eccentrics. In Cooper's novels, for example, Leatherstocking was initially presented as a self-made man, a child of nature. But in the series of novels about him, Cooper has him age and die. He was not self-made, and he had a life cycle. Bancroft had employed state-of-nature anthropology to support his vision of two worlds—one cultural, the other natural. These novelists, however, were implicitly using cultural anthropology to argue that there is no escape from artful and complex culture.[7]

Hawthorne, in *The Scarlet Letter,* explicitly rejected the theology of the English Puritan Roger Chillingsworth. When this Puritan leader came to America he declared that in this new world there would be no life cycles. There would be no sex. But his disciple Arthur Dimmesdale makes Hester Prynne pregnant. Since she does not name him as the father of her child, he can pretend he is loyal to Chillingsworth's theology. He can pretend that he has not participated in generational activity. When he does finally affirm his fatherhood, he proves that he is no longer loyal to Chillingsworth's antigenerational theology. He dies.[8]

Herman Melville in his *Moby Dick* does not present Anglo-Protestant sailors as superior to the other sailors on the whaling ship who came from Africa or islands in the Pacific. Indeed, an authentic American sailor, Ishmael, on the whaling voyage of the *Pequod,* falls in love with Queequeg, a man from the South Pacific who practices his traditional religion. It is Queequeg's responsibility to build a coffin for the death awaiting him at the end of his life cycle. He is committed to a tradition passed down from generation to generation. He embraces the mystery embodied in his tradition.

In contrast, Ahab, the Anglo-Protestant captain of the ship, hates the mystery that he sees embodied in the great white whale, Moby Dick. He is committed to killing whales so that their generational bodies can become commodities in the marketplace. He is, however, passionately committed to purging the world of the mystery embodied in Moby Dick. The fanaticism he brings to that task leads to the destruction of the ship and the death of everyone aboard except Ishmael. He is kept afloat by Queequeg's coffin. He is saved by his love of a traditional man. He is saved by the mystery expressed in the symbols that Queequeg carved on the coffin. I presented this counter reading in my book *The Eternal Adam and the New World Garden,* published in 1968, in which I discussed several generations of novelists who struggled with the Bourgeois Nationalist definition of the United States as nature's nation. My final generation included Norman Mailer, Saul Bellow, and James Baldwin.[9]

True to my childhood upbringing and academic education, I analyzed only male writers in this book. But like many in my generation, when we lost faith in the national landscape, we also lost faith in the exclusive democracy that supposedly had grown out of that landscape. I worked, therefore, in the history department and the American

Studies Program to move the study of American history and American literature in a multicultural direction. If we accepted the validity of cultural anthropology, we could no longer pretend that an American history or literature was expressed only by Northern white Protestant males. There were no timeless works of art that existed above the timeful art created by women, people of color, Catholics, and Jews. When members of these groups finally became members of English and history departments, they worked to desacralize the canons presented by Parrington and Matthiessen. They made the study of literature written by women, African Americans, Native Americans, Mexican Americans, Asian Americans, and Catholics and Jews respectable.[10]

I was sure that there was a connection between the disestablishment of the once-sacred economic boundaries of a supposedly isolated nation and the disestablishment of the once-sacred boundaries of an isolated literary canon. The academic term for the experience that I now had to learn was *deconstruction*. More and more of my colleagues throughout all the middle-class nations were implicitly rejecting the modern belief in negative revolution and replacing it with a belief in positive revolution. Modern nations did not represent an exodus from artful, timeful cultures to artless, timeless nature. Modern nations were artful and timeful. As Bruno Latour had stated, "We have never been modern."

I was greatly helped in creating this pattern by Bill Readings's book *The University in Ruins,* published in 1996. Readings claimed that when modern universities were being constructed in the 1840s, their purpose was to educate national citizens. For the middle classes in the nineteenth century, nothing was more important than the nation and its citizens. Starting in Prussia, a special education for professors was imagined that was implicitly clerical. As the clergy were supposed to be closer to the sacred than the laity, professors were now expected to be closer to the sacred essence of the nation than was the average citizen. In this revolutionary era higher education was to be disassociated from Protestant or Catholic theology. Central to universities, as redefined by the middle classes, was the implicit theology of nationalism. Civil religion was the core of bourgeois universities.[11]

Professors, in order to give the young men in their classes a full understanding of the good, true, and beautiful embodied in their nation, must receive an extraordinary education. They must become self-disciplined, so ephemeral things or irrelevant people would not distract them. A new pattern of graduate education was to give them the ability to discern the eternal aspects of their nation. In contrast to Catholic priests or Protestant ministers, who represented particular and subjective worlds, the new Ph.D.s spoke objectively about the universal national. For Readings this first group of professors who received the new doctor of philosophy degree were responsible for teaching a canon of texts that were more sacred than Protestant or Catholic texts. The souls of young male citizens would be saved when they were taught to see how novels and poems expressed the truth, goodness, and beauty of the national landscape. Literature, more than any other subject matter, provided a sacred body of national texts. Professors of literature, therefore, had the great responsibility of teaching young men how to interpret these texts.

Readings had given me an understanding of why the crisis of the national landscape in the 1940s was felt more intensely by men in English departments than by those in history departments. I could now go back and interpret my undergraduate and graduate education 1945–52 as designed to give me a sense of the exceptional truth, goodness, and beauty of my nation. I could see how I was being prepared to help undergraduates appreciate the spiritual and aesthetic gifts given to them by their nation. And, like Readings, I believed that this mission of higher education had lost its authority when the leaders of the modern bourgeois nations decided at the end of World War II that isolation must be replaced by internationalism. Readings mourned the death of this mission. But I was not in mourning, since I had rejected bourgeois nations because they claimed to be the end of history. I now believed that in a generational world, all antigenerational prophecies were false.

I had been trained—by my family, by my public education, by popular culture, by my undergraduate and graduate education—to focus on my nation. But as I came to doubt that the United States was nature's nation and I was encouraged to reject an isolated America and consider an international future, I theorized that there was a pattern of Bourgeois Nationalism shared by all the modern middle-class nations. I theorized that Bourgeois Nationalism had been created simultaneously by the middle classes in many European and American countries. I also theorized that the crisis in the United States caused in the 1940s by the official rejection of isolation was shared by all the middle-class nations. Everywhere, I thought, historians and literary critics must feel the loss of a sacred story in which each particular nation was the end of history.

English, French, or Italian historians must be bewildered that they were no longer expected to focus on how their particular nation became independent from an international community. And literary critics in many countries must be confused when they were no longer asked to guard the boundaries of a sacred canon of national literature. Everywhere scholars were surprised to learn that their particular country is an artful and timeful construction. When nations were defined as natural, one could not imagine analyzing how a nation was constructed. But nations constructed by humans could be deconstructed.

In this revolutionary situation American scholars in the humanities and social sciences suddenly were willing to read and learn from scholars in other countries. This was especially true in the field of literature. Much more than historians, professors of literature began to look abroad for help in understanding how to discuss literature as a product of artful, timeful culture rather than as the expression of a timeless national state of nature. Within the short space of a decade, literary critics went from the study of independent, eternal masterpieces to the study of a particular novel as an expression of a timeful culture. Almost overnight many literary scholars became professors of cultural studies.

The most influential voices in this dramatic move toward the analysis of culture came from France. And the culture they wanted to deconstruct was not that of France or any other particular nation. Paralleling the anthropologists who after World War II began to focus on a transnational modern culture, these literary critics also now wanted to deconstruct a transnational modern bourgeois culture.

It is probable that the French scholars, such as Michel Foucault, Jean Baudrillard, and Jean-François Lyotard, provided leadership for American scholars as well as those in other countries because they had been Marxists. They had learned to analyze a transnational bourgeois culture. Although they had renounced their commitment to Marxism, they were still able to make use of their international perspective. They were able to teach a perspective on the modern to professors in other countries who, until yesterday, had seen only their supposedly isolated national culture.[12]

It is my hypothesis that these former Marxist intellectuals shared the conversion of Bourgeois Nationalist academics to cultural anthropology. I believe that Marxists had made a variation on the middle-class metaphor of two worlds—one old, artificial, and ephemeral, the other artless and eternal. From the Marxist perspective a capitalist society had replaced traditional societies. But capitalist nations were not the end of history. Like traditional societies, they were artful and irrational. The end of history would come when a rational, scientific proletariat replaced an irrational, superstitious bourgeoisie.

The bourgeois revolution, for Marxists, then, had been positive. It had constructed an artificial society to replace artificial traditional societies. But the Marxist revolution would be a negative one. The final proletarian society would be built on scientific laws discovered by reason. After World War II these former Marxists could converse, therefore, with former Bourgeois Nationalists because neither group now had any idea of how to visualize an alternative to capitalism. Both Marxist and Bourgeois Nationalist scholars had embraced Plato's dichotomy between artful, timeful, irrational culture and artless, timeless nature. Both expected an exodus out of Plato's literary cave, the dark world of historical culture. Now after World War II both groups feared they were permanently trapped in Plato's cave. Neither group shared the faith of academic economists that the global marketplace was the alternative to the perpetual confusion of human cultures. Just when economists were celebrating their emancipation from such a fate, many humanists were lamenting their claustrophobic future.

In 1979 the French literary scholar Jean-François Lyotard published *The Postmodern Condition,* in which he announced that we in the modern world no longer had metanarratives in which we could believe. A metanarrative, for him, was something like the Idea of Progress that brought together a variety of narratives. Scientists, economists, humanists, artists, politicians could all have a particular version of Progress. But these particular concepts of Progress gained meaning only from a larger cultural commitment to Progress. Lyotard, when he was a Marxist, had believed that science predicted the victory of the proletariat over the middle class. When he lost that faith, he lost the metanarrative of Progress. He no longer believed in an exodus from a chaotic old world of capitalism to a harmonious new world of communism. There was no escape from the instability of the artful bourgeois world. In *The Postmodern Condition* he focused on the metanarrative of Progress as it was expressed in science. From the Renaissance to the Enlightenment, urban middle-class men had appealed to a new science as their authority to dismiss the medieval world as merely superstitious. In contrast to the irrational tradition of the Roman Catholic Church, the feudal aristocracy and the peasantry, the middle class believed it was using science to discover a rational natural environment.[13]

But now, in dramatic contrast to the academic economists who were his contemporaries, Lyotard no longer believed that science had an objective, universal language. Rather, he pointed to subjective, particular national languages that symbolized how bourgeois nations were subjective and particular. He now argued that Bourgeois Nationalists and Marxists had used their imaginations to construct the metanarrative of Progress. They had used their imaginations to create the narrative of science as the major way to map the exodus from an artificial and timeful old world to a natural and timeless new world. Speaking from his personal experience, Lyotard announced the death of this paradigm. If we are not moving from disunity to unity, he declared, we must see science as part of the existing disunity. We will never transcend the multiplicity of languages, he insisted, and so there will always be a multiplicity of scientific languages.

Lyotard, the disillusioned Marxist, made sense to the many academic humanists who were disillusioned Bourgeois Nationalists. They, too, had lost their master narrative that promised unity. They, too, were now confronted by an unexpected pluralism. Lyotard's claim was supported by the book *The Structure of Scientific Revolutions* by the physicist Thomas Kuhn. Published in 1962, it instantly became a major topic of discussion among many social scientists and humanists. I began to talk about it in my classes in the 1960s, and it has informed my subsequent writing. Unlike Lyotard, Kuhn did not self-consciously place his narrative within the culture of the modern world. He was only presenting a critique of the way in which the history of science had been written. Implicit in his book, however, is a critique of what I have called the modern metaphor of two worlds. And this implies that he was also criticizing the modern belief in negative revolution.

The history of science, Kuhn declared, has assumed a rational individual trapped in an irrational culture. Stepping out of that artificial world, the rational individual, working as a scientist, is supposed to discover an aspect of a timeless nature. Over time scientists will discover more aspects of this immutable nature. Finally they will know all aspects of nature, and the history of science as a progressive revelation of reality will be over. Scientists will have reached the end of history.

But Kuhn rejected what I call the concept of a negative revolution. Scientists, he argued, are always part of a community. They always participate in a group that shares hypotheses about the nature of reality. They are always within a culture created initially by imagination but one that becomes institutionalized. The period when hypotheses are created Kuhn called "revolutionary science." When scientists worked within an institutional structure, they were engaged in what he called "normal science." During this period of stability members of a community solved puzzles defined by their shared hypotheses.

Since this community was, for Kuhn, implicitly the result of a positive revolution, it had theories about reality, but it was not in direct contact with reality. Inevitably, according to him, the members of the community encountered anomalies that contradicted their shared paradigm. When anomalies became so numerous that they could not be ignored or repressed, some younger members of the community began to imagine a set of alternative hypotheses. They would then try to persuade other young members of the existing community to accept the new set of hypotheses. If the prophetic figures were successful, a new community would appear that self-consciously rejected the previous establishment. Scientists, therefore, experience struggles for power.

Kuhn emphasized that in this implicit positive revolution the language system of the new community was incompatible with that of the old community. The definition of reason was different for each community. One should not, for Kuhn, appeal to reason to justify one's movement from the old community to the new. Young scientists, Kuhn declared, experienced a leap of faith in converting from one scientific outlook to another. For many of us in the social sciences and humanities, who were influenced by Kuhn in the 1960s and 1970s, Lyotard's use of the term *postmodern* helped us understand our experience of moving from one intellectual world to another.

And, after we had been influenced by Kuhn in the 1960s, the writing of another French theorist, Michel Foucault, also made sense to many of us. Historians of science who remained committed to the metanarrative of Progress were particularly angry with Kuhn for his attack on their belief in an autonomous rational individual. Kuhn, implicitly using cultural anthropology, had placed all individuals within culture. He denied individual autonomy and the ability of an individual to participate in a universal rational. French theorists called this assumption that we get our identity from our community "the death of the subject."

To understand an individual, one had to understand her or his paradigmatic community. The French theorists said one must understand the particular and arbitrary language in which the individual was a participant.[14]

Kuhn's critics denounced him, then, for questioning science as a free marketplace of ideas. Instead of science as a space where the individual enjoyed liberty, Kuhn introduced power. If one were going to be part of a paradigmatic community, if one were not to be shunned by that community, one, as a scientist, solved puzzles as defined by the community. When, for Kuhn, this pattern of normal science was called into question, there was a power struggle between a potential new community and the existing community. And this struggle was between drastically different visions of reality, two dramatically different gestalts. And the victors would define the rational in their terms. They would deny the rationality of the defeated. Reason, for Kuhn, was a cultural concept. Power was involved with rationality as the victors segregated their definition of the rational from that of the vanquished.

Michel Foucault, in contrast to Kuhn, who limited the discussion of the model of revolution to scientific communities, placed it within the grand pattern of the transition from medieval Europe to modern Europe. For Foucault as a former Marxist and for many of us in the United States who were former Bourgeois Nationalists, it made sense to discuss a medieval, a modern, and a postmodern world in Eurocentric terms. Ironically, then, we assumed our particular Atlantic world was universal. Our new postmodern experience in the West must be the experience of all humanity.

In the 1960s Foucault published four books: *Madness and Civilization* (1961), *The Birth of the Clinic* (1963), *The Order of Things* (1966), and *The Archaeology of Knowledge* (1969). They all worked to subvert the bourgeois and Marxist metanarrative of Progress as an exodus from a world of irrationality and power to the world of rationality and liberty. These books implicitly presented the modern bourgeois world that was replacing the medieval world as the result of a positive revolution. For Foucault there was no essential rational individual to be liberated from an irrational culture. Instead, the individual gained his or her unstable identity from an unstable community. The language, rules, and practices of the community Foucault named a "discourse." I think it is clear that his discourse community was very similar to Kuhn's paradigmatic community.[15]

And, as Kuhn saw rationality not as a timeless identity but as a changing production of various scientific cultures, Foucault in *Madness and Civilization* was describing how modern bourgeois culture defined rationality in a very different way than medieval people had. Furthermore, in constructing a specific definition of rationality, modern Europeans were not moving toward liberty. Instead, they were using power to segregate rigidly those they defined as irrational from those they defined as rational. Seeking a uniform community, modern people, for Foucault, always created a dualistic world that contained a segregated other.

Next, in *The Birth of the Clinic,* he discussed how the modern professionalization of medicine created a specific form of this modern tension between the rational individual and the other, those who were not rational. Medical professionals were the rational people who looked at, who gazed at, those who were ill and abnormal. In the modern bourgeois world, where one expected that one had left the complexity of the old world behind and had arrived in a place of simple harmony, the ill symbolized a complexity that must be segregated.

Then, in *The Order of Things,* Foucault continued to describe the implicit positive revolution constructed by the bourgeoisie. He described how modern men compulsively organized a variety of disciplines, ranging from psychiatry to economics. By building strong and explicit boundaries around each of these disciplines, the bourgeoisie could pretend that their whole culture was one of uniformity. They could ignore the larger patterns of instability.

As he implicitly deconstructed the metanarrative of an exodus from a complex and unstable old world to a supposedly simple and stable new world, Foucault next criticized modern historians in *The Archaeology of Knowledge.* In order to construct a metanarrative of history as progress, both bourgeois and Marxist historians had to repress all the accidents, the discontinuities that characterize human experience. Foucault declared that he was not writing history but genealogy. Those who practiced genealogy expected that the human experience of time was one of discontinuity rather than continuity, instability rather than stability. In a close parallel to Kuhn's thesis that the history of science was characterized by periods of rapid change, revolutionary science, and periods of stability, normal science, Foucault argued that oscillation between periods of stability and periods of rapid change was true of all cultures.

Foucault was self-conscious that when he implicitly rejected the possibility of a negative revolution where an essential, rational individual was able to escape a complex and unstable culture, he was challenging the essential bourgeois belief. He explicitly wrote that this supposedly rational individual, the subject, was experiencing a cultural death. Our period, for him, was witnessing the death of man as an autonomous agent. Foucault was relieved to make such a report because he believed that the ideal of such an independent man led to the modern compulsion to classify, to dominate, to exclude. And he described such a self-destructive modern culture in his next book, *Discipline and Punish* (1975). The prison where criminals who contradicted the modern ideal of rational harmony were segregated was the invention of the middle class. Foucault was horrified at the way in which the modern search for order taught all individuals to discipline and punish themselves.[16] This concern led to his final project, unfinished at his death in 1984, a history of sexuality.

Foucault, in this project that was published as three volumes—*The History of Sexuality* (1976), *The Use of Pleasure* (1984), and *The Care of the Self* (1984)—was again implicitly challenging the modern concept of negative revolution in which the middle class had supposedly stepped out of timeful culture into timeless nature. Instead, Foucault wanted his contemporaries to understand that their attitudes toward sexuality were an expression of timeful, particular cultural values and not an expression of timeless natural patterns. And again his message was that instead of a modern world characterized by liberty, power had been used and was being used to enforce particular patterns of sexual behavior. Throughout all of these books there was an angry sense of irony. The bourgeoisie contrasted their Age of Enlightenment with the Dark Ages, but Foucault had found more cultural pluralism in the medieval era than in modernity.[17]

In rejecting his early commitment to Marxism, Foucault had come to see it as another expression of modernity. Marxists implicitly wanted a negative revolution leading to liberty but like the bourgeoisie, they engaged in the compulsive use of power in a vain attempt to build a rational society. Foucault had come to hate the modern world, this product of an implicit positive revolution. But he had rejected the modern hope in an implicit negative revolution. There was no alternative to complex and unstable societies. At the end of his life Foucault could only imagine local, small-scale resistance to modern power. If one went beyond guerrilla warfare, if one began to engage in the construction of an alternative culture, if one began a positive revolution, one would be explicitly using power. But did Foucault remain modern in his deep commitment to liberty? Had his culture taught him that the free individual was the ultimate value? Would he feel innocent if there could be a negative revolution? Did he secretly hope that men of feeling, men like himself, could be transported out of that world of power, out of the world of modernity?

It is my thesis that urban middle-class Greeks at the time of Plato invented the dichotomy between unreal, artful culture and real, artless nature. In Plato's parable of the cave, humans who believed in the reality of their artful cultures were trapped within a cave in which they failed to find meaning in constantly shifting shadows on the walls. They were unable to make a distinction between what was authentic and what was an illusion. Postmodernism, I have argued, marks that moment when most academic humanists and some social scientists lost faith in the metanarrative of progress. The story that had given meaning to their identity as Ph.D.s was that of an exodus from unstable culture to stable nature. With their loss of faith in that story, many felt they would be perpetually trapped in an unstable culture. No one expressed this terrible future more eloquently than another French academic, Jean Baudrillard.[18]

Like Lyotard and Foucault, Baudrillard was born around 1930. Like them he had believed in the Marxist vision of an exodus from an artful, timeful unstable capitalist society to an artless, timeless stable world of the working class, a world revealed by science. Like them he lost that narrative. Foucault filled this void with an explosion of scholarly activity, publishing many books in a short period. This was also true of Baudrillard, whose torrent of books included *The System of Objects* (1968), *The Society of Consumption* (1970), *For a Critique of a Political Economy of the Sign* (1972), *The Mirror of Production* (1973), *Symbolic Exchange and Death* (1976), *The Ecstasy of Communication* (1983), *America* (1988), and *Seduction* (1989).[19]

Marxists, Baudrillard declared, did not understand how current capitalist society is one of mass consumption. We always live, he continued, in the symbolic world of language. In this age of mass consumption, commodities have become an essential part of this artful world of language. And pride and status and love have also become commodities. We ourselves have been absorbed in the new networks of technology and communication. We as individuals are objects constantly circulating within the boundaries of the consumer society. Within this closed system, Baudrillard saw a world where nothing is real. He argued that we used places like Disneyland to reassure ourselves that there was a distinction between such a pretend world and our real world. But, for Baudrillard, the false impression about two worlds, fantasy and reality, masked the fact that there is only one world, that of fantasy, a world that has all of the characteristics of Plato's cave. As we watch the shifting patterns of shadows constantly projected by our communication technology, we have no way of distinguishing illusion from reality. We have, Baudrillard proclaimed, entered into a realm of hyperreality.

When Foucault lost his faith in a modern world in which all individuals were to be emancipated, he suggested that the medieval world had allowed more cultural pluralism than had the modern world. And Baudrillard also suggested that traditional people had a fuller grasp on reality than did modern people. For him the exodus from the traditional to the modern was an exodus from reality to fantasy, from reality to hyperreality. In his book *America* he argued that the signs of this transition to hyperreality were more advanced in the United States than elsewhere. But the advanced consumer society in America was an inevitable avant-garde leading all humans into a system in which they, as consumers, were interchangeable with the commodities they consumed. Permanently, perpetually, eternally trapped within the hyperreality of consumerism, we, Baudrillard lamented, can escape this one world only by dying. It would be difficult to evoke a more frightening, a more dehumanizing wasteland than that which emerges from Baudrillard's series of books.[20]

These early analysts of postmodernism seemed to agree with neoclassical economists that the surpluses in the marketplace that made mass consumption possible appeared by magic. They did not try to analyze the patterns of institutional power that were used to conscript surpluses throughout the world. Like the neoclassical economists, they did not look at continuing gender, ethnic, racial, and class hierarchies. And, of course, they did not see the tremendous vitality of the metanarrative of Progress. The bourgeoisie were enthusiastic revolutionists destroying the old worlds of Marxism and Bourgeois Nationalism. Look, the bourgeois converts to a global marketplace declared, look at the liberty and the plenty. Do not look at the continuing patterns of power and scarcity.

These were the supposedly radical intellectuals with whom the most important American Marxist academic, Fredric Jameson, wanted to disagree. His first book, *Sartre: The Origins of a Style,* was published in 1961. Jameson was aware that a strong community of Marxist intellectuals was present in France during the 1930s and that they remained active into the 1950s. This, he knew, was not the case in the United States, where the Marxist voices of the 1930s had been silenced by the 1950s. Jameson lamented, "I have frequently had the feeling that I am one of the few Marxists left." He was attracted to the study of Sartre because his writings were critical of the establishment. Jameson was trying to persuade his generation of graduate students that they should not accept the academic position dominant in the 1950s, the position expressed by Daniel Bell's *The End of Ideology* (1960). They must keep telling the story, the narrative, that there is a conflict between the oppressed and their oppressors. They must keep the faith that the oppressed will make a successful revolution. They can move from an old world to a new world. In his next book, *Marxism and Form* (1971), he asked his young colleagues in English departments to remember the many major European literary critics who were Marxists—Ernst Bloch, Walter Benjamin, Theodor Adorno, Herbert Marcuse, and, above all, Georg Lukács.[21]

But then he was dismayed when he saw that a number of the French intellectuals who had been Marxists were repudiating their belief in the possibility of a successful revolution. They were arguing that humanity was trapped within capitalist culture, a world from which there was no escape. The position of orthodox Marxists was that reality was found in the forms of economic production. This base of absolute reality was the foundation on which culture rested.

But now a number of French theorists were arguing that we define reality through the languages in which we have been initiated. All we know, therefore, is cultural. Culture does not rest on the foundation of economic means of production. The economy is within culture: the economy is defined by our language systems. Accepting the reality of the world of language, we only engage in an illusion when we dream of an exodus from an old world of oppressive capitalism to a new world of a workers' democracy. Jameson expressed his disappointment and anger at these pessimistic French theorists in his third book, *The Prison-House of Language* (1972).[22]

Jameson, however, faced a terrible dilemma. Marx had borrowed from Hegel the concept of history as a dialectic. As a new historical pattern was taking shape, it also was in the process of creating an alternative pattern that would succeed it. For Marxists, however, the dialectic that would liberate the working-class democracy developing within capitalist hierarchy was driven by the energy of the proletariat. The dialectic was set in motion by the commitment of the working class to experience an exodus out of capitalism. But where in the 1960s and 1970s was there any evidence of a militant working class? Jameson could write nostalgically about Marxist literary critics such as Lukács, but what relevance did theory have in a world in which one found no revolutionary avant-garde of workers?

To sustain hope within this stagnant status quo, Jameson moved to incorporate some of the outlook of the French thinkers who had abandoned Marxism. Marx had defined the individual in ways similar to those of bourgeois philosophers. The individual was an integrated and rational subject who would act constructively. This, however, was not how working-class people were acting. Jameson, in his next book, *The Political Unconscious* (1981), incorporated some of the concepts of his French enemies. These former Marxists had argued that the individual is complex, and our imaginations are profoundly influenced by our unconscious minds. While we current academics and workers have self-consciously accepted the status quo as a world in which we are forever imprisoned, at the level of the unconscious we, academics and workers, continue to imagine a utopia that exists beyond the current capitalist wasteland. At the present most of us are repressing our deep understanding of history as the story of progress from a limited old world to a limitless new world. We must, Jameson urged, free our unconscious from this pattern of repression. We must recover our vision of "a single great collective story, a single fundamental theme—for Marxism, the collective struggle to wrest a realm of Freedom from a realm of Necessity." We must, he shouted, "always historicize."[23]

During the decade following *The Political Unconscious,* in which he saw no signs that people were imagining a new and better world beyond capitalism, Jameson began to write a series of articles that explored the inertia of this postmodern status quo. These articles culminated in his book *Postmodernism, or, The Cultural Logic of Late*

Capitalism (1991). He borrowed from Ernest Mandel's book *Late Capitalism* (1975). He agreed with Mandel that capitalism has gone through three stages—market capitalism focused on national markets, then monopoly capitalism in which capitalist nations engaged in imperialism, and finally multinational capitalism dominated by multinational corporations. In this third, or postmodern, stage, capitalism has commodified all aspects of culture. This means that the Marxist belief in a distinction between economic base and cultural superstructure has become obsolete. The economy is the culture, and the culture is the economy. In this stage of late capitalism everything is fragmented. Postmodern art has no depth and no originality. Its lack of depth is expressed by pastiche and collage. Postmodern culture "ceaselessly reshuffles the fragments of preexistent texts, the building blocks of older cultural and social production, in some new and heightened bricolage: metabooks which cannibalize other books, metatexts which collate bits of other texts." And Jameson was angry with those of his colleagues who engaged in "the complacent (yet delirious) camp-following celebration of this aesthetic new world."[24]

Jameson did not talk about the parable of Plato's cave, but he did go back to antiquity for the image of the labyrinth. "The point," he declared, "is that we are within the culture of postmodernism to the point where its facile repudiation is as impossible as an equally facile celebration of it as complacent and corrupt."[25]

For Jameson the labyrinth in which we all are lost is the postmodern culture of late capitalism. This means, for him, that we are within a culture of fragments and that we see the world through a variety of language systems. We have no direct relationship to reality because "history is inaccessible to us except in textural form."

But if this is true, how can we gain an understanding of the culture in which we are living? "If we do not achieve some general sense of a cultural dominant," he insisted, "then we will back into a view of present history as sheer heterogeneity, random difference." And, he continued, "I do want to argue that without a conception of the social totality and the possibility of transforming a whole social system, no properly socialist politics is possible." This was the hope expressed in his book *Late Marxism: Adorno, or, The Persistence of the Dialectic* (1990).[26]

Jameson was also angry with the former French Marxists because they seemed to have become anarchists. Afraid of both capitalist and communist power, they celebrated a negative liberty for the individual.

Jameson was also disheartened by the way many artists in the United States were affirming their freedom: they were certain they were autonomous individuals. They had no commitment to the solidarity necessary for a political victory over capitalism. They felt that although they were within the system of capitalism they retained their ability to be creative. They could make meaningful choices within the economy of consumption.

Indeed, a sense of emancipation, a view of the consumer economy as providing unprecedented freedom to choose, was particularly strong among architects and architectural critics in the United States. For many architects the modern was an old world of scarcity and power, and the postmodern was a new world of abundance and liberty.

In the United States the term *postmodern* was first widely used by architects. I believe this was so because architecture was the most visible battleground between the culture of Bourgeois Nationalism dominant in the 1930s and the culture of international capitalism that had become dominant by the 1950s. For the academics who created American civilization programs in the 1930s, the architects Louis Sullivan and Frank Lloyd Wright were heroic figures. At the beginning of the twentieth century, Sullivan had moved from Boston to Chicago because he saw the East Coast as more European than American. The Midwest, he insisted, echoing Bancroft and Turner, was an America free from old-world influences. Sullivan was angry that most American architects felt comfortable imitating styles created in Europe. He wanted an organic architecture that grew out of the national landscape. He hoped that in Chicago he could develop such architecture. Influenced by Sullivan, Frank Lloyd Wright also committed himself to the task of ending the influence of old-world architecture. He committed himself to teaching his fellow citizens to see the need for an organic architecture that symbolized the segregation of America from Europe. Like his friends Charles and Mary Beard in their *The Rise of American Civilization,* he would show how there could be a synthesis of the national landscape and the urban-industrial landscape. Cities and factories could have an organic relationship to the national landscape. They could grow out of that landscape.

Again, like the Beards and literary critics Vernon Louis Parrington and F. O. Matthiessen, Wright saw international capitalism as the major threat to an isolated America. The United States was a spiritual expression of the national landscape. Since the Civil War, international capitalism had threatened to replace the nation's spiritual unity with a materialistic fragmentation. The issue for Wright, as for the professors in American civilization programs, was whether private property would be disciplined by national interest or whether it would express a chaos of self-interests.

Like the Beards and Matthiessen, Wright feared that the entry of the United States into World War II would mean the victory of international capitalism. It would mean that the national landscape would no longer keep Americans in organic unity with nature. They would fall back into an artful, timeful world. It must have been very painful for Wright to see his dream of an organic architecture that would express American exceptionalism replaced in the 1950s with a dream of the United States as the center of an international architecture that expressed the supposedly universal and rational values of international capitalism. And the final painful irony for Wright was that the founders of this school of international architecture were men who had fled from Austria and Germany. They had fled from Nazi Germany. They were exiles because they would not accept the Nazi orthodoxy that all art must express the exceptional German landscape.[27]

By 1900 a number of artists, philosophers, and architects throughout Europe had started to doubt that bourgeois nations were the end of history. They were aware of the great vitality of the urban-industrial landscape that was developing so quickly in Europe and seemed destined to spread throughout the world. For them the sacredness, the perpetual youth, of national landscapes no longer existed. Influenced by Marxist theory that linked the rational to the universal urban-industrial landscape, architects in a number of European countries were imagining an architecture that would express this rational universal. Architecture, for them, should not be an expression of the particular language of a supposedly autonomous nation. This was an irrational language that had no substance. Mathematics was the universal language of science, and it should be the language of architecture. A building that was an undecorated square would express the industrial value of productive efficiency. A building that expressed such mathematical purity had no relationship to particular places and particular cultures. It should and could be constructed everywhere and anywhere in the world. As Walter Gropius, one of the German exiles to the United States, declared, a building "must be true to itself, logically transparent, and virginal of lies and trivialities."[28]

As our political leaders began to construct a new United States that was to be the center of a new supposedly rational international capitalism, it was a great stroke of good luck for them to be able to define New York as the center of this style of international architecture. The European architects in America could transfer their vision of architecture as an expression of Marxist universalism to a vision of architecture as an expression of capitalist universalism.

And so this was the modern capitalist totality against which postmodern architects in the Unites States rebelled. They did not find international capitalism to be that system of fragmentation about which Jameson, Foucault, and Baudrillard were warning. American postmodern architectural rebels were rejecting the metanarrative of neoclassical economists who promised that the exodus from the chaos of Bourgeois Nationalism was culminating in a new world of absolute unity. Here all individuals speaking the rational language of mathematics would make the same choices. In place of Wright's hope for organic unity, here was a perfect mechanical unity.

In 1917 American Progressives had made a prophecy that our entry into World War I would instantly bring a utopia. Now World War II became the stage on which another apocalyptic prophecy was being proclaimed. But as the prophecies of Bancroft, of Turner, and of Charles and Mary Beard had failed, so did the international architects' prophecy of an end to history.

In his book *The Language of Post-modern Architecture* (1972), Charles Jencks, who had been initiated, as were most architectural students, into the supposedly timeless truths of international architecture, declared the death of this supposedly immortal art form. It died, Jencks declared, on July 15, 1972, at 3:32 P.M., when dynamite was used to destroy the Pruitt-Igoe housing project in St. Louis. This was a building that expressed the abstract functional ideal of the international style. It had won an architectural award. But it was a building in which people refused to live. Its death, for Jencks, marked the beginning of the era of postmodern architecture. Early major architectural critics such as Jane Jacobs, in her *The Death and Life of Great American Cities* (1961), and Robert Venturi, in his *Complexity and Contradiction in Architecture* (1966), had denounced the sterility of modern international architecture. Humans, they insisted, were complex and diverse. They needed buildings that expressed their humanity. Now Jencks in his book explicitly discussed a building as a language whose meaning could by read for its symbolic message as one reads a novel. Like

Jacobs and Venturi, he saw humans as "multivocal" beings who could not feel comfortable with the "univocality" of the international style of architecture. Jencks applauded the willingness of postmodern architects to design buildings that combined several styles. He applauded their willingness to combine the past and the future. Implicitly he was denying the possibility of an exodus from an old complex world to a new simple world. He praised these architects who were committed to "contextualism," who saw that a building was in a particular place at a particular time. He was delighted with postmodern architects who rejected the ideal of the genius, of an individual whose vision could inspire people to engage in an exodus from an old to a new world. Instead, they imagined the architect, like all artists, to be a member of a community. Architects engaged in "collaboration." Now that the moment of the modern, international style of architecture was dead and was replaced by the pluralism of postmodern architecture, Jencks looked forward to a future of "Radical Eclecticism." His implicit politics supposed what he imagined was a status quo of permanent diversity and tolerance. His politics had some similarity to the anarchism of Foucault and Baudrillard, but, unlike them, he did not feel trapped. Perhaps Foucault, Baudrillard, and Jameson might identify Jencks as a spokesman for the consumer culture that was becoming so persuasive and powerful after World War II. Jencks, indeed, was optimistic about the new consumer stage of capitalism. This was a space in which individuals could be creative. It was a space that encouraged pluralism. It was not an oppressive old world. Going from the modern to the postmodern, one had reached a new world of unprecedented freedom for the individual. The postmodern was not located within the modern, as the French theorists and Jameson insisted. It was an unprecedented alternative. Perhaps history was not to end when all people supposedly participated in a rational universal. Perhaps it was ending in a perpetually peaceful and prosperous pluralism.[29]

When America's leaders, along with those in other bourgeois nations, were making the monumental decision to desacralize national economies and place them within a sacred international marketplace, they were, without being self-conscious of what they were doing, desacralizing national citizenship. There was no concept of an international citizenship in the international marketplace. One supposedly left one's political identity behind when one transcended the boundaries of the nation. One had only an economic identity as a consumer in the global marketplace. As national citizenship lost its relationship to the universal national, the concept of first-class citizenship crumbled. Membership in the global marketplace was not to be exclusive as national citizenship had been. National citizenship, like national literature, was no longer something of transcendent meaning. Rationality in the marketplace was imagined as possible for everyone.

Bourgeois leaders by the end of World War II were redefining racism as an illegitimate cultural pattern rather than a legitimate natural pattern. They were redefining political hostility toward Catholics and Jews as a cultural rather than a natural pattern. They were redefining political prejudice against the working class as cultural rather than natural. But if everyone had an equal chance in the global marketplace, the economic hierarchy that clearly existed there must be based on individual ability. One had the rank in the hierarchy that one had earned. Again, most analysts of the global marketplace ignored the fact that middle-class white men monopolized most of the top of the economic pyramid.

The breakdown in the 1940s of the aesthetic authority of Bourgeois Nationalism as states of nature to be reached at the end of history coincided with unprecedented prosperity from the Western European nations through Canada and the United States to Australia and New Zealand. There was a huge increase in the number of white-collar jobs, and many middle-class women began to work outside the home. This changing pattern was related to large-scale changes in cultural attitudes toward the division between the public and private spheres. But it also became necessary for many married women to work outside the home if their families were to have a middle-class lifestyle. A self-conscious women's liberation movement developed out of this revolutionary experience of moving from an old world where women were defined as biologically inferior to a new world where women could claim equality. In 1970 Kate Millett's *Sexual Politics* and Shulamith Firestone's *The Dialectic of Sex* were published. Both books were attempts to analyze and describe the ongoing revolution.[30]

Like the male theorists of postmodernism, female intellectuals participating in this transnational feminist movement were self-conscious that they were denying that bourgeois cultural patterns rest on a foundation of timeless natural laws. The women argued that cultural patterns were relative, not absolute. Like the male postmodernists who insisted that individuals internalized these patterns and policed themselves, women leaders advocated "consciousness-raising" so that women would become aware of how they had been conditioned to expect that they would be passive followers of male leaders. The taboo in Bourgeois Nationalism against women professors had been broken. Women were no longer irrational and particular people who threatened the identity of male students as participants in a universal national.

Many of these new women professors could see parallels between postmodernism and feminism. Both denied that a universal male subject had ever existed. Both denied that any universal subject could exist. But what did such relativism mean for the success of feminism as a dynamic political movement demanding the liberation of women from their subordinate position? Some women scholars, such as Judith Butler, announced that to talk about a women's movement implied the acceptance of a natural rather than a cultural definition of woman. Butler, working with the postmodern theory that all identities are complex and shifting, insisted that the current political movement of women was still working with the discredited modern belief in fixed identities. She was in a position, therefore, comparable to that of Foucault, who argued that there could not be a postmodern politics. Politics, for him, was built on the fiction of a unified body of actors. This myth contradicted the postmodern truth that we, as actors, are complex and contradictory and are always in the process of changing our identities.[31]

But other women professors, such as Alice Jardine, pointed out that modern men had defined what women could or could not do. Jardine reminded her readers that all the major theoreticians of postmodernism were men. And they also seemed to be telling women what they could and could not do. Certainly women were struggling to change the patterns of political power in higher education, and many of these academic activists refused to accept the idea of limited guerrilla warfare recommended by many postmodern theorists. This refusal to give up academic politics was also true for the first generations of African American, American Indian, Asian American, and Chicano scholars now able to teach in major universities. They too recognized the parallels between their deconstruction of the white male claim to have a monopoly on the universal and the critique of the Enlightenment by the postmodernists.[32]

And as women academics recognized how much postmodernism was a male creation, these new professors who represented a variety of racial backgrounds insisted that it was significant that the postmodernist theorists were white men. White men who were modern had told the peoples of color whom they had conquered that they should be passive. Now white men who were postmodern were telling peoples of color that they were trapped forever within the boundaries of international capitalism. Like the many academic women who refused to give up their roles as political activists, many of the academics who represented a variety of racial and ethnic groups remained committed to political activism.

Participating in this revolutionary change in the academic worlds of the bourgeois nations, male historians of my generation and subsequent generations became increasingly self-conscious of how our teachers represented a powerful racist, sexist, and classist tradition. Male literary critics also became aware of how the boundaries of the literary canon of their particular nation expressed a pattern based on class, gender, and race. There now was a cultural war between the white male defenders of a privileged Bourgeois Nationalism and those who wanted to affirm and celebrate the long-repressed cultural pluralism that had always characterized their nations. By the 1980s the war had been won by the advocates of pluralism. Those whose paradigm had been discredited would now attack what they defined as a new oppressive orthodoxy. *The Closing of the American Mind* (1987), by Allan Bloom, and *Tenured Radicals* (1990), by Roger Kimball, expressed the anger and frustration of those who continued to be loyal to the defeated paradigm and its affirmation of timeless truths. Bloom and Kimball mounted an attack on what they saw as the totalitarian rules imposed by the academics who had embraced all of the peoples who supposedly lived within the darkness of unstable, timeful cultures. Such professors had rejected Western civilization and identified with "barbarians." They were imposing patterns of "political correctness" that imposed alien values on the remnant of academics who remained loyal to the truths of Western civilization.[33]

By the 1980s the successful revolution that proposed to replace the Bourgeois Nationalist ideal of a uniform, homogeneous people with the ideal of a pluralistic people was being institutionalized. For the first time in the history of universities there were departments of women's studies and of African American, American Indian, Asian American, and Chicano studies. This new pattern symbolized the replacing of state-of-nature anthropology by cultural anthropology. In this postmodern academic world the humanities had established the new paradigm that humans are always within culture. Now Kuhn's moment of revolutionary science was being institutionalized as normal science. Important parts of this new academic world, therefore, were programs or departments of cultural studies. Implicitly the outlook of those involved in cultural studies was a rejection of the pattern of segregated departments established in the bourgeois universities of the nineteenth century. Cultures were not something one could break down into separate parts as one could with a machine. One could understand cultures only by looking at them simultaneously from a variety of perspectives. All the departments in colleges should become interdisciplinary.

In a way this had been the perspective of the men who began American studies programs in the 1930s. But they had seen a national culture isolated from the rest of the world, and they had seen a national culture that was male, middle-class, and Anglo-Protestant. They wanted an interdisciplinary approach to their segregated and exceptional culture. Now this new generation of scholars in cultural studies wanted to overcome this antidemocratic outlook. Many of the leaders of cultural studies were white men. But they felt that they, too, like academic women and academics who were members of racial and ethnic departments, were engaged in a liberation movement. Perhaps some of these men felt that their liberation movement was more important than those of women and minorities because their outlook was broader. They were concerned with all aspects of their nations, and of the larger culture of international capitalism.

This liberation movement was momentous because, for these men, they were participating in the creation of the first American democracy, one that was inclusive of all classes, all genders, all ethnic and racial groups. This was the message of the historian Lawrence Levine in his book *Highbrow/Lowbrow* (1988). He wanted his readers to recognize the class, racial, and gender prejudices of the men who were the leaders of the so-called American democracy in the nineteenth century. And he celebrated the authentic pluralistic democracy developing in the late twentieth century in his *The Opening of the American Mind* (1998). Another cultural critic, Andrew Ross, echoed these sentiments in his *No Respect: Intellectuals and Popular Culture* (1989), in which he also demonstrated how antidemocratic Anglo-Protestant cultural leaders had been. Ross believed they had nothing but contempt for the people.[34]

Scholars in England and America who were in cultural studies in the 1980s and 1990s focused, therefore, on popular culture, the culture of the people. They were self-conscious of themselves as revolutionists, and by 1990 were producing a number of books that were chronicles of the historical development of cultural studies. Among these were Patrick Brantlinger's *Crusoe's Footprints* (1990), Laurence Grossberg's *We Gotta Get Out of This Place* (1992), Stanley Aronowitz's *Roll over Beethoven* (1993), John Fiske's *Power Plays, Power Works* (1993), and Angela McRobbie's *Postmodernism and Popular Culture* (1994), as well as Simon During's edited volume *The Cultural Studies Reader* (1993) and Jeffrey Williams's edited collection *PC Wars* (1995).[35]

These academic leaders in cultural studies implicitly accepted the position of a Baudrillard or a Jameson that the capitalist world after World War II was characterized by mass consumption. They, like Baudrillard and Foucault, implicitly retained the centuries-old bourgeois faith that an environment of permanent economic plenitude would be reached. They implicitly agreed, then, with the official spokesmen for the new order of international capitalism, the neoclassical economists, that their promised land had been reached after World War II.

Many of the academic spokesmen for cultural studies in the 1990s emphasized, therefore, how much freedom of choice and how much cultural creativity the average consumer had in the new worldwide democracy. Much of the scholarship analyzing the movies, television, and popular music demonstrated the agency exercised by consumers: they were actors, not passive receivers. As one scholar remarked, "Watching television is almost frantic with creative activity."[36]

In the segregated university both the humanists who hated the consumer culture and those who loved it were not aware of what ecologists were saying about the future of the global marketplace. They were not aware that scientists had also participated in the paradigm revolution of the 1940s. Like historians, economists, and literary critics, scientists interested in ecological issues now put them in a global context. Suddenly they saw the earth as the home of human beings. They saw that humans were engaged in shaping their home. Human history was within the history of nature. Human cultures were timeful and unstable. Nature also was timeful and unstable. The bourgeois paradigm that insisted the middle classes were engaged in an exodus from timeful, unstable culture to timeless, stable nature was false. And the bourgeois belief in perpetual surpluses in the marketplace also was false. A timeful, unstable nature meant that there were limits to economic growth. From the 1940s to the present, ecologists have rejected the politics of nature identified by Latour that rested on the foundation of a timeless, stable nature. Bourgeois intellectuals had seen a future in which we would share surpluses. Ecologists since the 1940s have seen a future in which we will share scarcity.

As I write in 2012, I have seen little evidence that any significant number of humanists have considered the possibility of using ecology to criticize a capitalist consumer culture. They are so committed to culture as the only reality that they cannot imagine a new politics of nature in which culture plays an active role within nature. Perhaps this is why the book *Postmodernism and the Environmental Crisis* by Australian culture critic Arran Gare seems to have disappeared down a deep well after its publication in 1995. Gare was implicitly using a model similar to that developed by Kuhn in *The Structure of Scientific Revolutions*. For postmodernists the modern metanarrative of Progress is false. Leadership by the middle classes has not brought liberty and plenty in a timeless space. Postmodernists, according to Gare, emphasized the anomalies, the contradictions of the modern bourgeois paradigm.[37]

Postmodernists had demonstrated that this bourgeois world was artful, not natural. But, they said, because everything is ephemeral, they could not construct an alternative metanarrative to replace that of middle-class Progress. They refused to help create a revolutionary party. Gare was frustrated and angry that Marxists and postmodernists had not chosen to "theorize the links between the ecological crisis, the globalization of capitalism, and the fragmentation of the modern world." Gare wanted to replace the metanarrative of Progress with the metanarrative of sustainability. But in his history of the academic left from 1990 onward, *The Left at War* (2009), Michael Bérubé found no significant interest in ecological issues. No creative energy by humanists has gone into creating an alternative politics of nature in which culture is within nature. Bérubé, a professor of literature, seems himself to be so uninterested in climate change, global warming, and shortages of water and food that he does not comment on the insignificance of these issues among antiestablishment academic-humanists. These humanists had not paid attention to the book *Planet of Slums* (2004), by Mike Davis. Using statistics gathered by the United Nations, Davis spotlighted the tragedy of a billion people now living on the edges of the cities of Latin America, Africa, and Asia. Most were part of the huge population growth that took place from 1970 to 2000.[38]

In a parallel to the way in which the economic boom of the 1990s became an economic bust after 2000, the book by Davis may have been symbolic of a boom–bust cycle among the academic humanists who had written during the 1990s as if there were no limits to the new consumer culture. It seemed, to them, as if all the people of the world were becoming affluent consumers in a worldwide shopping mall that was not constructed in time and, therefore, could not be deconstructed in time.

Andrew Ross was one of the most important figures trying to lead his fellow academics out of the fading utopia. His first book was *The Failure of Modernism: Symptoms of American Poetry* (1986). He then joined a number of his fellow literary critics in exploring cultural criticism. He edited *Universal Abandon: The Politics of Postmodernism* (1988) and wrote *No Respect: Intellectuals and Popular Culture* (1989). But, then, he saw a future shaped by the debates about popular culture that were obscuring a pattern in which multinational corporations were increasing their ability to control and exploit working people everywhere in the world. Having changed from literary critic to cultural critic, Ross now became an economic historian. Economists and historians were not telling the truth about the global marketplace. They were not telling that it was a space of liberty and a space of prosperity only for a privileged few. Ross would have to tell this story himself.[39]

In his next book, *The Celebration Chronicles: Life, Liberty, and the Pursuit of Property Values in Disney's New Town* (1999), he discussed how popular culture was used to obscure the growing world tragedy of impoverished workers. In 1997 he had edited *No Sweat: Fashion, Free Trade, and the Rights of Garment Workers,* which explored the ironic relationship between a world of beauty and a world of exploitation. Now his books illuminating the dark side of the global marketplace appeared with great rapidity—*No-Collar: The Humane Workplace and Its Hidden Costs* (2002), *Low Pay, High Profile: The Global Push for Fair Labor* (2004), *Fast Boat to China: Corporate Flight and the Consequences of Free Trade* (2006), and *Nice Work If You Can Get It: Life and Labor in Precarious Times* (2009). At this point Ross must have felt that the postmodern critique of the metanarrative of Progress was irrelevant. Clearly men in many powerful modern institutions were motivated by that metanarrative. And they were creating a global tragedy. The crucial question, then, was how Ross and other academic humanists could create an alternative metanarrative that would help people escape an ever-greater tragedy.[40]

Walter Benjamin and other members of the Frankfurt school were critics of the Nazi Party that was taking over their Germany in the 1930s. Like Ross more than seventy years later, they saw their nation and their world moving toward a terrible tragedy. But why did so many of their fellow citizens ignore the dramatic danger signs? Why did they see stability where there was only instability? Benjamin's answer was that his fellow Germans acted as if they were in a movie theater. They were observers of a story on the screen. They were not actors; they were not participants. A movie might have a tragic conclusion, but the members of the audience would return to homes that were eternally stable.[41]

Perhaps Ross had developed a similar vision after 2000. He could look back at those cultural critics in the 1990s who rejoiced in a popular culture where many television programs and many movies had happy endings. In such a positive environment, how could scholars imagine that they were participating in a flow of events that was leading to a tragedy that would be more destructive than World War II? Look, Ross now shouted, at growing poverty. Look at how the powerful are dominating and controlling the majority of people in the world. Ross wanted his colleagues to stop defining themselves as viewers of a feel-good movie. They were participants in a world characterized by pain, fear, and frustration. They must become actors if they hoped to limit the impending tragedy.

5 ECOLOGISTS ON WHY HISTORY WILL NEVER END

THE RELATIONSHIP OF SCIENCE to the current middle-class world is one of monumental irony. From the Renaissance to the Enlightenment, bourgeois men in Europe and in their American colonies appealed to the authority of their new science to demonstrate that they and they alone were rational. They contrasted themselves to what they were beginning to define as the European "Dark Ages." But, for them, all traditional cultures were irrational, unstable, and timeful. Once urban middle-class men had been trapped within such an oppressive old world, but their science showed them that there was an alternative new world. This was the timeless space of nature, where the rational individual could escape the complex, unstable systems that characterized traditional societies. Here in the endless plenitude of nature one was free of generational experience; one was free from the cycles of birth, death, and rebirth; one was free from the limits of renewable resources. Today orthodox economists present the marketplace as such a magical space. There one can transcend interdependence with neighbors, family, and a living nature and act as an autonomous individual. There one can leave behind such emotions as love and hate, pride and humility, sadness and joy. There one is supposedly able to be a purely rational individual. There one can transcend concern for children or illness or old age. If one believes in this middle-class magical kingdom, nature and the marketplace are timeless. They are outside history.

But since the early nineteenth century scientists in a variety of fields have been creating a picture of the earth that directly contradicts this bourgeois vision of an independent individual in harmony with a timeless space. Supposedly rational modern people have not denied the claims of the scientists who present a nature with a history. They have, however, segregated them. This compartmentalization has allowed modern middle-class people to keep their master narrative. They are moving or will move from timeful complexity to timeless simplicity. They are moving from scarcity to plenty. They are moving from the flux of history to the end of history.

The first magic trick that modern middles classes had to perform to make scientific evidence disappear was with the new science of geology, which was created in the first half of the nineteenth century. In stark contrast to Newton's affirmation that space is timeless, geologists argued that the supposedly timeless earth imagined in the eighteenth century had existed for millions of years. But certainly this news that the earth had been changing constantly during its long life span had to be hidden in a closet. Over the years, new generations of geologists provided detailed pictures of those changes. Mountain ranges appeared and disappeared. Inland areas once had been oceans. And finally they presented the theory that all of the continents had once formed a single land mass that had, over a long period, drifted apart to form our current group of separate continents.

Our political and economic leaders today, however, continue to believe there is a space—the marketplace—without time, a space that allows endless economic growth. I assume that geology departments in universities, therefore, are intellectual ghettos that are isolated from the mainstream. Perhaps Foucault's argument that we internalize cultural norms and police ourselves explains why most geologists during the past century and a half have not identified themselves as heretics. They have not pointed out that the modern, middle-class hope of straight-line economic expansion cannot be fulfilled on a planet with a timeful history.[1]

This pattern also fits the science of biology as it developed in the nineteenth century. The Enlightenment, with its abstract philosophers and abstract businessmen, affirmed a new world of timeless nature as a refuge from timeful culture. But biologists, like geologists, defined a nature that was timeful. Newton and the capitalist members of his generation saw a nature without generations. But generations, of course, were central to the new science of biology. Humans were linked to their ancestors. They were linked to the animals and plants that had sustained the members of traditional cultures. They were part of a changing and unstable natural history. All living things experienced mutations. The future was unpredictable.[2]

Since most modern people today continue to believe they can predict endless economic growth, biologists are, at best, eccentrics or, at worst, enemies of the modern. But until recently they, like the geologists, have identified themselves as modern. When the urban middle classes on both sides of the Atlantic converted to Darwin's theory of evolution in the late nineteenth century, they were able to do this easily because they co-opted Darwin into their exodus narrative. Evolution guaranteed that the middle classes were moving from an inferior to a superior world. Belief in evolution, therefore, did not return modern individuals to the views of traditional societies. Evolutionary theory did not imply that nature was unstable and mysterious. Natural history, as the economist Walt Rostow had argued in his book *The Stages of Economic Growth* (1960), was leading to a utopian end of history. And many biologists, like many geologists, did relate their science to the modern narrative of Progress. They were learning more and more about the world. They, as scientists, were pathfinders for their society as it moved out of darkness into light. But because of their implicit heresy that affirmed generational continuity, they, like geologists, were in an academic ghetto. Certainly Akerlof and Shiller, with their B.A. and Ph.D. degrees, seemed ignorant of an extensive body of biological scholarship linking us to animals. At the beginning of the twenty-first century, these economists felt the need to reinvent themselves as pioneering biologists.[3]

If geology and biology were implicit threats to the bourgeois belief in the self-made man escaping a complex, timeful old world to find a simple, timeless new world, this was also true of the psychological theories of Sigmund Freud. The ideas he presented in the early twentieth century were a direct attack on the concept of the self-made man who became independent and rational when he left home. Biologists argued that we cannot escape our genetic links to our parents. Freud argued that we cannot escape our psychological links to our parents. The complex love–hate relationship that children have with their parents and siblings remains part of their adult identity forever.

Furthermore, for Freud, all individuals have a complex relationship between their conscious and unconscious minds. We cannot escape being a mystery to ourselves. We cannot be completely modern.

We cannot be either rational or irrational, as we are always both. But Freud ironically saw himself as a modern scientist helping us move from ignorance to knowledge. He did realize, however, that his theories cast doubt on the future of modern middle-class civilization. But seeing himself as a man of science, he did not see the possible parallels between psychiatrists and the individuals who were healers in traditional societies. Since, for Freud, we cannot escape our complexity, our constructive and destructive impulses, we should go to psychiatrists who will help us achieve a balance. This balance is temporary, and individuals will always need help in their search for balance. Traditional societies have such a both/and outlook, and their healers help individuals to restore balance. But since the balance is temporary, a traditional person must participate in healing rituals throughout the life cycle. One cannot be born again. One cannot leave the old world that is our only world.[4]

Freud was a contemporary of the physicist Albert Einstein. Throughout his long life, Einstein always considered himself a modern scientist. Scholars have focused on Einstein as the representative figure for his generation of physicists. At the beginning of the twentieth century, this generation discovered for itself the message of geologists and biologists. Nature is timeful; nature has a history. When Einstein said that Newton was wrong because there is no timeless space, he, of course, as part of the segregated university, did not point out that he was echoing what geologists and biologists had been saying for more than half a century. He did not see himself as part of a larger revolution.[5]

It did not occur to Einstein, therefore, that the superiority of his modern civilization could be called into question if one doubted the modern faith that there are two worlds, an old timeful one and a new timeless one. But, of course, Einstein's reconnection of time and space did challenge the middle-class metaphor of two worlds. This also was true of his argument that space is curved, not flat. What did this imply for the modern claim to be moving in a straight line after escaping the cycles of traditional society?

During the first three decades of the twentieth century, a group of physicists, including Einstein and Max Planck, expanded the revolution that challenged Newton. The atom as defined by Newton was an immutable individual object with parallels to a modern rational immutable individual. This ideal bourgeois man had escaped the mutability and irrationality of traditional culture. But for this new quantum physics the atom was a community containing a variety of particles. These atomic communities were full of energy; their particles were in constant motion. There was no stable material world. Everything in the universe was vibrating. Particles were disappearing; other particles were appearing.[6]

Oh, no! The commitment of the traditional world to cycles that had been denounced by the middle-class science of the Renaissance might be escaping its relegation to the dustbin of history. Seeing dynamic and unstable atoms, physicists spoke the unspeakable: they described our solar system as having been born in time, and sometime in the distant future it would die in time. They spoke of our whole universe as being born. They spoke of the universe as one in which suns were constantly being born and constantly dying.

But, for neoclassical economists in the 1960s and the 2010s and for most of the middle-class public, all of this was not relevant knowledge. It certainly did not cause them to consider that the marketplace was born in time and would die in time. All of these exotic cycles did not mean there were limits to the energy of the marketplace. Suns might die, but not the marketplace. Soon after Thomas Kuhn had suggested in *The Structure of Scientific Revolutions* that the history of science was characterized by the creation of unexpected hypotheses, the anthropologist Loren Eiseley's book *The Unexpected Universe* (1964) was published. Unlike his colleagues in economics, Eiseley did take the revolution in physics seriously. During "the early years of modern science," he wrote, in "the late eighteenth and early nineteenth centuries," men were "basking comfortably in the conception of the balanced world machine. Newton had established what appeared to be the reign of universal order in the heavens." But, then, Eiseley reported, this stable world had been demolished. "From the oscillating universe, beating like a gigantic heart," he wrote, "to the puzzling existence of antimatter, order, in a human sense, is at least partially an illusion. Ours, in reality, is an order of a time, and of an insignificant fraction of the cosmos, seen by the limited senses of a finite creature." "This," he concluded, "is why the unexpected will always confront us." This dramatic revolution in perception is expressed in the title of a recent history of physics—*From Clockwork to Crapshoot* (2007) by Roger Newton.[7]

Eiseley was aware of the metaphor of two worlds expressed in Newtonian physics, and he stated that the current rejection by physicists of a timeless natural world should cause us to consider that we have not left the traditional world behind. We should consider, Eiseley concluded, that there is only one world shared by both nature and culture.

In 1975 the physicist Fritjof Capra published his book *The Tao of Physics,* in which he argued that post-Newtonian physics is very similar to Eastern mysticism. If all matter is made up of atomic communities that are in constant motion, then the universe can be said to be participating in the "cosmic dance" envisioned in Hindu tradition. Physicists such as Einstein and Planck had seen themselves in dialogue with nature. They needed hypotheses created by their imaginations to direct their investigations of nature. In the segregated university, academic humanists were not aware that some scientists were interested in language. As these humanists began to move toward postmodernism, they were not aware of the publication of such books as *Science as Metaphor* (1973), edited by Richard Olson, and *Physics as Metaphor* (1982), by the physicist Roger Jones.[8]

Indeed, this understanding of matter as dynamic and capable of dramatic change encouraged several physicists to argue that quantum physics had parallels to early Christian miracles. Some of the books that present this thesis are *Modern Physics and Ancient Faith* (2003), by Stephen Barr; *The Physics of Christianity* (2007), by Frank Tipler; and *Quantum Physics and Theology: An Unexpected Kinship* (2007), by John Polkinghorne.[9]

These physicists had moved decisively away from the politics of nature that Bruno Latour had seen stretching from classical Greece to the present. That politics had judged unstable culture by the standards of a supposedly stable nature. And certainly neoclassical economists continue to pass judgment on an unstable political culture from what they claim are the immutable laws of the marketplace. They, of course, do not want to learn that many physicists no longer see a stable nature that is superior to unstable cultures. Implicitly their alternative politics of nature is critical of the middle-class utopianism whose goal is to end instability and bring about the end of history.

I became an academic historian in the 1940s and 1950s at that moment when historians were losing their faith that the national landscape made their nation an island of timeless stability in a worldwide sea of instability. I have no memories of talking with my colleagues in history or in American studies about our participation in a major spatial crisis. And in the segregated university we humanists were not

aware of a spatial crisis in economics and physics. Historians and literary critics in the last decades of the twentieth century did not join the
neoclassical economists in defining the global marketplace as a timeless and immutable space. But as we struggled with an unexpected history of unpredictable change, we also did not see a parallel between our
confusion and that of our colleagues in physics such as my colleague
at Minnesota, Roger Jones. We historians certainly were not saying
that we wrote about complex and confusing cultural patterns because
we lived within complex and confusing patterns of nature. An English
scientist, C. P. Snow, lamented this separation of the humanities and
physical sciences into two worlds in his book *The Two Cultures and
the Scientific Revolution* (1959). Little has changed in the half century
since he asked his colleagues to erase their intellectual boundaries.[10]

When I began my graduate studies at Wisconsin in 1948, I had
just read two recently published books, *Road to Survival* (1948), by
William Vogt, and *Our Plundered Planet* (1948), by Fairfield Osborn.
I, of course, did not imagine that I was witnessing a confrontation
between two politics of nature. I had been initiated into the politics of
nature expressed by Vernon Louis Parrington and Charles and Mary
Beard. They saw the United States as the end of history because people
leaving Europe for America had left an artificial, timeful, and unstable
culture behind in the old world. In the American new world these pil-
grims found harmony in a timeless and stable national landscape that
must remain isolated from the timeful old world. Parrington and the
Beards became pessimists because they feared that the United States
could not remain isolated and would fall back into the chaotic old
world.[11]

I have argued that economists in all the bourgeois nations faced this
crisis of a nation becoming timeful, and they responded by inventing
another new timeless world, the global marketplace. Particular bourgeois nations were not the end of history. The end of history meant the
triumph of the universal. In this new transnational world every human
being would escape the limits of time. Everyone would enjoy endless
plenitude.

And just as we historians were unaware that economists were proph-
esying that a universal worldwide utopia of limitless plenitude was
about to be reached, we were unaware that scientists in a variety of fields
were also responding to the collapse of Bourgeois Nationalism. Their
response was the direct opposite of that of the economists. They now

saw the earth as a whole. They saw a universe. But this earth was a living body, and, like all living bodies, it had limits. This was an earth where humans had experienced scarcity and would experience scarcity.

For conservationists at the end of the nineteenth century both in Europe and in the Americas it was clear that population explosions in their nations demanded increasing amounts of lumber to meet the demand for housing. The answer was to create a scientific management of the forests owned by national governments. The training of such experts began in Germany, but soon several American universities had schools of forestry. These managers would keep forests in equilibrium with a calculated balance between the harvesting of old trees and the planting of new trees.

These conservationists were Bourgeois Nationalists who assumed that their timeless national landscapes could provide endless plenitude. As they came into the twentieth century, these scientific foresters certainly did not share the view of their colleagues in physics that an unstable and timeful nature should be described by the uncertainty principle put forward by Werner Heisenberg. In her book *The Culture of Wilderness* (1996), Frieda Knobloch has evoked the almost hysterical response of the U.S. Forest Service to wildfires. In the natural harmony of the national landscape there should be nothing as destructive and unpredictable as wildfires. For decade after decade it was expected that these scientific managers would soon permanently eliminate such unnatural aberrations. These were men committed to a timeless utopia.[12]

But these national utopians had lost their credibility in the 1940s. The choice now seemed either to be an international utopia, a universal new and limitless world, or to be an international old world, a universal, unstable environment with limits. It would be very difficult for modern people to imagine a universal that was not stable and rational. But I have argued that developments in geology, biology, and physics during the nineteenth century contradicted the Enlightenment hope of a universal utopia, a timeless space with endless plenitude. Most modern middle-class people, however, were able to ignore these heretical scientists. They ignored how these scientists were creating a nature that had a history. It was timeful. It was mutable. Perhaps this is the context for the recent book *Unscientific America: How Scientific Illiteracy Threatens Our Future* (2009), by Chris Mooney and Sheril Kirshenbaum.[13]

It is my hypothesis, then, that when environmentalists, like economists, were pushed out of their focus on national landscapes, they, unlike economists, were pushed into an international world that had many of the characteristics of the old traditional world. Environmentalists had entered into a world that emphasized sustaining life within a communal home. The bourgeois dream, expressed by the economists, was to escape a generational home and find endless plenitude in a new world that had no generations.

But what if there were no magical new world with unlimited resources? What if modern history were the record of middle classes so enchanted by their magic that they ignored the way in which they were using up the resources that sustained life at home? What if the bourgeoisie were so enchanted by their belief in a utopian future that they ignored the problem of how their children and grandchildren would survive when their homes had been stripped of their resources?

Living at home, one did think about how one would feed, clothe, and provide shelter for all the members of the family. If one were able to leave the limits of home, however, for an unlimited new world, there would be no reason to be concerned about population growth. As I stated earlier, my youthful experiences with the Great Depression and World War II had caused me to doubt the modern faith in progress from an imperfect old world to a perfect new world. When I read the books by Vogt and Osborn, therefore, I found them plausible. But when I talked to the history faculty at Wisconsin about these books, they all told me that every intelligent person knew that Thomas Malthus, who had concerns about population growth, was an eccentric. Progress in technology and science, they assured me, would guarantee perpetual economic growth. In our modern world one did not worry about food, clothing, and shelter for members of the family. After all, in the marketplace there were only individuals. And since the decisions they made were within the timeless space of the marketplace, their actions were not connected to the past or to the future. What, then, were Osborn and Vogt saying that caused my teachers to dismiss them as deluded followers of a discredited Malthus?

Vogt and Osborn, both participants in conservation organizations, were writing so they could share the revelations they had just experienced. Losing their Bourgeois Nationalism, they were able to see and feel the heretical argument of geologists, biologists, and physicists that humans are part of the history of a living nature. Nature is our only home, our only world. One can feel the shock when Vogt and Osborn suddenly confronted the issue of population from the perspective that we are within the circle of the earth. Continual population growth within this limited space with its limited resources must lead to catastrophe.

They had turned their backs on the bourgeois belief in a timeless nature that provided endless surpluses in the marketplace. As biological creatures we need food, water, and shelter. For Vogt and Osborn, we get these resources from the earth. There is a limit to the amount of fertile land available on which to grow crops. There is a limit to the amount of freshwater, which is essential for life. There is a limit to the forests that provide materials for shelter.

For them, therefore, our modern world is moving toward a tragic collapse because we do not see our interdependence with a living nature. Instead, we have come to believe in an unlimited world made possible by our science and technology. Again, Vogt and Osborn agreed that we could not sustain this illusion much longer. Both pointed to cultures in Europe, Asia, Africa, and South America whose members felt they had no limits. All of them collapsed. As Jeremiahs, Vogt and Osborn were asking all the peoples of the world to reject the belief in perpetual growth and to learn to live in dignity with limited renewable resources.

As converts, both expected that people would listen to them. When Osborn's book was reprinted in 1968, however, he expressed deep disappointment. The peoples of the world were still living beyond their means. They were still marching toward the edge of the cliff. As we listen to major voices in ecology from 1948 to the present, I think it is apparent that they all share the alternative politics of nature expressed by Vogt and Osborn. We must accept our place in a nature that is timeful, unstable, and limited. We must reject the illusion of independence and recognize the reality of interdependence. This alternative politics of nature was expressed in a collection of essays published in 1973, *From Conservation to Ecology: The Development of Environmental Concern.* The contributors argued that the resources within the earth as our home must be conserved for future generations. The biologist Barry Commoner, in his essay "Can We Survive?," and the heretical economist Robert Heilbroner, in his essay "Ecological Armageddon," both emphasized that modern people had been able to sustain a population explosion because they had utilized nonrenewable resources such as coal and oil. Commoner and Heilbroner asked modern people to consider what will happen when nonrenewable sources of energy begin to dwindle. It was obvious to them that modern people would bid up the prices of these commodities, and then people would begin to experience a future of severe inflation. This would, at first, cause starvation among the poorest people, and then hard times would begin to move upward into the middle classes. In their fanatical quest for constant economic growth, the middle classes, for Heilbroner and a few other heretical economists such as Nicholas Georgescu-Roegen and Herman Daly, had ignored renewable sources of energy. The middle classes had not been concerned about how the huge population made possible by the use of nonrenewable sources of energy was reducing the fertility of the land and the availability of freshwater. Imagining that they were leaving their limited home and entering a magical unlimited world, the middle classes felt no responsibility for conserving the renewable resources that sustained life at home.[14]

By the 1970s, the small group of physical scientists and social scientists who had come to believe modern people were self-destructive had also come to identify the world defined by Newton as the major source of the illusions leading modernity toward suicide. The Newtonian paradigm described nature as a perpetual-motion machine. One did not ask where energy came from. In this outlook, one did not talk about either renewable or nonrenewable resources. This certainly was the attitude of neoclassical economists. But when scientists in the nineteenth century began to imagine the universe as dynamic and full of energy, one now could construct a paradigm in which it was necessary to be concerned about both nonrenewable and renewable sources of energy. The creation of such a paradigm had to wait, however, until the weakening of Bourgeois Nationalism in the 1940s made it possible for one to write about the global patterns of a timeful nature. But, of course, another new global perspective made it possible for neoclassical economists to revitalize the Newtonian vision of a universal nature that was immutable. And the voices of the neoclassical economists who were speaking for the dominant political and economic culture drowned out the voices of the handful of heretical economists and the minority of scientists who were warning about a future where nonrenewable sources of energy were diminishing and renewable sources of energy were neglected.

The 1970s was a decade, then, in which there was a new self-consciousness about the difference between conservation at the national level and ecology at the global level. Barry Commoner published two important books, *The Closing Circle* (1971) and *The Poverty of Power:*

Energy and the Economic Crisis (1976). Nicholas Georgescu-Roegen published *The Entropy Law and the Economic Process* (1971). Herman Daly edited a collection of essays titled *Toward a Steady-State Economy* (1973). It was clear to these scholars that most economists in the 1970s were not aware that Newton's concept of a timeless space had been replaced by a physics that defined space as full of energy and always in motion.[15]

Georgescu-Roegen, in *The Entropy Law and the Economic Process*, directly attacked the belief of orthodox economists that the marketplace, like nature, was timeless. He asked them to go back to the mid-nineteenth century, when the first and second laws of thermodynamics were constructed. The first law states that energy cannot be created or destroyed. It can, however, be transformed from one state to another. The second law of thermodynamics is that every time energy is transformed from one state to another there is a loss in the amount of energy that can be used to do work. Entropy is a measure of the amount of energy no longer able to do work. Finally, all of the sun's concentrated energy will be diffused throughout the universe. The sun and its surrounding planets will be dead. In 1980, *Entropy: A New World View* was published. The author, Jeremy Rifkin, who had academic training as an economist and as an ecologist, wanted to make Georgescu-Roegen's analysis available to a wider audience. Rifkin emphasized that time is meaningful to us as an expression of the change in energy from a concentrated state to a diffuse state, from order to disorder.[16]

The urban middle-class Greeks of antiquity and their heirs in the Renaissance had, of course, rejected the generational perspective of traditional culture. Traditional people measured time by the rising and setting of the sun, by the appearance and disappearance of the seasons, by the yearly cycle. They measured time by the birth, death, and rebirth of generations of animals and humans. They measured time by the waxing and waning of the sun's energy available to them. They lived with rhythms of concentrated energy becoming diffuse. Now in 1980 Rifkin was announcing that entropy provided a new worldview. Neoclassical economists must see that the marketplace is an expression of the energy it contains. Orthodox economists must learn that they are permanently limited by the finite amount of concentrated energy that can be used to drive machines and automobiles, heat houses, make fertilizer. They are not in the Land of Oz, where no one ever ages and dies.

But, of course, in the segregated university no one asked orthodox economists why they were able to ignore the laws of thermodynamics. Certainly the presidents of universities, like the presidents of the United States and other political leaders throughout the world, knew it was common sense that economies would expand forever. Barry Commoner in 1970 had imagined an integrated university. If culture is within nature and nature is within culture, we must see, he insisted, that the humanities, social sciences, and physical sciences are all studying the same world. Integration, not segregation, he concluded, must come to characterize education. The Newtonian world, with its mechanical metaphors, could justify studying isolated parts, but if we see a living world in which everything is related to everything else, we should, he continued, use organic metaphors that define parts as having meaning only in relationship with the whole. But when I retired in 2009, I left the world of higher education still divided into autonomous departments. As we experienced the entropy of the winter of 2009–10, Commoner's dream, like that of Snow, seemed impossible of fulfillment.

In his 2002 book *Down to Earth: Nature's Role in American History,* the historian Ted Steinberg described the 1960s and 1970s as revolutionary decades in which many people were inspired to proclaim "a declaration of interdependence." The biologist and nature writer Rachel Carson had written *Silent Spring* (1962), which became a national best seller in the year it was published. She wanted to teach her readers that the world is not made up of separate parts. We should learn that all life is interrelated. Because we do not think in terms of interdependence, we have not seen the danger caused by our indiscriminate use of chemicals, especially pesticides. DDT, for example, was being used to kill mosquitoes. But in an interdependent world, Carson pointed out, chemical poisons cannot be segregated. Many birds were dying. Most dramatically, the insecticide DDT was destroying the eagle population. We humans should also understand that we are poisoning ourselves.[17]

Since the dominant culture assumed a timeless nature, Carson's arguments contradicted established common sense. *Time* magazine was condescending and sexist in its comments about her when it said, "Many scientists sympathize with Miss Carson's love of wildlife and even with her mystical attachment to the balance of nature. But they fear her emotional and inaccurate outlook." Her appeal to her fellow citizens to understand how their actions had an impact on their natural environment was reinforced, however, by a four-year drought in the Northeast and Midwest. As the levels of the Great Lakes declined, the impact of pollution on these bodies of water was dramatized. Detergents discharged from washing machines were destroying many forms of life, especially in Lake Erie. Photos of the earth sent back by the astronauts also emphasized how we were within the boundaries of a circle. By 1970, then, there seemed to be a national movement to save the environment. Twenty million people participated in the first observance of Earth Day on April 22, 1970.

President Richard Nixon and the U.S. Congress responded by creating the Environmental Protection Agency (EPA), which quickly became one of the largest federal agencies. Similar agencies were established in a number of U.S. states. A torrent of legislation was passed in response to this new and vigorous expression of national concern for the health of the environment. The Clean Air Act was passed in 1970. The Water Pollution Control Act was passed in 1972. Eight more major acts dealing with the environment and conservation were passed by Congress between 1972 and 1980. Because of this legislation, air and water quality improved throughout the nation.

During the 1960s and 1970s, combined membership in the variety of organizations in the United States committed to conservation grew from half a million to 2.5 million. Then in the 1980s and 1990s most of this momentum seemed to disappear. Why? In his book *From Apocalypse to a Way of Life* (2003), the literary critic Frederick Buell hoped to answer this question. His first publications were on poets and poetry, but, like his fellow literary critic Andrew Ross, he felt that he was participating in a major cultural and environmental crisis. Ross believed that economists were not addressing the deteriorating position of workers throughout the world, and so he made himself into an economist. Now Buell found no historians engaged in explaining why the expanding ecology movement of the 1960s and 1970s had been shrinking in the 1980s and 1990s. And so he made himself into a cultural historian. An answer that he developed at length was that "a strong and enormously successful antienvironmental disinformation industry sprang up." The relationship between this disinformation movement organized by corporations and the Republican Party was analyzed a few years later by Chris Mooney in his book *The Republican War on Science* (2005).[18]

The declaration of interdependence that Steinberg saw as a major characteristic of the environmental movement in the 1960s and 1970s was now challenged by a revitalized declaration of independence. Between Republican president Richard Nixon, elected in 1968, and Republican president Ronald Reagan, elected in 1980, their party moved away from its support in the 1940s and 1950s of the commitment to government activism and regulation of the economy developed by the Democratic Party under the leadership of President Franklin Roosevelt in the 1930s.

When Reagan was elected in 1980, however, the Republican Party had embraced the neoliberal, neoclassical position expressed in academic economics. The marketplace made rational decisions. Government made irrational decisions. Government regulation, therefore, must be removed. As the Republicans led the way back to trusting the laws of the marketplace, the Democrats followed. When Bill Clinton became president in 1993, he, too, was opposed to government regulation. Both parties, then, were participating in the transnational patterns of neoliberalism and neoclassical economics. The global marketplace was understood as a natural space in which the individual could be independent of irrational governmental actions. How, then, could an ecological movement committed to increasing governmental regulations of many aspects of the economy keep its momentum after 1980? Converts to the neoliberal–neoclassical position saw conservationists as dangerous heretics. Their science was seen as irrational.

The hostility of a neoliberal Republican Party toward the scientific authority claimed by conservationists was intensified by the movement of most Southern whites from the Democratic Party to the Republican Party in the 1970s. From the Civil War to World War II, Southern whites were loyal to a national Democratic Party committed to defending white supremacy in their region. Then, from President Truman's order to desegregate the military in 1947 to President Johnson's support of civil rights legislation in 1964, Southern whites felt betrayed by the national Democratic Party. By the 1970s they had fled to the Republican Party. From 1896 to 1968, there really was no Republican Party in the South. Since the 1970s, however, Southern whites have been the most loyal voting bloc in the Republican Party.

And many of these white Southern Republicans were fundamentalist Protestants. By the 1830s, Southern Methodists and Baptists were defining themselves as better Christians than Northern Methodists and Baptists. They saw themselves as obeying the Bible's sanctification of slavery while Northern Protestants disobeyed the Bible when they criticized slavery. When many Northern Protestants after the 1870s accepted Darwin's theory of evolution, Southern Protestants again claimed spiritual superiority. They, unlike the Northerners, continued to accept the biblical story of creation. Now, after the 1970s, Southern fundamentalist Protestants were in a position to make an alliance with the neoliberal–neoclassical fundamentalists who saw the marketplace as a timeless space. Both the Protestant and the secular fundamentalists would denounce the idea that nature is timeful.

These Southern fundamentalist Protestants also had allies throughout the nation. As Americans entered the twenty-first century, polls indicated that half of them did not believe in evolution. Steinberg in his book saw the environmental legislation of the 1970s as the beginning of a new era. Buell's book, in contrast, was more of an obituary. This also was true of *Losing Ground: American Environmentalism at the Close of the Twentieth Century* (1995), by the journalist Mark Dowie, whom Buell had cited frequently. Perhaps, then, we should consider the possibility that the environmental legislation of the 1970s marked the end of an era of governmental action that began in 1933 with the presidency of Franklin Roosevelt. That activism was a response to the collapse of the marketplace. It had betrayed its premise of a timeless, natural equilibrium that classical economists believed was its major characteristic. But by the 1970s, faith in the timeless stability of the marketplace was revitalized. In the magical world of the global marketplace, with its supposedly perpetual surpluses, there was no place for the doom and gloom of heretical economists such as Nicholas Georgescu-Roegen and Herman Daly. When one anticipated the thrill of perpetual economic growth, their talk of entropy and limits seemed to be esoteric gibberish.[19]

There is the ironic possibility, therefore, that, just when neoclassical economists, popular pundits, and much of the public expected a sudden and dramatic escape from complexity and scarcity, ecologists hoped for a sudden and dramatic escape from this self-destructive modern illusion. They expected widespread conversions to their vision of a natural history that was characterized by change, complexity, and scarcity. For ecologists, natural history was primarily a history of slow change, but there were occasionally periods of rapid change. These expectations that the public would instantly embrace their vision of natural history did not take into account how current social, cultural, economic, and political patterns are organized to move into a future of endless growth. It would be outrageous, for example, to suggest that children should be interdependent with their parents. For the middle class, it was a law of nature that children became independent of their parents. This social expectation was interrelated with the economic expectation that children leaving home would find a new world of surpluses. It was interrelated with the bourgeois fear of generations that suggested we cannot escape time and its limits.

But the English scientist Mike Hulme has argued in his book *Why We Disagree about Climate Change* (2009) that science is always part of culture. People will not embrace their participation in natural history until they see that world as good and beautiful. For Hulme, truth segregated from the good and beautiful is meaningless. And most modern people in 2010 found the good and beautiful in the timeless utopia of the global marketplace. Many current ecologists, such as the biologists Paul and Anne Ehrlich, in their book *One with Nineveh: Politics, Consumption, and the Human Future* (2005), still defined two worlds (Here we go again!), one rational, the other irrational. They, in contrast to contemporary neoclassical economists, do not see an old irrational traditional world that is giving way to a new rational modern world. For the Ehrlichs, the modern world is completely irrational. Rational ecologists, like themselves, see that all life depends on renewable resources. But modern people believe they can have security in an economy that depends on nonrenewable sources of energy. Using and depleting these resources, they have created a population explosion that fills expanding cities. Those cities are dependent on nonrenewable sources of energy. When those resources are depleted, cities across the world will collapse.[20]

Paul Ehrlich had issued a major warning about this inevitable collapse in his book *The Population Bomb* (1968). Now, in their more recent book *One with Nineveh,* the Ehrlichs take an in-depth look at the rise and fall of the city of Nineveh, the capital of the ancient Assyrian empire located on the Tigris River. Prisoners of hubris, according to the Ehrlichs, the rulers of Nineveh believed they could bring in surpluses from the empire forever to sustain their city. Focused on those distant resources, they neglected the agricultural world that surrounded the city and provided it with food. The collapse of their empire and the disappearance of their city under the shifting sands of a desert came when both nonrenewable resources from the edges of the empire and the renewable resources right outside the city walls became scarce.[21]

Writing in 2005, the Ehrlichs expressed bitterness toward the wasteful lifestyles of the rich in the United States but also everywhere in the world. And they were even more bitter toward those who told the public they could ignore the warnings of the ecologists that there are limits to growth. The most influential and dangerous of those false prophets were those who promised that new developments in technology would overcome any shortages of both nonrenewable and renewable resources. Technological progress supposedly would provide endless prosperity. For the Ehrlichs, then, modern people had turned their backs on the essential role of renewable resources for their survival. They had put their faith in an endless supply of nonrenewable resources that supposedly made perpetual growth possible. We must, they declared, escape the irrational faith of modern people. "The time has come for what Sam Harris called an 'End of Faith.'" And so they concluded, we must engage in "a rational search for a sustainable future."

I am suggesting, then, that the Ehrlichs represent a particular group of ecologists who use modern categories to criticize the modern world. At the beginning of this book, I argued that the urban middle-class Greek men who were Plato's contemporaries saw their movement away from the renewable resources of the traditional agricultural societies as a negative revolution. They said they were not creating a new culture. They were only stepping out of irrational artful traditional cultures. They were achieving an artless natural relationship with timeless nature. This dichotomy of a rational and an irrational world also was the vision of the Ehrlichs and a particular group of ecologists. They had stepped out of an artful, irrational modern culture and had achieved a rational relationship with nature. They had experienced a negative revolution.

They did not see, therefore, that in rejecting the modern paradigm they, like Plato's generation, were using their imaginations to create an alternative paradigm. They did not see the need to make their implicit visions of a good and beautiful world explicit. There was, however, another group of ecologists who did believe it was necessary to present an alternative to the modern world that explicitly linked the true, the good, and the beautiful. A founding text for this school of ecologists committed to a positive revolution was E. F. Schumacher's *Small Is*

Beautiful (1973). And many younger ecologists are now explicitly arguing that there was and is greater social justice in a number of traditional societies than in our modern society. Raj Patel, for example, in his book *The Value of Nothing: How to Reshape Market Society and Redefine Democracy* (2009), presents the case that societies that share the resources of a commons are morally superior to our self-centered world. They have a strong foundation of social justice. And as theologians begin to discover ecology, some of them now appreciate Charles Dickens's position in *A Christmas Carol*. Scrooge can have a rich spiritual life only when he rejects the values of the marketplace. *Christian Faith and the Environment* (1998), by Brennan Hill, and *Religion and the New Ecology: Environmental Responsibility in a World in Flux* (2006), edited by David Lodge and Christopher Hamlin, are two of the books that represent this belated discovery by theologians of the ecological position expressed by Vogt and Osborn in 1948.[22]

In an essay published in 1996, the heretical economist Herman Daly pondered why it was only ecologists who were writing jeremiads warning that the modern world faced a future of shortages and great instability. Why were religious, cultural, and political leaders not joining ecologists such as the Ehrlichs in issuing jeremiads? We should remember, however, how thoroughly most of us are initiated into the modern metaphor of two worlds. We expect, therefore, that leaving the status quo should inevitably take us into a new and more prosperous world. For the many Catholics, Protestants, and Jews who had converted to the idea of evolution by 1900, Charles Darwin seemed to promise that the future would be more abundant than the past. Darwin's natural history, as it was understood by the middle classes in a number of nations, guaranteed a happy ending as we participated in an exodus from an old world of scarcity and complexity to a new world of plenty and simplicity.

Instead, ecologists such as the Ehrlichs, therefore, were asking middle-class people to abruptly renounce their bourgeois culture. They must recognize that capitalism cannot expand forever. They must recognize that when their children leave home they will not find a future full of surpluses. They must see that in a future characterized by scarcity and complexity there will be no place for the bourgeois ideal of the autonomous, self-made individual. If one takes interdependence seriously, there will be no place for a fragmented economy of separate pieces of private property. Plato's metaphor of two worlds had made sense to the members of this new cultural group who exchanged surpluses in the urban marketplace. The new science of the Renaissance had made sense to the middle class as a way to free markets from the authority of medieval restrictions.

If today we find ourselves with a science that denies there is a sound foundation for middle-class expectations about the future, where does one find a revolutionary group that will use this heretical science to overthrow the bankrupt authority of bourgeois culture? Ecological scientists remain isolated heretics because they cannot mobilize a group of heretical followers. The middle classes from Plato to Newton to Friedman have been revolutionists. The goal of the middle-class revolutionists is to destroy the traditional cultures that assumed renewable resources were the sacred source of life. The social scientists of the 1960s, such as Daniel Lerner and Walt Rostow, were justifying the assault when they compared the irrational use of resources by traditional people to the rational use of resources by modern people. Obviously the middle classes do not worry about any threat from a revitalization of traditional cultures. Then the United States became the symbolic center of international capitalism during the Cold War and had purged a potentially revolutionary American working-class politics inspired by Karl Marx. Working-class radicalism also disappeared in the Western European countries. And, of course, the Soviet Union in 1989 had ceased to be a center of anticapitalist internationalism, and then Communist China also soon followed the path to a market economy. Karl Marx had been relegated to the dustbin of history as his former followers embraced the bourgeois faith in the marketplace as that magical space where economic growth had no limits. This is what Francis Fukuyama meant by "the end of history."[23]

It had seemed to the historian Ted Steinberg and to other observers that significant numbers of middle-class people were moving from their orthodox commitment to independence to a heretical commitment to interdependence. They seemed to be moving toward a new green politics. But then by 1980 many middle-class Americans seemed to be intensifying their commitment to independence. And so there was no significant growth of green politics. The sociologist Andrew Szasz has an explanation of how middle-class Americans apparently could accept the reality of air, water, and land pollution in the 1960s and 1970s and still preserve their sense of independence from the 1980s to the present. In his book *Shopping Our Way to Safety: How We*

Changed from Protecting the Environment to Protecting Ourselves (2007), he points to shifting middle-class attitudes toward regulation. He sees an attitude favorable to regulation giving way to one of increasing hostility.[24]

For Szasz, middle-class Americans had accepted the reality of pollution in the 1960s and 1970s. If, however, they had turned their backs on regulation in the 1980s, then they would have to deal with ecological problems as individuals. For Szasz, these middle-class citizens had, since the 1980s, engaged in what he calls an "inverted quarantine." Quarantines, he argues, express the sense that our environment is sound and healthy. Its people must be protected from particular diseases. They and their sound environment must be kept from contamination. After a period of quarantine, of segregation of the healthy majority from the unhealthy minority, one expects that the threat will disappear.

But, for Szasz, when the middle class converted to an ecological perspective, they came to see the larger environment as polluted, as diseased. Rejecting collective action after 1980 as the way to deal with pollution, they resigned themselves to living in an environment that is unhealthy. This is his definition of an inverted quarantine. Individuals must segregate themselves from the unhealthy environment to avoid air pollution. Middle-class individuals can move out of fume-filled cities to the cleaner air of the suburbs. Learning that the water that comes out of the tap contains dangerous chemicals, they can protect themselves by drinking bottled water. Learning that most foods contain dangerous chemicals, they can protect themselves by buying organic food. For Szasz, however, who believes that we are in a global ecological crisis, this behavior is like the proverbial ostrich putting its head in the sand. He is angry at the sense of resignation that he sees in this middle-class behavior. These individual efforts to free their personal bubble of space from larger environmental patterns indicates, to me, that most of the middle-class converts to ecology in the 1960s and 1970s did not imagine that they had become participants in natural history. They did not see themselves as interdependent within a chain of generations. They continued to see themselves as self-made and independent. Implicitly nature must continue to be the timeless foundation for the timeless marketplace.

I propose, then, that we work with the hypothesis that many middle-class Americans by 1990 had constructed a profound dichotomy between a secondary nature that is timeful and unstable—a nature with a history—and a primary nature that is timeless and stable. This is the nature expressed in the immutable laws of the marketplace. Ecological problems existed in the complex and unpredictable secondary nature, but the primary nature promised a marketplace of perpetual prosperity. Middle-class citizens would deal with the ecological issues as private individuals. Middle-class politics, the politics of public life, would focus on the marketplace and rising standards of living. This hypothesis provides an explanation for the failure of politics in the United States and elsewhere to address the dangers of global warming as presented by the scientific community. Most scientists since the 1990s have been recommending large-scale government regulation of industry and automobiles to reduce the amount of greenhouse gases that we are releasing into the atmosphere.

As we have seen, geologists had challenged Newton's definition of space as timeless. And they argued that in the lengthy history of the earth there had been long-term patterns of warming and cooling. From Plato to Newton, the orthodox view of nature as timeless included climate. But now in the nineteenth century physicists and chemists could ask the question, What causes climate to change? Working in England in the 1850s, John Tyndall proposed that it was the changing pattern of gases in the atmosphere. As these patterns changed, more or less of the sun's energy would be trapped within the atmosphere. And in the 1890s a Swedish scientist, Svante Arrhenius, had proposed that emissions from factories could change the mixture of gases in the atmosphere.

I also have argued that it was the dramatic shift in perspective in the 1940s, related to the desacralization of national space, that provided the context for Vogt and Osborne to propose a major role for humans in changing their natural environment. This may be why Charles Keating began to measure the amount of carbon dioxide in the atmosphere at two stations, one in Hawaii, the other in Antarctica, in 1957. He now had statistical evidence of the rapidly increasing amount of carbon dioxide in the atmosphere. This was a greenhouse gas that trapped the sun's heat and accelerated global warming.

By the 1970s, as we have seen, many in the scientific community had accepted the perspective presented by Vogt and Osborn in 1948. We are within the circle of a finite, living earth. Within the circle, we cannot experience perpetual growth. Instead, we will experience self-destruction if we continue our efforts at endless growth. One of the first of the many warnings that appeared in the 1970s was the Report of the Club of Rome, which marshaled evidence to support the thesis of the limits to growth. It was within this context that the scientist Wallace Broecker published an article in 1987 titled "Unpleasant Surprises in the Greenhouse." He argued that because of the huge increases in the amount of carbon dioxide entering the atmosphere, there was a probability of a sudden, dramatic increase in the earth's temperature.

In the artless world of the marketplace, with its immutable laws guiding rational individuals, there are no ironies. But those of us who are outside this perfect space frequently experience irony. I see a major one in the confrontations in the 1990s between the fear expressed by scientists about the consequences of global warming and the widespread euphoria expressed by much of the public about the consequences of a global economy.

In 2009, William O'Neill published *A Bubble in Time: America during the Interwar Years, 1989–2001*. In this book, O'Neill, a well-known historian, argues that never before and never since the period 1989–2001 have Americans been so free from fear. The Cold War and the threat of nuclear war were gone. The economy was booming, and a future of perpetual growth in the global marketplace seemed guaranteed. If, as Szasz argues, many Americans were afraid of a polluted natural environment, this fear was insignificant in contrast to fears of war and economic decline. In his analysis of this period of widespread positive thinking, O'Neill includes no material on environmental issues. The index of his book includes no entries for the topics of climate change, conservation, ecology, environmentalism, or global warming. In this brief era of good feelings, most Americans seemed self-confident that they had quarantined themselves from a dangerous environment, including global warming.[25]

When the war on terror became a major source of fear in 2001, and when fear of a collapsing economy grew between 2001 and 2007, these new fears seemed to overshadow completely fears about the environment. A poll taken in 2006 asked Americans whether they were concerned about global warming. Then a similar poll taken in 2009 revealed that global warming was of less concern to Americans than it had been in 2006. Reality for most political, economic, and cultural leaders in the United States and throughout the world was a perpetually expanding marketplace. Implicitly these leaders were committed to the metaphor of two worlds, a timeful, unstable old world of culture and a timeless, stable new world of nature in which the market operated. Implicitly, they denied or ignored the view of nature as timeful and unstable that had become increasingly persuasive in the scientific community since the early nineteenth century.

Starting in the 1980s, nations came together in conferences about global warming. National leaders were concerned enough about the warnings of scientists regarding the destructive consequences of unlimited emission of greenhouse gases into the atmosphere that periodically they sent representatives to international meetings to discuss the problem. Always at these conferences the issue of growth was raised. It would cost money to limit emissions from factories and automobiles. This was money that should be used for economic growth. How could a nation agree to limit its emissions of greenhouse gases unless all nations agreed? If only some agreed, they would lose their competitive advantage. As professional economists were discovering by 2000, a global marketplace had not caused nationalism to disappear.

In 1988, the World Meteorological Organization created the Intergovernmental Panel on Climate Change (IPCC), which soon gained support from the United Nations Environment Programme. The IPCC quickly called a conference that met in Montreal in 1989. This was followed by a conference at Rio de Janeiro in 1992 and one in Kyoto in 1997. The purpose of these conferences was to persuade the nations of the world to agree on limiting their emissions of greenhouse gases. But the representatives from each nation were aware that national economic growth was a much higher political priority than controlling global warming. As President George H. W. Bush stated in response to the meetings in Rio, "The American way of life is not negotiable." Little progress had been made, therefore, in reducing the emissions of greenhouse gases. Still, many scientists were hopeful that a meeting of the nations in Copenhagen in 2009 would result in a treaty that would finally establish strict standards. But these scientists were bitterly disappointed by the continued gap between their vision of a transnational crisis of global warming that must be contained and the vision of most political leaders that economic growth was their national priority. At Copenhagen the industrialized nations agreed only that each would publicly list its individual actions to limit emissions of greenhouse gases.

In 2009 a scientist, Tim Flannery, published *Now or Never: Why*

We Must Act Now To End Climate Change and Create a Sustainable Future. He hoped that his book would help persuade the political leaders meeting at Copenhagen that a profound crisis exists. He hoped he could persuade them that if they did not act decisively, humans would face a tragic future. "From mid-2007 onward," he wrote, "I've found it increasingly difficult to read the scientific findings without despairing." From the warnings of Vogt and Osborn in 1948 to 2010, scientists had been trying to convince their fellow citizens that their commitment to perpetual growth was self-destructive. Now, however, with the failure of participants in international conferences from the 1980s to 2009 to accept the argument that the movement toward self-destruction was accelerating, one heard a tone of sadness and resignation in the writings of many scientists. This was true of Flannery, who expressed both hope and despair.[26]

In 2010 the ecologist Bill McKibben published *Eaarth: Making a Life on a Tough New Planet.* In this book he does not express hope that governments will act to control global warming. He also does not express despair at their inaction. Instead, he announces that global warming has already ended the world dominated by the middle classes since the eighteenth century. There is now, he declares, a new earth. Listen to our commentators, he says, listen as they announce an unprecedented drought in Russia or unprecedented floods in Iowa and Pakistan. In 2010 they define these catastrophes as aberrations from normal weather patterns. But, McKibben declares, the temperature of the earth has risen. This, therefore, is a new earth where frequent floods and droughts are the normal pattern. It is to be expected that storms will be more frequent and violent. Warmer temperatures have changed major air currents, and new patterns of airflow, therefore, are now keeping moisture from reaching areas where grass and trees had grown. New deserts are emerging.[27]

The authors of three books published in 2011 agree with McKibben that we have indeed entered a new world of limits. These books are Paul Gilding's *The Great Disruption: Why the Climate Crisis Will Bring on the End of Shopping and the Birth of a New World,* Richard Heinberg's *The End of Growth: Adapting to Our New Economic Reality,* and Chris Martenson's *The Crash Course: The Unsustainable Future of Our Economy, Energy, and Environment.* Their arguments contradict the orthodox economists who continue to define the Great Recession of 2008 as a fleeting exception to our normal pattern of perpetual growth. These establishment economists point out that from the 1950s to the present all downturns in the business cycle were brief. We have quickly returned to the normal pattern of economic expansion. They predicted, therefore, that the downturn of 2008 would end in 2009. Then they predicted it would end in 2010, 2011, 2012, or ?[28]

For Gilding, Heinberg, and Martenson, however, the Great Recession of 2008 was indeed unprecedented for the period from 1950 to 2000. But the limits of the earth are now making that half century abnormal. Slow growth or stagnation is now normal. Thomas Friedman, a columnist for the *New York Times,* wrote in his October 11, 2011, review of Gilding's book, "When you see spontaneous protests erupting from Tunisia to Tel Aviv to Wall Street, it is clear that something is happening globally that needs to be defined." Gilding's *The Great Disruption* is, for Friedman, an important attempt at defining this global crisis. Gilding's major thesis, as Friedman sees it, is "that these demonstrations are a sign that the current growth-obsessed capitalist system is reaching its financial and ecological limits."[29] No longer a prophet, Gilding in 2011 presents himself as a reporter. "We've been borrowing from the future, and the debt has fallen due," he declares. "We have reached or passed the limits of our current economic model of consumer-driven economic growth. We are heading for a social and economic hurricane that will cause great damage." Gilding hopes his readers will listen to his suggestions on how they can re-create their economic lives in order to survive in a no-growth economy.[30]

Richard Heinberg also presents himself as a reporter, not a prophet. He mocks the orthodox economists who refuse to see that the marketplace is within time and that our natural environment is unstable. Only by isolating the marketplace can they argue that the Great Recession is a temporary and abnormal situation. These economists ignore the continued high levels of unemployment, the continued decline of real estate values, the terrible burden of debt crushing individuals and governments. In contrast to the optimism of orthodox economists, Heinberg sees our present situation as characterized by scarcity, not plenty. We have reached the maximum peaks in available oil, water, and arable land. We are now sliding down from those peaks. We must learn to celebrate survival, not growth. We must cherish our renewable resources in order to sustain our community. Like Gilding, Heinberg suggests dramatic changes in lifestyles.

Chris Martenson is also sure that the Great Recession of 2008 provides evidence that our modern history of constant expansion is over.

Our next twenty years will be dramatically different from the previous twenty. He footnotes this prophecy with evidence from our current crisis. Like Gilding and Heinberg, he points to the years from 2008 to 2011 to show the challenge of limited energy and food resources to our expectation of unlimited growth. This faith in the inevitability of increasing wealth encouraged us to borrow. Future growth supposedly would give us the added wealth needed to eliminate the debt. But the debt crisis currently being experienced in the United States by the national government, most state governments, and many individuals dramatizes our economic stagnation. And, of course, many governments in Europe, Africa, Asia, and Latin America also cannot pay their debts because the global economy is stagnant. Instability, therefore, is global. Martenson, like Gilding and Heinberg, hopes that we will contain the crisis by renouncing our modern faith in limitless growth.

Perhaps the recognition by economic leaders that the Great Recession of 2008 is unprecedented for the period since 1945 explains why corporations have intensified their efforts to discredit the science that identifies and explains global warming. Capitalism depends upon confidence that there will be a future of increasing plenitude; the scientific presentation of the reality of global warming threatens to undermine that confidence. Our future will be unpredictable.

I do not find it surprising, therefore, that James Lawrence Powell's *The Inquisition of Climate Science* should have been published in 2011.[31] Powell explicitly wants his readers to think about the parallels between the war waged by the medieval church against modern science at the time of the Renaissance and the current war against modern science. The statement on the dust jacket of his book reads:

> Modern science is under the greatest and most successful attack in recent history. An industry of denial abetted by news media and "infotainment" broadcasters more interested in selling controversy than presenting facts has duped half the American public into rejecting the facts of climate science—an overwhelming body of rigorously vetted scientific evidence showing that human-caused, carbon-based emissions are linked to warming the earth. The industry of climate-science denial is succeeding. Fuller acceptance has declined even as the scientific evidence for global warming has increased.

I believe, however, that Powell misinterprets the current war on science. I see much of the public engaged in a war against heretical science. This public is trying to save modern science. During the

Renaissance and Enlightenment modern scientists, as the historian of science Carolyn Merchant has pointed out in her *The Death of Nature*, killed the medieval view of nature as a living body. And when modern Europeans came to the Americas, they wanted to eradicate the Native American understanding of nature as a living body.[32]

Imagining nature as a lifeless–deathless machine, the middle classes were certain they were in an eternally youthful environment in which capitalism could perpetually expand. Newton was a Protestant fundamentalist as well as a physicist. Both the Bible and nature were, for him, God's timeless creations. Recent polls show that more than half of Americans today do not believe in Darwin's theory of evolution. They remain loyal to Newton's timeless universe, the universe of modern science. This has been the timeless universe of neoclassical economists from the 1950s to the present. From the appearance of geology in the first half of the nineteenth century down to the present, modern people have wanted to turn a deaf ear to any message that suggests the earth is timeful.

In the next chapter I will analyze several of the optimistic prophecies propounded in the 1990s. These millennial predictions were, of course, much more popular than the dark future forecast by scientists. And then, after 2000, the utopian prophecies failed. Would this unpleasant shock bring the paradigm revolution that ecologists so hoped for? But the old world of instability and complexity in which we dwell reminds us that we should expect to encounter irony and contradictions at least as often as we experience constructive revolutions. One of these ironies is that the politics of the bourgeois nations has become even more committed to the magic of the marketplace.

Still, a number of individuals after 2000 were searching for alternative narratives that involved defining the earth as our home. And in politics one found groups in the Republican Party and to the right of that party who seemed to be retreating toward the pre-1940 belief that only the United States was an expression of timeless space. It will be interesting to observe the developing debate between those who continue to hold their international faith in the millennial promise of the global marketplace and those who are falling back on the tradition of an exceptional and isolated space that is immutable. Once again there are groups who define the United States as the only sanctuary from the flux of history.

6 WHEN PROPHECY FAILS

IRRATIONAL EXUBERANCE is the title of a book published in 2000. The author, Robert Shiller, is an economist. He was responding to what he called the "herd behavior" of people in the 1990s. Why, he asked, did so many intelligent people believe they were entering a "New Era" with a "New Economy"? Why, he asked, did they believe that in this "New World" the stock market boom was to last forever? Listen to me, he cautioned. This boom is about to burst. And it did.[1]

Unlike the many orthodox economists who imagine they are in the timeless and stable space of the marketplace, a heretical Shiller remembered that capitalism has a timeful history. One can see that capitalism has always been characterized by cycles of boom and bust. This unstable history of capitalism contradicts the faith of capitalists that they can transcend generational time.

In the revised edition of his book published in 2005, Shiller predicted that the boom in real estate values would soon collapse. And it did. He then looked back at his cross-country book tour in 2000. He expressed disappointment that so many of the people who came to hear him speak became angry. They had not come to hear him challenge their faith that the New Economy was the end of history. They wanted only confirmation of that faith.

The purpose of my book is to answer Shiller's questions. I have argued that ever since the construction of the cities of ancient Greece, middle-class men have imagined two worlds. There is the old world of farmers and hunters. These backward people assume their economy is limited to the plants and animals born each spring. They imagine a world in which life is sustained from generation to generation by this yearly cycle. But urban middle-class men in 400 B.C.E. and in 2000 C.E.

have believed they will experience an exodus from that old timeful world to a new timeless world free from cycles. In such a world surpluses are permanent and available to the self-made men who have escaped generational continuity. Why shouldn't people who hold this worldview expect that each boom is a doorway leading to an earthly paradise free from complexity and scarcity? Perhaps it is difficult for modern scholars like Shiller to imagine that the exuberance of the 1990s is part of a two-thousand-year tradition. Since the booms as doorways to new worlds of simplicity and plenty have always closed before the new Eden is reached, it has been necessary for the bourgeoisie to revitalize the tradition by repeatedly imagining another promised land.

Anthony F. C. Wallace, an anthropologist, has written extensively about revitalization movements. I see important parallels between his model and Kuhn's model of a sequence of cycles from revolutionary science to normal science and back to revolutionary science. I also see parallels between Wallace's model and the model of *The American Jeremiad* presented by Sacvan Bercovitch. His model was that of a promise of a timeless space, declension from the promise into time, and then a prophecy of the restoration of the promise of a timeless space. But Bercovitch found that in the cycle the Promised Land was continually redefined. And I have argued that when bourgeois nations failed to be the end of history the bourgeoisie began to replace them with the new promised land of the global marketplace.[2]

The sense of participation in a mass exodus into this supposedly timeless paradise grew stronger from the 1940s until the 1990s. For early prophets of this exodus such as Walt Rostow, a global economy that expressed the rational principles of international capitalism was challenged by the Marxist vision of a global economy that expressed the rational principles of international communism. But then, in 1989, the Soviet Union collapsed, and Moscow was no longer the ideological center of the prophecy of a forthcoming universal triumph of communism. There now seemed to be no doubt that international capitalism with Washington, D.C., as its ideological center was the wave of the future. This, as Francis Fukuyama reminded us, was "the end of history." And many Americans experienced exuberance. At last the prophecy of an exodus from an old to a new world was being fulfilled.

No one gave expression to this widespread euphoria more eloquently than Thomas Friedman, a Pulitzer Prize–winning columnist for the *New York Times*. His best-selling book *The Lexus and the Olive*

Tree: Understanding Globalization (1999) was constructed around the metaphor of two worlds. The olive tree symbolized traditional cultures rooted in particular places and dependent on limited local resources. In this old world the individual had no independence. But modern technology, symbolized by the Lexus, a luxury car, was making it possible for individuals to uproot themselves from generational continuity. They could be self-made. Here at last was the long-awaited exodus into the promised land of simplicity, plenty, and perpetual harmony.[3]

In 2005 a group of anthropologists contributed essays to the book *Why America's Top Pundits Are Wrong*. Two of the essays analyzed *The Lexus and the Olive Tree*. Implicitly these anthropologists were contrasting their commitment to cultural anthropology to Friedman's commitment to state-of-nature anthropology. Implicitly they were using their cultural anthropology to criticize Friedman's belief in negative revolution. How, these anthropologists asked, could Friedman believe that individuals can stand outside of complex culture? How could he believe that there are autonomous individuals? They did not ask, however, why Friedman's use of a metaphor of two worlds was so popular. Although they were aware of Anthony F. C. Wallace's work on revitalization movements, they did not imagine that Friedman was an important figure in the current revitalization of a long-held exodus narrative. Why did they not use their cultural anthropology to discuss Friedman's role in the dominant culture?[4]

Working with the essential elements of the politics of nature that Latour had identified in classical Greece, Friedman described the old world of the olive tree as artful, ephemeral, subjective, and irrational. In the new world of the Lexus, a rational, independent individual found immutable laws. When one entered this new world, one's imagination must be repressed. Here only reason should operate as the individual chose to obey the laws of nature embodied in the global marketplace. Friedman defined this rejection of subjectivity and the embrace of objectivity as the "Golden Straitjacket" and asserted that if we live without emotions in the global marketplace, we, of course, will all become rich.

Friedman, therefore, was in complete agreement with neoclassical economists and with the antipolitics of neoliberalism. All politics was artful and limited to emotion and imagination. Politics entering the artless marketplace was an alien and corrupting presence. And Friedman insisted repeatedly that the exodus taking place from particular, timeful cultures to the universal, timeless global market-place was moving humans from complexity to simplicity.

The anthropologists who were analyzing his popular book expressed astonishment that this Pulitzer Prize–winning columnist for the *New York Times* could imagine a future without complexity. They were not aware, then, of Bruno Latour's identification of a middle-class politics of nature that had been created in the cities of classical Greece. They had not imagined that bourgeois culture for more than two thousand years assumed an old artful, complex world of scarcity and a new natural, simple world of plenty. And the middle classes had believed that there would be a redemptive exodus from the hellish old world to the earthly heaven of the new world. They had read the theories of their fellow anthropologist Anthony F. C. Wallace about revitalization movements. But even in 2000 it seemed to be difficult for anthropologists to consider that their culture experiences moments of crisis. They did not see how Thomas Kuhn's theory that the history of science is the record of a series of paradigm revolutions had possible parallels to Wallace's model of revitalization movements. The anthropologists analyzing Friedman discussed him as a particular individual rather than as a symbolic figure who was expressing a powerful cultural outlook. In contrast, I am arguing that Friedman did express exuberance in his book because he knew that now, after centuries of expectation, a miraculous exodus was taking place. And many readers of his book shared his belief that they were the chosen generation to experience the end of history.

These critical anthropologists, therefore, did not see themselves as heretics who no longer shared the dominant paradigm of their community. They used the word *incantations* when they discussed Friedman's writing, but they did not see his sentences in a context of ritual call and response. He was not teaching his readers something new. He was engaged in a ceremony that gave substance to their long-held dreams.

In 2005 Friedman published another exuberant book, *The World Is Flat: A Brief History of the Twenty-First Century.* Like *The Lexus and the Olive Tree,* it expressed the orthodox middle-class expectation of an inevitable exodus from a complex old world of scarcity to a simple new world of plenitude. Reviewers in major newspapers expressed gratitude for Friedman's exceptional ability to describe this new world. One wrote, "The metaphor of a flat world, used by Friedman to describe the next phase of globalization, is ingenious." Another declared that Friedman had presented "a brilliant, instantly clarifying metaphor for the latest, arguably the most profound conceptual mega-shift to rock the world in living memory."[5]

In this book Friedman expressed astonishment that in *The Lexus and the Olive Tree* he had spent so much time discussing traditional cultures. He had known that it was inevitable that all people would leave their bounded traditional homes and move into the boundless new world of the global marketplace. But he confessed that he had not realized how many people already had been lifted up from the world of the olive tree by 2000. He had not realized how many had entered the world of the Lexus. We are in a "New Era," he declared, one that "empowers the individual." "It is now possible," he proclaimed, "for more people than ever to collaborate and compete in real time with more other people on more different kinds of work from more different corners of the planet and on a more equal footing than at any previous time in the history of the world."

The sociologists Roberto Patricio Korzeniewicz and Timothy Patrick Moran, in their book *Unveiling Inequality: A World-Historical Perspective* (2009), are extremely critical of this triumphalist story. They call it "the Official History of Globalization," which "insists that our past, present, and future are marked by the growing triumph of individual achievement over ascription." Instead, they see a modern world in which, from the Renaissance to the present, nations, not individuals, are the primary actors.[6]

In rejecting the official history of globalization, they are implicitly rejecting the fundamental bourgeois myth that the marketplace allows all individuals to escape from power and enjoy liberty. Instead, for them, marketplaces are always defined by the political and military power of particular nations. The evidence, for them, is overwhelming: most wealthy people in the world are born in nations with high standards of living. Most poor people are born in nations with low standards of living. And, within the wealthier nations, most wealthy individuals have wealthy parents. Most poor individuals, in contrast, are the children of poverty-stricken parents. Friedman had to repress massive amounts of evidence to claim that the world is flat.

John Kampfner, in his book *Freedom for Sale: Why the World Is Trading Democracy for Security* (2010), agrees with Korzeniewicz and Moran. He points out that the history of the large nations—China, India, and Russia—in the 1990s was a complete contradiction of the neoliberal dream that the entire world was converting to free-market capitalism. These nations were committed to markets but to ones that were regulated and directed by the national government. For Kampfner, the neoliberal prophecy that market economies inevitably create democracy no longer has authority. And where in Latin America and Africa the United States had used the World Trade Organization, the World Bank, and the CIA to force national governments to open their borders to foreign investments, most of these governments have remained or become dictatorships. Only an extremely strong faith could have kept Friedman and his readers from seeing these glaring contradictions to their prophecy of the emancipation of all individuals within the redemptive space of the global marketplace.[7]

Friedman had used India as an example of the way in which technology was liberating individuals and creating a flat world. He described the marvelous new centers of technology that were freeing this huge country from its ancient traditions. He wrote in loving detail about the new forms of communication. He did not mention that the new middle class in India connected to these developments lived within walls that segregated them from vast urban slums. Friedman would not want to know about the Mike Davis book *Planet of Slums*. He would not want to know about *Unveiling Inequality,* by Korzeniewicz and Moran, or about Kampfner's *Freedom for Sale.*

I describe Friedman, then, as a latter-day Frederick Jackson Turner. Turner had seen the history of the United States as a series of frontier experiences. Home was a place of generational hierarchy. A frontier was a doorway into a space in which sons found liberty as they escaped the power structures of their fathers. Each frontier was supposedly a flat world. For Turner it took a generation before the frontier ceased to be flat as sons became fathers and constructed hierarchies. It had taken historians who studied the United States more than a half century after 1890 to decide that there had never been any frontiers where society was flat.

Finally, by the 1960s and 1970s, however, many historians were ready to say that patterns of class, gender, ethnic, and social hierarchy coming from Europe had been transformed into European American patterns of hierarchy. This new world had never been flat. Turner had dwelled in a world of illusion. It is ironic, then, that just as neoclassical economists, political leaders, and many public intellectuals such as Friedman were proclaiming that the global marketplace was a frontier where hierarchy and power were replaced by equality and liberty, many scholars, including Korzeniewicz and Moran, were refuting the thesis that the global marketplace was a new frontier, a new flat world. For these heretical scholars, this international community was only the most recent phase of a bourgeois world that, since the Renaissance, has always been characterized by hierarchy and power. By 2000 a significant number of social scientists, therefore, were heretics. They no longer believed in the metaphor of two worlds and the exodus narrative.

Turner's vision of a sequence of frontiers, for me, should be interpreted as a sequence of revitalization movements. If the current bourgeois world is not flat, a space of liberty, it supposedly will soon leave hierarchy behind as we experience an exodus into the Promised Land. For me, it is evidence of the power of the bourgeois revitalization pattern in the 1990s that Friedman not only ignored class hierarchy and widespread poverty in India to proclaim the existence of a flat world but also ignored growing class hierarchy in the United States. And many of his readers certainly shared that ability to repress contrary evidence. But historians, political scientists, and sociologists, as well as anthropologists, now are instantly challenging the new-frontier thesis propounded by neoliberal politicians, neoclassical economists, and public intellectuals.

Sociologist Douglas Massey directly challenges that repression of class hierarchy in the United States that Friedman shares with neoclassical economists. In his book *Categorically Unequal: The American Stratification System* (2007), Massey presents evidence that neoliberal politics in the United States, the politics of the "Golden Straitjacket," has not created a classless society. Instead, when President Reagan began urging anti-union legislation, lowered taxes on the rich, reduced the buying power of the federal minimum wage, and cut social welfare spending, the standard of living also began a long decline. These are some of the contraindications to Friedman's belief that the "Golden Straitjacket" would cause rising standards of living everywhere in the world. Massey points out that these neoliberal policies have especially harmed women, African Americans, and Mexican Americans in the United States. These groups make up a disproportionate share of the 20 percent of Americans living in poverty. And African Americans and Mexican Americans make up a disproportionate share of the American prison population.[8]

Ha-Joon Chang was born in South Korea. He now teaches economics at Cambridge University in England. He represents a growing minority of young economists who have rejected neoclassical economics.

In his book *Bad Samaritans: The Myth of Free Trade and the Secret History of Capitalism* (2008), he places economics within the complex web of particular economic patterns. He sees no universal laws of the marketplace that can be expressed only in the language of mathematics. Like Massey, Chang wants to look at the record of neoliberal politics. He, however, is analyzing worldwide patterns. In his chapter "The Lexus and the Olive Tree Revisited," he, like many scholars, finds declining standards of living in our current world. In South America and Africa he finds that in the 1960s and 1970s the growth rate in per capita income was 3 percent. After the World Trade Organization, the International Monetary Fund, and the CIA forced many countries in these continents to move from government planning to unregulated economies, the average growth rate in per capita income dropped to 1.7 percent. Neoliberal globalization, he writes, "has failed to deliver on all fronts of economic life—growth, equality, and stability." He points out that the rapid growth of the economies of India and China has come with government regulation and supervision of the marketplace. Chang, like the anthropologists, has difficulty in understanding why the myth of globalization put forward by neoliberal spokesmen such as Friedman has been so persuasive. Why do so many intelligent people believe in a global utopia?[9]

But the conclusion of *The World Is Flat* reveals a Friedman who was losing the faith that he expressed so vigorously in his opening chapters. His flat world may no longer be flat. His simple world may no longer be simple. His harmonious world may no longer have harmony. Here in this new utopia at the end of history he encounters terrorists! In this suddenly complex frontier, there are powerful men who are passionately committed to preserving the world of the olive tree. And they support their reactionary commitment to an old world by using the latest communications technology. Their successful attack on the World Trade Center in New York was made possible by a sophisticated communication system.

In *The Lexus and the Olive Tree* and in most of *The World Is Flat*, Friedman had argued that it is technology that is opening the door through which the exodus from an old to a new world will take place. But here were some men who were using the most modern technology to preserve the world of their fathers. Suddenly Friedman's sunny optimism that technology was making the exodus from complexity to simplicity inevitable was shattered. He seemed to find himself in an unstable and unpredictable world. History had not ended.

The influential literary critic Fredric Jameson had lost his faith in the promise of Karl Marx that it was inevitable that a harmonious world inhabited by the working class would replace the chaos and conflict of the bourgeois world. Unable to retain the Marxist faith that reason would inevitably reveal a path leading to social redemption, Jameson had turned to art and imagination to provide a vision of a beautiful world that could replace the ugliness of capitalism. Now at the conclusion of *The World Is Flat,* Friedman urged all those loyal to the new global world that free-market capitalism hopefully was leading toward to develop more powerful and creative imaginations than those being used by the evil men who wanted to preserve an old world full of boundaries. Perhaps, then, we should not expect that Friedman in his next book could sustain his role in the revitalization of the middle-class exodus narrative.

The historian Frederick Jackson Turner had imagined America as a new world, a virgin land without generations. For him and for the European American culture that he represented, Native Americans had never existed. Then Turner announced in 1890 that this heaven on earth had vanished. An old world now stretched from sea to sea. L. Frank Baum was one of the many writers in the 1890s who imagined new utopias to replace Turner's lost virgin land. Baum created a young girl, Dorothy, who at the beginning of her story is living on the farm of her elderly uncle and aunt in Kansas. Yes, generations have come to a frontier Kansas and also scarcity. It is difficult for Dorothy's aunt and uncle to meet the mortgage payments on the farm. But suddenly a tornado lifts Dorothy out of an old world, Kansas, into the new world of Oz, where no one ages. She, like Friedman, finds evil in what seems to be a beautiful alternative to the drabness of Kansas. She is confronted by a wicked witch. Although she defeats the witch, she comes home. In his next book, *Hot, Flat, and Crowded: Why We Need a Green Revolution—and How It Can Renew America* (2008), Friedman also was coming home.[10]

He had discovered that the global marketplace as a new world was an illusion. It was not a utopia of liberty and plenty for all individuals. Friedman was experiencing a dramatic conversion. He no longer saw two worlds. Listening now to ecologists, he saw only one world, the earth—our home. After celebrating the bourgeois exodus narrative in *The Lexus and the Olive Tree* and in *The World Is Flat,* he now seemed to be retracing his steps toward the rootedness symbolized by the olive tree. After experiencing this paradigm revolution, Friedman became committed to sustainable resources. New-world plenty had been replaced by old-world scarcity.

Self-conscious that he had converted from one worldview to a totally different worldview, Friedman now desperately wanted to share his transformation with his readers. It had been revealed to him that human cultures are within nature and that our cultural activities are changing our earthly home. He no longer had faith in the bourgeois exodus narrative that imagined leaving unstable culture to live with the stable nature that was expressed in the laws of the marketplace. Now, for him, there was only a single world of unstable cultures within unstable nature.

When he was a true believer in the bourgeois exodus narrative, Friedman had not asked where the resources necessary to support a worldwide population of emancipated individuals would come from. He therefore had not asked how the use of these resources might affect the natural environment, our home. But soon after 2005 he became a participant in the tradition of ecological jeremiads that went back to the warnings issued by William Vogt and Fairfield Osborn in 1948. Our use of oil and coal is causing global warming. Coal and oil also are limited resources. As their availability shrinks, the world economy will become destabilized. But Friedman affirmed that we have the technology to replace coal and oil with wind and solar power. Their use will end our contribution to global warming. And, as sustainable resources, they will stabilize the world economy.

Seeing himself for the first time within a closed system, Friedman joined the long tradition of ecologists who warned against population growth. In a world with finite food, water, and energy supplies, continued population growth must lead to a worldwide catastrophe. Americans, Friedman implored, you must see that the world and we are in an unprecedented crisis. To gain perspective on the magnitude of this terrifying situation, Friedman advised, remember World War II, when we were locked in a life and death struggle with the Fascist nations, Germany, Italy, and Japan. To win that war our leaders mobilized the economy to produce the weapons and supplies necessary for victory. Now Friedman was asking that Americans mobilize themselves to defeat the ecological crisis that threatened them and the entire world. The national government acted in 1941 to direct corporations to work for the national good. Now our government must act to see that corporations produce the wind-powered generators and solar panels necessary to replace the oil and coal that put so much greenhouse gas into the atmosphere. The government must provide leadership so that in the immediate future all cars and trucks will be powered by electricity.

Friedman also saw a parallel between the ecological crisis and the civil rights movement. In the 1950s Americans knew, according to him, that patterns of racial discrimination were morally unjustified, but they complacently accepted this bankrupt status quo until brave prophets confronted the contradiction between citizenship and segregation. Today, our moral issue, for Friedman, is the contradiction between an irresponsible consumer culture and an earthly home that is clean, healthy, and capable of sustaining its household community. Our morally inferior society is leading us to self-destruction.

In this book, then, Friedman expressed his hope that brave prophets will be able to clarify the moral superiority of a green society to the self-centered consumer culture. When Americans see the truth about this bankrupt status quo, they will demand a drastic change, and, as in 1941, we will move into a planned national movement that will mobilize resources to create a green America that will inspire all other nations.

Friedman's message was popular when he participated in the bourgeois exodus narrative and called for the final negative revolution that would end history. But now he was calling for a positive revolution in which the government would play a creative, an artful, role. Friedman was no longer speaking within the framework of the dominant culture. Instead, he was a revolutionist trying to subvert the dominant paradigm. He had joined the scientists whose jeremiads had been ignored, mocked, and repressed for more than half a century. A poll in April 2010 found that 75 percent of Americans did not trust the national government and thought it was too big. Clearly, the majority clung to the virtuous new world of the marketplace.

Friedman in his first two books was participating in a long-term political revolution. When the vision of the global marketplace as a timeless space replaced the vision of the nation as a timeless space, the tradition of an activist national government that was dominant from the 1930s to the 1960s came under attack. If American politics was to be in harmony with the natural laws of the global marketplace, it must express Friedman's "Golden Straitjacket." It must protect the virtuous marketplace from the corrupt laws made by the government. This outlook became dominant in American politics in the 1980s. It has remained dominant down to the present. Friedman, then, in his *Hot, Flat, and Crowded,* hoped to have his fellow citizens suddenly reject a dominant political paradigm that still had momentum. He had no understanding that the political culture that made national planning possible during World War II had been killed by 1980.

I have argued that this worship of a global marketplace began during World War II. The dominant culture coming into the 1940s was that of Bourgeois Nationalism. This culture insisted that all private property must work within the national interest. The major threat to Bourgeois Nationalism came from international capitalism. Believers in that false faith wanted their property to be independent of national boundaries and national politics.

In this world of national interest, politics involved words such as *community, equality, social justice,* and *compassion.* The New Deal of Franklin D. Roosevelt that began in 1933 used these words. They were the context for legislation to regulate corporations, to tax the rich, to support labor unions, to feed the poor, and to establish social security as a floor for the elderly. National interest was the justification for government mobilization of the economy in World War II. For President Truman it was also in the national interest to order the desegregation of the armed services in 1948.

Presidents Kennedy and Johnson in the 1960s also appealed to the values of community, equality, and justice in their support of both the civil rights movement and civil rights legislation. Justice and compassion again were used in the creation of Medicare and Medicaid. Richard Nixon, the Republican president elected in 1968 and reelected in 1972, believed it was in the national interest to create the Environmental Protection Agency. He also argued that every family should have a minimum income.

Bourgeois Nationalists had defined international corporations as the major artful and aggressive threats to particular national states of nature. National governments protected virtuous peoples from the corrupting influence of the corporations. But now in the global marketplace, international corporations were no longer artful; instead, they were part of a universal state of nature. National governments were now the major threat to corrupt the international marketplace and the virtue of its free-floating consumers.

Within a generation, bourgeois cultures rejected the heroic role of national governments that protected national peoples from destructive international corporations. Within a generation, national governments became the dangerous enemies of the global marketplace. This is the ideological context for the triumph of neoliberalism in the United States. Conservative Republicans and their hero, Ronald Reagan, led this revolution.[11]

This is why, between the Republican president Nixon and the Republican president Reagan, conservative Republicans were able to seize control of their party from the liberal and moderate Republicans still committed to national government. For conservatives the sacred was the global marketplace in which individuals could be independent. Here they would be in harmony with universal and immutable laws. Here they were free from artful, particular, and ephemeral political patterns that threatened their autonomy. From this perspective, artful governmental activism from the 1930s to the 1970s had been a threat to the natural laws of the marketplace. It had been a declension from the republic created by the Founding Fathers—a republic based on natural law.

It was only when these laws were uncontaminated by government regulations and taxation that they could provide independence for the individual in a perpetually expanding economy. The sacred language of the marketplace, therefore, could not include the words *community, equality, social justice,* and *compassion.* These words expressed irrational emotions that contradicted the rational objectivity of the marketplace. The most sacred words in the marketplace, therefore, were *freedom* and *efficiency.* They expressed the essence of independence, rationality, and objectivity.

This ideological revolution within the Republican Party was soon imitated by the Democratic Party, which also accepted the sacredness of the global marketplace. The movement of first the Republican Party and then the Democratic Party to the position that government activism is immoral was part of a transnational pattern. Politicians and cultural leaders in all the bourgeois nations were engaged in replacing the bourgeois nation with the global marketplace as the end of history. The neoliberal celebration of free-market capitalism appeared in the bourgeois nations from New Zealand and Australia to France and Germany, but it was strongest in the United States and Great Britain, led by Ronald Reagan and Margaret Thatcher. In these two countries free-market capitalism became part of national identity.

In the United States competition with the Soviet Union in the Cold War was used to label critics of free-market capitalism as un-American. They were supporting our Cold War enemy. This revolution in political paradigms has been analyzed by a political scientist, Mark Smith, in his book *The Right Talk: How Conservatives Transformed the Great Society into the Economic Society* (2007). But Smith, like most academics, does not consider that American culture is similar to all cultures in having an implicit commitment to a foundation of space and time. He, like most of his colleagues, therefore, does not try to identify a new dominant politics of nature from the 1980s to the present.[12]

It is my argument, however, that Friedman, in *The Lexus and the Olive Tree* and in *The World Is Flat*, was participating and rejoicing in the victory of a politics of nature that saw the true, good, and beautiful embodied in a universal global marketplace and the false, evil, and ugly embodied in the political and social patterns of all particular national cultures. Friedman in 2000, therefore, was echoing the arguments of neoliberal Republicans and Democrats, who had rejected the tradition of government activism dominant from the 1930s to the 1970s. Both Republican and Democratic presidents were committed to the "Golden Straitjacket" before Friedman coined the phrase. The Democratic president in the 1990s, Bill Clinton, worked to reduce government regulation of the economy. He worked to reduce government funding for welfare. He did not criticize the reduction of taxes for the rich. In pushing for American participation in the North American Free Trade Agreement (NAFTA), he ignored the opposition of organized labor and environmental groups. Instead, he criticized the Republican Party for its inefficacy that enlarged the national debt.

Clinton was followed by the Republican president George W. Bush, who was also opposed to government regulation of the economy. He won support from Democrats as well as Republicans in Congress to further lower taxes on the wealthy and corporations. He too was speaking for the politics of nature that defined the international marketplace as a timeless space. He also hoped to tighten the "Golden Straitjacket" when he advocated the privatization of Social Security. A Democrat, Barack Obama, replaced him in 2008. Although the economy had fallen into a deep recession, Obama expressed his continued commitment to the post-1980 politics of nature by choosing men to be his economic advisers who had played that role in the Clinton administration. Obama moved decisively to lend billions of dollars to major banks and corporations. This policy was designed to keep the economic status quo from collapsing.

Obama, therefore, did not define unemployment and poverty as his highest priorities. And he angered teachers' unions across the country by giving support to charter schools rather than public schools. Like Clinton, however, he did support health care reform. Reaction to the Great Recession of 2008 had increased the Democratic majority in Congress, and Obama was able to get a health care bill passed in March 2010. It did not directly provide government support of health care but, rather, worked through private insurance companies.

Although the United States continued to stand outside the pattern of government-subsidized health care found in all the other industrial countries, Republicans shouted that now the country had socialized medicine. Democratic members of Congress arriving at the Capitol to vote on the health care bill were cursed and spat upon by protesters. After the vote, several of them received death threats, and their offices were vandalized.

In March 2010 Obama reversed his campaign opposition to offshore drilling for oil and gas. He now supported it as he opened up the Atlantic and Alaska coastlines to such methods. This was a position loudly advocated by Republicans. But he then angered many Republicans by demanding that auto manufacturers produce cars capable of getting better gasoline mileage.

Perhaps conservative Republicans reacted so violently to the passage of health care legislation because they had come to fear that America was not leading the world to a global marketplace characterized by free-market capitalism. Perhaps the United States was not going to redeem the world and end history. Republican politicians began to express a strident jeremiad warning that most of the world was trapped in artful and corrupt cultures. This profane chaos might creep across our borders and cause a declension from the free-market values of the Founding Fathers. Thomas Frank, in his book *The Wrecking Crew: How Conservatives Ruined Government, Enriched Themselves, and Beggared the Nation* (2008), described the self-confidence of Republicans since the 1990s in their ability to purge artful government. Their promised land of the free marketplace was about to be cleansed of all corrupting influences of artful government.

Conservatives had rallied in the 1990s to quarantine the scientific heresy that human activity was altering the climate of the earth. This was heresy because the natural laws embodied in the marketplace were timeless. Nature did not change. Conservatives had to save the public from this heresy because if it spread it could encourage Americans to engage in the secular sin of government regulation of the economy. There were anti-Americans who were arguing that the government should control emissions from factories and automobiles. Fourteen conservative think tanks began in the 1990s to provide materials to magazines, newspapers, and radio and television news programs questioning the validity of the science that identified global warming. This disinformation campaign was still in motion in 2010. The defense of the purity of the market demanded eternal vigilance.

In pushing for health care legislation, the Democrats, however, had not abandoned their commitment to the marketplace that had become central to their party in the 1980s. Clinton had argued in his proposal for health care in the 1990s and Obama argued in his presidential campaign of 2008 that our health care system is inefficient. We spend more money per capita for health care than any other industrial country. And our public health patterns are lower than in these countries. For Republicans, however, even the limited role for government in health care established by the legislation of 2010 had a corrupting influence. Identifying America with the free marketplace, conservative Republicans such as Sarah Palin described Obama and his advisers as "anti-American socialists."

Masking this fear that the United States has failed to make its market system universal, there is a deep taboo in both major political parties against any public discussion of the decline of the United States as a great power. Many Americans had arrogantly claimed since the 1940s that the twentieth century was the American century. Now at the beginning of the twenty-first century, many political scientists and historians are pointing out the dramatic decline of American power and influence. The historian Andrew Bacevich has written *The Limits of Power: The End of American Exceptionalism* (2008). His critique, perhaps a majority outlook among academic historians, sociologists, and political scientists, is, of course, an unacceptable discourse in the world of mainstream politics. A political scientist, David Mason, in his book *The End of the American Century* (2009), echoes Bacevich. "The United States," he writes, "has been the dominant power in the world, in almost every sense, for the six decades since the end of World War II." "Yet," he continues, "in the past decade . . . every aspect of this American predominance has begun to wane. The U.S. economy is riddled with debt and unsustainable obligations—by both government and households—presaging at least long-term economic decline if not general collapse."[13]

In 2010 two other political scientists, Steven Weber and Bruce Jentleson, published *The End of Arrogance: America in the Global Competition of Ideas*. They point out that the United States stands alone in advocating free-market capitalism. Most of the emerging world powers, such as China and India, have government-directed marketplaces. They also point out that most governments today are authoritarian. In 1990 many American political and academic leaders expected that all nations would move toward our form of political democracy. Between 1990 and 2010 their expectations were contradicted by dominant economic and political trends. Weber and Jentleson hope that Americans will admit that their expectation of a worldwide acceptance of American leadership has failed. They advise their fellow citizens to move from a Ptolemaic perspective to a Copernican one. The Ptolemaic theory was that the earth was the center of the solar system—that is, the sun and the planets revolved around the earth. But Copernicus argued that the sun is the center and the earth, like the other planets, revolves around it. Americans, Weber and Jentleson urge, should stop thinking that their country is the center with all other countries revolving around it. Americans should see themselves as merely one country among other countries. We are not the sacred center of the planet earth.[14]

During the economic and psychological boom of the 1990s, jeremiads warning against a pattern of living beyond sustainable resources were an art form expressed almost exclusively by ecologists. But with the economic and psychological bust of the first decade of the new century, academics in many of the social sciences and humanities joined the ecologists. Thomas Friedman, therefore, is not alone in becoming a participant in these warnings that we must become prudent and live within limits.

Once scientists began to theorize that humans live within the circle of a finite earth, they were able to imagine that resources could be

depleted as Fairfield Osborn had predicted in 1948 in his *Our Plundered Planet*. Soon scientists began to discuss oil in particular as a
finite resource and began to speculate on when the discovery of new
oil fields would no longer keep ahead of the use of oil.

In 1988, an Englishman, Colin Campbell, hoped to bring the perspectives of these scientists to the wider public in his book *The Coming
Oil Crisis* (1988). He was largely ignored in the United States, but this
attempt to reach the public gained momentum around 2000 as the psychological boom of the 1990s collapsed. John Mitchell published *The
New Economy of Oil* in 2001 and Vaclan Smil published *Energy at the
Crossroads* in 2003. Richard Heinberg also published his *The Party's
Over: Oil, War, and the Fate of Industrial Societies* in 2003. And then
a journalist, Paul Roberts, published *The End of Oil: On the Edge of
a Perilous New World* (2004). But these popular jeremiads seemed to
reach only a few more readers than those written by the scientists of a
generation earlier.[15]

Commercial publishers, however, did seem to believe that there was
an audience who took seriously the concept that there are limits to
growth. James Howard Kunstler, a novelist and journalist, did find
many readers for his *The Long Emergency: Surviving the End of Oil,
Climate Change, and Other Converging Catastrophes of the Twenty-
First Century* (2005). Another journalist, Thom Hartmann, also had
modest sales for his *Threshold: The Crisis of Western Culture* (2009).
Here he warned about "three critical breaking points—economic, de-
mographic, and environmental—that we've reached." Much more than
Friedman, Hartmann is aware of the power of the dominant paradigm
that combines "religious fundamentalism, capitalism run amok, male
domination, and militarism."[16]

One gets some feeling of the persuasive power of the dominant
worldview that has faith in the marketplace as the end of history by
analyzing the column written by David Brooks that appeared in the
March 25, 2010, *New York Times*. In addition to his position as a columnist at the newspaper, Brooks is a regular commentator on PBS
(Public Broadcasting Service) news programs. He has always proudly
identified himself with the center of the political spectrum. The *New
York Times* column is titled "The Return of History." Here Brooks
implicitly rejects his longtime faith in a timeless marketplace based
on the immutable laws of nature. Now he is mocking "the era of economic scientism when economists based their work on a crude vision of

human nature (the perfectly rational, utility-maximizing autonomous individual) and built elaborate models based on that creation."[17]

Brooks, therefore, no longer shares the bourgeois orthodoxy that there is a stable individual trapped within an unstable culture. He no longer believes there can be an exodus of that supposedly stable individual out of the history of unstable cultures. The unstable individual cannot reach a stable nature and escape timeful cultural instability. He quotes approvingly those current heretical economists who say, "People aren't perfectly rational"; "they don't act out of narrow self-interest" but sometimes behave "altruistically." And then he points out that orthodox economists theorized that the market has immutable stability. Their models, therefore, "did not predict the financial crisis as it approached." Their false prophecies helped "wipe out $50 trillion in global wealth . . . causing untold human suffering."

In 2010 Brooks, an admired mainstream columnist and TV commentator, seems to be where postmodern theorists were in the 1970s. Economists, he declares, deal with unstable individuals within unstable cultures. Economists had wrongly believed that they are superior to historians, sociologists, political scientists, or anthropologists because they supposedly study stable individuals in the stable environment of a market with natural laws. But, for Brooks after his conversion, economists, like all academic humanists and social scientists, cannot get outside of culture.

But like the postmodernists of 1970 and like most of his academic contemporaries in 2010, he does not imagine that unstable culture is within an unstable nature. He continues to believe that physicists study a timeless universe similar to the one theorized by Newton. In contrast to his colleague at the *Times* Thomas Friedman, Brooks, therefore, does not correlate the market's loss of the magical qualities of immutability and immortality with a worldwide crisis of overpopulation, dwindling resources, and global warming. He, then, like the postmodernists, cannot create an alternative politics of nature that envisions one world. He, like them, can criticize the long-held bourgeois politics of nature. But again, like them, he cannot say, here is the new paradigm that offers a way to explain the anomalies and contradictions that the existing paradigm is repressing.

Although the dominant culture's faith that perpetual growth is normal remains common sense, for most people the visibility of ecology since the 1970s has caused a variety of individuals to convert to a belief that the future will be one of scarcity. This vision that modern civilization is limited has inspired the writing of books that discuss the cyclical nature of civilizations. In contrast to the urgency and anger expressed in the antimodern jeremiad *One with Nineveh,* by the biologists Paul and Anne Ehrlich, an archaeologist, Joseph Tainter, created a tone of scholarly objectivity in his *The Collapse of Complex Societies* (1988). On the surface, his book was not a jeremiad. He was merely pointing out that there is a shared pattern in the rise and fall of civilizations. The implication, however, was that our modern world, like these earlier societies, might collapse. Tainter was casting doubt on the immortality of our civilization. And a geographer, Jared Diamond, in his *Collapse: How Societies Choose to Fail or Succeed* (2005), also did not explicitly define his book as an antimodern jeremiad. He too was making a scholarly analysis of the parallel patterns in past societies that had caused them to collapse. But he was asking if our modern society exhibited any of those patterns, and the answer was yes.[18]

In the December 2009 issue of *Time,* editors of the magazine expressed their view of the first decade of the new century with a cover that read "The Decade from Hell." The article declared, "The first 10 years of this century will very likely go down as the most dispiriting and disillusioning decade Americans have lived through in the post-World War II era." They were not, however, writing about a crisis of modern civilization, but only about our national crisis. "If you live in Brazil or China," they continued, "you have had a pretty good decade economically. Once, we were the sunniest and most optimistic of nations. No longer."[19]

Newsweek, the major competitor with *Time* for readers from the center of the political spectrum, also recognized how the psychological boom of the 1990s had become a psychological bust at the beginning of the new century. But, again, in contrast to the ecologists who warned about a worldwide crisis, the editors of *Newsweek,* like those at *Time,* chose to focus only on an American national crisis. Their December 2009 cover read "How Great Powers Fall." The issue contained a lengthy essay by historian Niall Ferguson, "An Empire at Risk," that focused on this problem. Ferguson, who teaches at Harvard, is the author of *The Ascent of Money* (2009). His explanation for how great powers fall is simple and direct. They fall when their expenditures become greater than their incomes. They create debts that lead to bankruptcy. Then they can no longer afford the large militaries that made them great powers.[20]

Ferguson then pointed out that since the 1980s our national debt has been growing rapidly, and projections in 2009 are that it will continue its unhealthy expansion into the foreseeable future. This also is true for projections since 2009.

In focusing on particular countries in the past and now on the United States, Ferguson expressed no curiosity about how ecological issues might have played a role in why our national debt went out of control in the 1980s and has remained out of control. He did not join the Friedman of *Hot, Flat, and Crowded* in discussing why energy was becoming more expensive or why food was becoming more expensive. He, unlike the latter Friedman, did not discuss the relation of population growth to limited resources. He did not discuss the parallel between declining incomes for the average American between 1980 and 2010 and the increase in the national debt.

He did say that to avoid bankruptcy the national government must both raise taxes and reduce spending for Social Security, Medicare, and Medicaid. But he did not discuss whether current political patterns make either of these choices probable in the immediate future. These issues did come up in March 2010 on a television program devoted to discussion of the current political scene. Several of the commentators said that the nation was like a speeding train about to fall off the rails. They did not think it was possible to raise taxes or reduce spending. They could only imagine counting the days until the debt crisis would explode. Although the dominant paradigm continues to predict an expanding market and increased prosperity, there is widespread recognition that this paradigm cannot explain our current experiences. But, so far, we have not been able to create an alternative paradigm.

Instead, the Republican Party increasingly employs a jeremiad that an artless, timeless, virtuous American Eden based on the marketplace is threatened by an artful, timeful, and corrupt government. For a significant number of Americans this jeremiad makes sense. Using Sacvan Bercovitch's model in his *The American Jeremiad,* the Republicans assert that the promise of America is the timeless marketplace. Here, if everyone lives by its eternal and immutable laws, the American people will live in perpetual harmony and plenitude.

But, according to this jeremiad, the Democrats are causing a declension by creating artful, timeful government patterns. They are corrupting the market given them by claiming that their artificial laws are more useful than those found in the state of nature, the market. They are dragging Americans back down into a timeful, ephemeral, unstable

culture no different from those in other profane nations. This is a fundamentalist expression of the politics of nature created by urban middle-
class men in classical Greece. It assumes a stable individual trapped in
unstable old-world culture. It assumes this individual can escape that
culture and achieve harmony in a marketplace that expresses the timeless and universal natural laws of an American new world.

In 1990 it had seemed as if the United States could lead all the
peoples of the world out of timeful cultures into a timeless global marketplace. But if the global marketplace was not going to express the
universal laws of nature, if artful cultures were to remain the fate of
most human beings, Americans must segregate themselves from the
chaos existing outside the nation's boundaries. Liberal bad sons said
that we should move in the direction of the European welfare states,
but we must resist these false prophets and save American exceptionalism. We must see that the Unites States remains true to the natural
principles of free-market capitalism. Republicans had lost the optimism of President Reagan in the 1980s that the United States was a
"Beacon to the World" and would persuade all other nations to embrace our free-market philosophy. Many Republicans in 2010 seemed
to have become isolationists. Since we are no longer redeeming the
world, our focus must be on saving ourselves from a profane world.

In February 2009 the so-called tea party movement began to organize across the country. Its leaders asked Americans to remember
why patriots had started the Revolution against England. They should
remember the brave Sons of Liberty, who went out into Boston Harbor
to destroy tea brought from England. These men understood the difference between American liberty and European tyranny. The Americans
were free individuals living by the laws of nature. The English were
unfree individuals, and they were acting to destroy American freedom
by imposing a pattern of unjust taxation.

Here in 2009 the many people joining the tea party movement were
imagining that the government in Washington was as alien to them
as the English government was to the colonists in 1776. This alien,
un-American government was a dangerous enemy. This hostile view
of the national government gives added meaning to Thomas Frank's
title *The Wrecking Crew*. In 2010 a representative of the tea party in
Arizona was running in the Republican U.S. Senate primary against
Senator John McCain. McCain had been the Republican presidential
candidate in 2008. From the perspective of many tea party members,

some Republicans, such as McCain, were not fundamentalist enough in defense of the eternal laws of the marketplace against ephemeral human legislation. Pressure from the tea party may explain why Republicans in Congress voted as a solid bloc against the health care legislation proposed by the Democrats.[21]

Given this widespread political hostility toward government activism, Friedman's expressed hope in *Hot, Flat, and Crowded* seems to have been wishful thinking. This powerful pattern of antipolitics seems to block any possibility of legislation to control greenhouse gases into the foreseeable future.

The tea party movement has divided people in the United States into patriotic good sons loyal to the laws of the market and anti-American bad sons loyal to the ephemeral laws they have created. In April 2010, members of the tea party in Oklahoma proposed the formation of an armed militia. They felt that the crisis of 1776 was about to be repeated. But there already were Americans who found the conspiracy of the anti-Americans even more threatening than did members of the tea party.

In the two years from 2008 to 2010, militia groups grew by 200 percent. If, for them, America was the promised land where each independent individual was supposed to live forever in harmony and plentitude, how did one explain all the economic hardships and all the social instability? There must be a conspiracy by anti-Americans to destroy the national Eden. And the anti-Americans were for the most part in control of the government. Loyal Americans must arm themselves and create local military units. One day those groups could rise together from the Atlantic to the Pacific and create a people's army. They would purge the country of impure aliens and restore the original republic. In 2009 and 2010, popular culture, in the form of a TV series and several Hollywood movies about aliens invading the earth, seemed to tap into a long tradition of political paranoia. These militia groups also expressed a fear of what they considered aliens already living in the United States—African Americans, Mexican Americans, and Asian Americans.

The political paranoia of these military groups is an expression of the politics of nature that, from the time of Plato to the present, has divided the world into artful unstable cultures and artless stable nature. Like the other conservative groups in 2010 the militia groups see themselves protecting a stable American nature against unstable anti-American cultures. They are protecting the purity of the artless virtuous market from an artful corrupt government.

Another expression of how conservatives increasingly feel the need to defend themselves from an anti-American establishment can be found in the conflict within the Texas School Board. A group of conservative Republicans has been able to marginalize liberal members of the school board, and since January 2010 the conservatives have been able to demand dramatic changes in the textbooks used in Texas public grade schools and high schools. They want the text on U.S. history to start with a focus on a major Protestant theologian of the Reformation, John Calvin. I interpret this demand as an expression of their commitment to a timeless earth created by the divinity less than ten thousand years ago. And, for them, Calvin recommended that humans should obey the laws of the timeless Bible and of God's timeless earth. This is why they want the history texts to relate our timeless free enterprise system to the timeless Bible. They, of course, agree with Calvin that Protestant fundamentalists have rejected Catholicism, Judaism, and other false religions because they are artful, human creations. Only fundamentalist Protestants obey God's laws.

The history text they envision will be an alternative to those written by professional historians who are anti-American leftists. "Academia," they write, "is skewed too far to the left." One of the falsehoods issued by these "secular humanists" is that the Founding Fathers did not want the government based on the principles of Protestant fundamentalism. As one of the conservatives stated, "I reject the notion of the left of a constitutional separation of church and state."[22]

Although Protestant fundamentalists in 2010 were a minority in the United States, the conservative school board members saw themselves and their proposed textbook as evidence that Protestant fundamentalists were regaining control of God's republic. They were helping to end the declension and restore the promise. Their textbook, then, would remind young students that the United States was established as a republic with a government of limited power. It is a leftist lie that the United States is a democracy with a government of unlimited power. Surely students would understand the implication that in 2010 members of the Republican Party were loyal sons to the Founding Fathers, while the Democratic Party was made up of disloyal sons.

This group of conservative Republicans wanted a U.S. history textbook from which Thomas Jefferson was absent. Jefferson, for them, was not an authentic Founding Father because he believed in the separation of church and state. He also engaged in vigorous criticism of Protestant fundamentalists. Given their commitment to limited government, it is not surprising that their text would give as much space to Jefferson Davis as to Abraham Lincoln. Leaders of the Confederate States of America in 1861 were critical of the growing tyranny of the national government. And Lincoln had acted to expand that national power.

Like all the major historians from George Bancroft to Charles and Mary Beard, these amateur historians on the Texas School Board imagined a uniform national people. They, therefore, also wanted a text that would minimize cultural pluralism. Racial and ethnic minorities would be kept at the fringes of our national story. These Protestant fundamentalists would also put liberal Protestants, Jews, and Catholics on the fringe.

The conservative school board members wanted a text that would be very critical of government activism from President Roosevelt in the 1930s to President Johnson in the 1960s. And the text should emphasize how the election of Ronald Reagan in 1980 marked the end of this tragic period of declension. Reagan, then, was leading a conservative Republican Party back to the principles of limited government embodied in the republic of 1789. They wanted the text to illustrate how this was a populist movement led by grassroots groups such as the Moral Majority and the National Rifle Association.

These grassroots historians on the Texas School Board, for me, illustrate the continued power of the cultural tradition of American exceptionalism. The United States is a timeless space. If we remain artless and innocent in this God-given state of nature, we will dwell in perpetual peace and plenty. Among us, however, are relatives and neighbors who are not content to live by the laws of nature and the Bible. They are artful and corrupt. These anti-Americans must be identified and contained. Jill Lepore captures this perspective in her book *The Whites of Their Eyes: The Tea Party Revolution and the Battle over American History* (2010). If tea party members were aware of how current scientists insist that space and time are interrelated, they would define such scientists as sharing the un-American outlook of academic historians. They would denounce the heresy expressed in Ilya Prigogine's book *The End of Certainty: Time, Chaos, and the New Laws of Nature* (1996).[23]

Many Americans today, then, are responding in a variety of ways to the collapse of the prophecy that the 1990s would mark the end of history. The global marketplace was supposed to be the timeless space in which all the peoples of the world would enjoy perpetual plenitude and harmony. Responding to the failure of that prophecy, some conservatives have fallen back on the tradition that was so powerful from the Revolution to World War II. America is a timeless space isolated from a world full of timeful cultures.

These conservative groups see themselves reversing a dangerous declension taking the United States from that virtuous space back to corrupt timeful culture. For many conservatives the major impetus into the declension had come from the government activism led by Democratic presidents—Roosevelt, Truman, Kennedy, and Johnson during the period 1930–70. The declension, then, was checked by the conservative resurgence led by Ronald Reagan and continued by the Republican presidents George H. W. Bush and George W. Bush. Then, however, in 2008 a Democrat, Barack Obama, became president and threatened to renew the declension by artfully creating more government agencies. Republicans must mobilize to defeat this threat and save the nation. For tea party members, the success of their revolution would come from the triumph of their will. They would save the soul of the nation because of the purity of their cause. They were the true sons of the Sons of Liberty. The Revolution of 1776 was their revolution in 2010.

Supercapitalism: The Transformation of Business, Democracy, and Everyday Life (2007), by Robert Reich, provides an example of how a response by a liberal Democrat to the failure of the 1990 prophecy differs from that of a conservative Republican. Secretary of labor in the Clinton administration, Reich is now a professor at the University of California, Berkeley. He too sees a pattern of promise and declension. For him the period from the 1940s to the 1970s was an "almost golden age."[24]

In those years, he reports, power was balanced among government, labor unions, and corporations. There was great faith in democracy and government. The income of the average American was rising, and the gap between the rich and the poor was closing. Reversing the conservative Republican view of declension and restoration, Reich defines the 1980s as the beginning of our current decline. As government and union power waned, corporations became all-powerful. Income for the average American began to decline, and the gap between the rich and the poor widened. Americans became less hopeful about democracy and their government. In contrast to the conservative Republicans, who blame the current declension on bad sons, Reich reports that technology caused the erosion of the "almost golden age."

Thomas Friedman in 2000 had declared that technology was the redemptive force energizing the worldwide exodus from complexity to simplicity. Reich in the 1990s, like Clinton and Friedman, was a strong advocate of globalization. He too saw a future that would be much better than the past. Technology would play a major role in creating progress from the particular national to the universal global.

Like the Friedman of *The Lexus and the Olive Tree,* Reich believed he was transcending the artfulness and the boundaries of national government. But with the failure of the global utopia to become reality, Reich, again like the disillusioned Friedman, began to focus on signs of declension within his particular nation. And, again like Friedman, he saw a necessary role for the national government in restoring limits on corporate power. He argues that when technological advances in communication and transportation made it possible for national corporations to become international corporations, they were freed from regulation by the national government, and there was no international government to regulate them.

There being no global community, Reich reports another irony: Americans imagined themselves as consumers in that global marketplace. They imagined they were outside of national politics. They saw themselves as autonomous atoms of self-interest when they searched for the cheapest goods produced throughout the world. They had lost their identity as rooted citizens in a national community. They could not make the connection that by shopping for low prices at Wal-Mart they were helping to drive down wages for themselves and their neighbors.

Supercapitalism provides an explanation for the changing patterns discussed by Mark Smith in *The Right Talk.* In this world of self-interested individuals, words such as *community, social justice,* and *compassion* are not sacred. Indeed, they are profane. Reich, like Andrew Ross, came to believe that the global marketplace is leading toward a dystopia rather than a utopia. Its consequences are destructive rather than constructive. Like Thomas Friedman, he expects that his personal conversion is being shared by many of his fellow citizens. But he has told us that our sense of community has been shattered. Like Friedman, he is participating in a political world in which self-interest is celebrated while cooperation is criticized. Today, all the major leaders of the Republican Party denounce government intervention in the economy. All denounce proposals for social justice as un-American. Such proposals are socialist and European. Reich's book, therefore, helps explain why, as the income of the average American declines, the salary of every corporate CEO has shot up to unprecedented heights.

In hoping for a miracle that will lift his fellow Americans out of this declension into being selfish consumers, Reich, like Friedman, does not identify the politics of nature that they had shared in the 1990s. He is unable to describe the continuing authority of that cultural paradigm. This politics of nature has defined two worlds—ephemeral, timeful culture and an immutable, timeless nature embodied in the marketplace. The major challenge to this orthodoxy has come from a marginalized scientific community. From the 1940s to the present there has been a heretical politics of nature. Here culture is defined as within nature. There is only one world that we must sustain for future generations. Within this circle everyone and everything is interrelated. The jeremiad of this politics of nature warns against those who pursue self-interest. Selfishness threatens the social and physical survival of the community.

For Reich the dominant paradigm, the dominant politics of nature, is bankrupt. But like so many who share his rejection of the current establishment, he does not join the ecologists in constructing an alternative politics of nature. He is not ready to renounce the modern bourgeois world.

In his book *Ill Fares the Land,* published in the spring of 2010, Tony Judt, a historian, laments the unwillingness of critics from Australia and New Zealand to France and Germany to give up their faith in the market. For him the economic collapse of 2007–9 demonstrated that the marketplace was an emperor who has no clothes. The prophecy that the market has eternal stability had failed, "and yet," he declares, "we seem to be unable to conceive of alternatives." Judt suggests an alternative in which we no longer worship the independent individual. He would like us to find our individual fulfillment as interdependent parts of a community. He would like us to see government as an expression of community. He would like us to create an alternative value system. He would like us to follow the advice of Richard Wilkinson and Kate Pickett in their book *The Spirit Level: Why Greater Equality Makes Societies Stronger* (2009). But this would mean a miraculous mass conversion from the patterns described by Robert Putnam in his

Bowling Alone: The Collapse and Revival of American Community (2000) and by Robert Frank and Philip Cook in their *The Winner-Take-All Society: Why the Few at the Top Get So Much More Than the Rest of Us* (1995).[25]

I do not share the hope in such an immediate revolution in values. I have written this book in the hope that I can persuade a few of my colleagues in the humanities to participate in replacing the modern metaphor of two worlds with the new but traditional metaphor of one world. I hope that some humanists will begin to teach and write that our unstable cultures are within an unstable nature. I hope that they will identify and renounce the bourgeois exodus narrative. I hope that they will participate in the creation of a politics of nature in which the resources of the earth, our home, are sustained for future generations.

Given my sense of the continuing cultural authority of the bourgeois belief in ephemeral, artful, timeful traditional old worlds and the artless, timeless new modern world, I do not know what to make of the popularity of the movie *Avatar,* released in 2009. Selling more tickets in the United States and around the world than any previous film, it presented a bitter critique of our capitalist status quo.

In February 2010 the creator of the film, James Cameron, was interviewed on television by Charlie Rose. Cameron revealed that he has been influenced by ecologists and shares their view that there will be a worldwide crisis in about twenty years. It will be caused by overpopulation, global warming, and rising energy costs. Our modern problem, for Cameron, is that we do not see the consequences of our actions. We think we are independent. We ignore that we are interdependent. In his movie he presents a traditional culture that is aware of the interrelatedness of all things. This community is invaded by a corporation whose officers can see only specific things outside of their contexts. These modern invaders, therefore, inflict great damage on the home of the traditional people, who struggle to sustain a balance in their complex, organic world. Cameron stated that he hoped the viewers of his film would become self-critical of their destructive value system. At this point, however, all we can do is wonder if Cameron's jeremiad, warning that there are limits to growth, is an anomaly or an indication of an emerging alternative narrative. Will we heretics be able to celebrate living at home as much as modern people have celebrated leaving home?

NOTES

1. Two-World Metaphors, from Plato to Alan Greenspan

1. Carl Becker, *The Heavenly City of the Eighteenth-Century Philosophers* (New Haven, Conn.: Yale University Press, 1932).

2. David W. Noble, *The Paradox of Progressive Thought* (Minneapolis: University of Minnesota Press, 1958).

3. J. G. Pocock discusses the efforts of Renaissance thinkers such as Machiavelli to find a timeless space. See his *The Machiavellian Moment: Florentine Political Thought and the Atlantic Republican Tradition* (Princeton, N.J.: Princeton University Press, 1975).

4. David W. Noble, *The Eternal Adam and the New World Garden* (New York: Braziller, 1968).

5. David W. Noble, *The End of American History: Democracy, Capitalism, and the Metaphor of Two Worlds in Anglo-American Historical Writing, 1880–1980* (Minneapolis: University of Minnesota Press, 1985).

6. David W. Noble, *Death of a Nation: American Culture and the End of Exceptionalism* (Minneapolis: University of Minnesota Press, 2002).

7. Bruno Latour, *We Have Never Been Modern* (Cambridge, Mass.: Harvard University Press, 1993); and *Politics of Nature* (Cambridge, Mass.: Harvard University Press, 2004).

8. Joseph Meeker, in *The Comedy of Survival* (New York: Scribner's, 1974), argues that all cultures have the art form of comedy but only the classical world and the post-Renaissance modern world have the art form of tragedy.

9. I discuss the desacralization of bourgeois nations after World War II and the sacralization of the global marketplace in the first chapter of *Death of a Nation*, "Introduction: Space Travels."

10. The hostility of the English colonists toward the communal property of the Native Americans is linked to the hostility of the English middle classes to the communal property in Michael Perelman, *The Invention of Capitalism: Classical Political Theory and the Secret History of Primitive Accumulation* (Durham, N.C.: Duke University Press, 2000). For the bourgeoisie, communal property was

generational and timeful. Private property, in contrast, was antigenerational and timeless.

11. Genevieve Lloyd, *The Man of Reason: "Male" and "Female" in Western Philosophy* (London: Routledge, 1984).

12. Arlene W. Saxonhouse, *Fear of Diversity: The Birth of Political Science in Ancient Greek Thought* (Chicago: University of Chicago Press, 1992).

13. Carolyn Merchant, *The Death of Nature: Women, Ecology, and the Scientific Revolution* (New York: Harper & Row, 1980). The triumph of the bourgeois worldview is discussed in Karl Polanyi, *The Great Transformation* (New York: Farrar & Rinehart, 1944). It is also discussed in Alan MacFarlane, *The Origin of English Individualism* (Oxford: Basil Blackwell, 1978); in C. B. MacPherson, *The Political Theory of Possessive Individualism* (Oxford: Oxford University Press, 1963); and in Benjamin Nelson, *The Idea of Usury: From Tribal Brotherhood to Universal Otherhood* (Princeton, N.J.: Princeton University Press, 1949). Also see Donald Lowe, *The History of Bourgeois Perception* (Chicago: University of Chicago Press, 1982).

14. The many ways in which the European middle classes created the vision of a timeless new-world utopia are discussed by Durand Echeverria in *Mirage in the West: A History of the French Image of American Society to 1815* (Princeton, N.J.: Princeton University Press, 1957); by Charles L. Sanford in *The Quest for Paradise: Europe and the American Moral Imagination* (Urbana: University of Illinois Press, 1961); and by Edmundo O'Gorman in *The Invention of America* (Bloomington: Indiana University Press, 1961). William Cronon, in his *Changes in the Land: Indians, Colonists, and the Ecology of New England* (New York: Hill & Wang, 1983), discusses how the English colonists were committed to replacing the communal property of Native Americans with the new system of private property. It was after the desacralization of a supposedly isolated United States in the 1940s and 1950s that European American historians could see that the middle-class quest for liberty in the New World was interrelated with the violent use of power to remove Native Americans from the national landscape. Walter A. McDougall exposes this hidden contradiction in bourgeois culture between liberty and power in his *Promised Land, Crusader State: The American Encounter with the World since 1776* (Boston: Houghton Mifflin, 1997). The fact that Europeans were conquering the homelands of the Native Americans is expressed by Francis Jennings in *The Invasion of America: Indians, Colonialism, and the Cant of Conquest* (Chapel Hill: University of North Carolina Press, 1975); and by Ian K. Steele in *Warpaths: Invasions of North America* (New York: Oxford University Press, 1994). Kerwin Lee Klein discusses the ways in which Europeans and then European Americans focused on their experience of liberty rather than their use of power in *Frontiers of Historical Imagination: Narrating the European Conquest of Native America, 1890–1990* (Berkeley: University of California Press, 1997). The European American commitment to ethnic cleansing is discussed by Richard Drinnon, *Facing West: The Metaphysics of Indian-*

Hating and Empire-Building (Minneapolis: University of Minnesota Press, 1980); and by David E. Stannard, *American Holocaust: Columbus and the Conquest of the New World* (New York: Oxford University Press, 1992). Several recent books have focused on how the Founding Fathers expressed the contradiction between the middle-class promise of liberty and the middle-class practice of power. These include Christopher Tomlins, *Freedom Bound: Law, Labor, and Civic Identity in Colonizing English America, 1580–1865* (Cambridge: Cambridge University Press, 2010); and Aziz Rana, *The Two Faces of American Freedom* (Cambridge, Mass.: Harvard University Press, 2010).

15. J. G. A. Pocock, *The Machiavellian Moment: Florentine Political Thought and the Atlantic Republican Tradition* (Princeton, N.J.: Princeton University Press, 1975).

16. Ibid.

17. See my discussion of these issues in "Introduction: Space Travels" and in the epilogue of my *Death of a Nation*.

18. See Shlomo Arineri, *Hegel's Theory of the Modern State* (Cambridge: Cambridge University Press, 1972); Raymond Plant, *Hegel: An Introduction* (Oxford: Basil Blackwell, 1983); and Jonathan Boyarin, ed., *Remapping Memory: The Politics of TimeSpace* (Minneapolis: University of Minnesota Press, 1994). The movement away from Bourgeois Nationalism and Hegel is discussed in Prasenjit Duara, *Rescuing History from the Nation: Questioning Narratives of Modern China* (Chicago: University of Chicago Press, 1995); Ernest Gellner, *Nations and Nationalism* (Ithaca, N.Y.: Cornell University Press, 1983); E. J. Hobsbawm, *Nations and Nationalism since 1780* (Cambridge: Cambridge University Press, 1990); Jean-Marie Guéhenno, *The End of the Nation-State* (Minneapolis: University of Minnesota Press, 1995); and Kenichi Ohmae, *The End of the Nation State: The Rise of Regional Economies* (New York: Free Press, 1995). Benedict Anderson, in his *Imagined Communities* (London: Verso, 1983), interprets bourgeois nations as timeful cultural constructions.

19. Jennifer Burns, *Goddess of the Market: Ayn Rand and the American Right* (New York: Oxford University Press, 2009); Anne Heller, *Ayn Rand and the World She Made* (New York: Doubleday, 2009); Leonard Peikoff, *Objectivism: The Philosophy of Ayn Rand* (New York: E. P. Dutton, 1991).

20. Ayn Rand, *Atlas Shrugged* (New York: Random House, 1957).

21. Quoted in Burns, *Goddess of the Market*, 43.

22. Steven Shapin, *Never Pure: Historical Studies of Science As If It Was Produced by People with Bodies, Situated in Time, Space, Culture, and Society, and Struggling for Credibility and Authority* (Baltimore: Johns Hopkins University Press, 2010).

23. Books about Greenspan's career include Alan Greenspan, *The Age of Turbulence* (New York: Penguin, 2007); Jerome Tuccille, *Alan Shrugged: The Life and Times of Alan Greenspan, the World's Most Powerful Banker* (Hoboken, N.J.: John Wiley & Sons, 2002); Ravi Batra, *Greenspan's Fraud: How Two Decades*

of His Policies Have Undermined the Global Economy (New York: Palgrave Macmillan, 2008); and Paul Krugman, *The Return of Depression Economics and the Crisis of 2008* (New York: W. W. Norton, 2009).

24. See Justin Martin, *Greenspan: The Man Behind Money* (Cambridge, Mass.: Perseus, 2000); and also Krugman, *The Return of Depression Economics*.

25. Compare Greenspan's belief in a timeless marketplace with the view of a natural world that is changing rapidly expressed by the ecologist Bill McKibben in his recent book *Eaarth: Making a Life on a Tough New Planet* (New York: Henry Holt, 2010).

26. Robert Collins, *More: The Politics of Economic Growth in Postwar America* (New York: Oxford University Press, 2000).

2. Historians against History

1. See the discussion of Bancroft in Noble, *Death of a Nation,* 6–35.

2. See discussion of Bancroft's Protestantism in ibid., 1–5. Other books that discuss Bancroft's Protestantism and racism are David Levin, *History as Romantic Art* (Stanford, Calif.: Stanford University Press, 1959); Richard Hofstadter, *The Progressive Historians* (New York: Alfred A. Knopf, 1968); Philip Wayne Powell, *Tree of Hate: Propaganda and Prejudices Affecting United States Relations with the Hispanic World* (New York: Basic Books, 1971); and Robert Young, *White Mythologies: Writing History and the West* (New York: Routledge, 1990).

3. Noble, *Death of a Nation,* 1–15.

4. Ibid., 1–6, 79.

5. See the discussion of Turner in ibid., 16–58. Other books that discuss Turner are Hofstadter, *The Progressive Historians*; Jack Forbes, *Frontiers in American History* (Reno: University of Nevada Press, 1968); and Gene Wise, *American Historical Explanations* (Homewood, Ill.: Dorsey Press, 1973).

6. Noble, *Death of a Nation,* 6–16.

7. Ibid., 10.

8. See Ralph Brauer, *The Horse, the Gun, the Piece of Property* (Bowling Green, Ohio: Popular Press, 1975).

9. See the discussion of Beard in Noble, *Death of a Nation,* 38–71. Other books that discuss Beard include Ellen Nore, *Charles A. Beard: An Intellectual Biography* (Carbondale: Southern Illinois Press, 1983); Bernard Bosing, *The Political Thought of Charles Beard* (Seattle: University of Washington Press, 1963); Hofstadter, *The Progressive Historians*; David Marcell, *Progress and Progressives: James, Dewey, Beard, and the American Idea of Progress* (Westport, Conn.: Greenwood Press, 1974); and Cushing Strout, *The Progressive Revolt in American History: Carl Becker and Charles Beard* (Ithaca, N.Y.: Cornell University Press, 1958).

10. Noble, *Death of a Nation,* 17–19.

11. Ibid., 1–19.

12. Ibid., 23–25, 156–59.

13. See the discussion of lost-generation novelists in my book *The Eternal Adam and the New World Garden.*

14. Ibid., 144–60.

15. Ibid., 163–76.

16. Becker, *The Heavenly City.*

17. See the discussion of this debate in my *Death of a Nation,* 198–201, 213–14.

18. See the discussion of Benton and American scene painting in ibid., 158–64.

19. See the discussion of Wright in ibid., 177–82.

20. Charles A. Beard and Mary R. Beard, *The Rise of American Civilization* (New York: Macmillan, 1927), 2:516–17.

21. Ibid., 2:198.

22. See Charles A. Beard and Mary R. Beard, *The American Spirit* (New York: Macmillan, 1942).

23. Richard Hofstadter, *Social Darwinism in American Thought* (Philadelphia: University of Pennsylvania Press, 1945).

24. Richard Hofstadter, *The American Political Tradition and the Men Who Made It* (New York: Alfred A. Knopf, 1948).

25. Richard Hofstadter, *The Age of Reform* (New York: Alfred A. Knopf, 1955).

26. Reinhold Niebuhr, *The Irony of American History* (New York: Scribner's, 1952).

27. Richard Hofstadter, *Anti-intellectualism in American Life* (New York: Alfred A. Knopf, 1963); and *The Progressive Historians.*

28. Richard Hofstadter, *The Idea of a Party System* (Berkeley: University of California Press, 1971); and *America in 1750* (New York: Alfred A. Knopf, 1971). Hofstadter is discussed in Susan Stout Baker, *Radical Beginning: Richard Hofstadter* (Chicago: University of Chicago Press, 2006); and Marian J. Morton, *The Terrors of Ideological Politics: Liberal Historians in a Conservative Mood* (Cleveland, Ohio: Press of Case Western Reserve University, 1972).

29. Peter N. Carroll and David W. Noble, *The Free and the Unfree* (New York: Penguin, 1977).

30. William Appleman Williams, *American-Russian Relations* (New York: Rinehart, 1952); and *The Tragedy of American Diplomacy* (Cleveland, Ohio: World, 1959).

31. William Appleman Williams, *The Contours of American History* (Cleveland, Ohio: World, 1961.

32. William Appleman Williams, *The Great Evasion* (Chicago: Quadrangle Books, 1964).

33. William Appleman Williams, *Some Presidents: Wilson to Nixon* (New York: New York Review, 1972); and *America Confronts a Revolutionary World* (New York: Morrow, 1976).

34. William Appleman Williams, *America in a Changing World* (New York: Harper & Row, 1978); and *Empire as a Way of Life* (New York: Oxford University

Press, 1980). For perspectives on Williams and his influence on the writing of diplomatic history, see Paul Buhle and Edward Rice-Maximin, *William Appleman Williams: The Tragedy of Empire* (New York: Routledge, 1995); Robert Tucker, *The Radical Left and American Foreign Policy* (Baltimore: Johns Hopkins University Press, 1971); and Joseph Siracusa, *New Left Diplomatic Histories and Historians* (Port Washington, N.Y.: Kennikat Press, 1973).

35. Andrew J. Bacevich, *American Empire: The Reality and Consequences of U.S. Diplomacy* (Cambridge, Mass.: Harvard University Press, 2002); *The New American Militarism: How Americans Are Seduced by War* (New York: Oxford University Press, 2005); *The Limits of Power: The End of American Exceptionalism* (New York: Macmillan, 2008); *Washington Rules: America's Path to Permanent War* (New York: Macmillan, 2010); and Bacevich, ed., *The Imperial Tense: Prospects and Problems of American Empire* (Chicago: Ivan R. Dee, 2003); *The Long War: A New History of U.S. National Security Policy since World War II* (New York: Columbia University Press, 2007).

36. David S. Mason, *The End of the American Century* (Lanham, Md.: Rowman & Littlefield, 2009); Peter Beinart, *The Icarus Syndrome: A History of American Hubris* (New York: Harper, 2010).

37. Donald Worster, *Nature's Economy: A History of Ecological Ideas* (New York: Cambridge University Press, 1985); and *The Wealth of Nature: Environmental History and the Ecological Imagination* (New York: Oxford University Press, 1993); Ted Steinberg, *Down to Earth: Nature's Role in American History* (New York: Oxford University Press, 2002).

38. Carolyn Merchant, *The Death of Nature*; and *Ecological Revolutions: Nature, Gender, and Science in New England* (Chapel Hill: University of North Carolina Press, 1989).

39. Carolyn Merchant, *Radical Ecology: The Search for a Livable World* (New York: Routledge, 1993); and *Earthcare: Women and the Environment* (New York: Routledge, 1995).

40. Carolyn Merchant, *Reinventing Eden: The Fate of Nature in Western Culture* (New York: Routledge, 2003).

3. Economists Discover a New New World

1. Sacvan Bercovitch, *The American Jeremiad* (Madison: University of Wisconsin Press, 1978).

2. Benjamin G. Rader, *The Academic Mind and Reform: The Influence of Richard T. Ely in American Life* (Lexington: University of Kentucky Press, 1966); Robert M. Crunden, *Ministers of Reform: The Progressives' Achievement in American Civilization, 1889–1920* (New York: Basic Books, 1982); Paul K. Conkin, *Prophets of Prosperity: America's First Political Economists* (Bloomington: Indiana University Press, 1980); Joseph Dorfman, *The Economic Mind in American Civilization* (New York: Viking Press, 1949).

3. Yuval Yonay, *The Struggle over the Soul of Economics: Institutional and Neoclassical Economists in America between the Wars* (Princeton, N.J.: Princeton University Press, 1998); Mary Morgan and Malcolm Rutherford, eds., *From Interwar Pluralism to Postwar Neoclassicism* (Durham, N.C.: Duke University Press, 1998); J. Ronnie Davis, *The New Economics and the Old Economists* (Ames: Iowa State University, 1971).

4. Dorothy Ross, *The Origins of American Social Science* (Cambridge, Mass.: Harvard University Press, 1991); Michael Bernstein, *A Perilous Progress: Economists and Public Purpose in Twentieth-Century America* (Princeton, N.J.: Princeton University Press, 2001); C. P. Snow, *The Two Cultures and the Scientific Revolution* (Cambridge: Cambridge University Press, 1959).

5. Philip Mirowski, *More Heat than Light: Economics as Social Physics, Physics as Nature's Economy* (Cambridge, Mass.: Harvard University Press, 1989).

6. See the discussion in Noble, *Death of a Nation,* xxvi–xlv.

7. Thomas Kuhn, *The Structure of Scientific Revolutions* (Chicago: University of Chicago Press, 1962).

8. See the discussion of logical positivism in Noble, *Death of a Nation,* 198–214.

9. See the discussion of architecture in ibid., 177–82.

10. See the discussion of Benton and Pollock in ibid., 158–95.

11. E. Roy Weintraub discusses the commitment of neoclassical economists to mathematics as their only language in his *How Economics Became a Mathematical Science* (Durham, N.C.: Duke University Press, 2002). At the same time Geoffrey M. Hodgson criticizes this choice in his *How Economics Forgot History: The Problem of Historical Specificity in Social Science* (New York: Routledge, 2001).

12. Liah Greenfeld, *The Spirit of Capitalism: Nationalism and Economic Growth* (Cambridge, Mass.: Harvard University Press, 2001).

13. F. M. Barnard, *Herder's Social and Political Thought: From Enlightenment to Nationalism* (Oxford: Oxford University Press, 1965).

14. Bernstein, *A Perilous Progress,* 87; Mona Harrington, *The Dream of Deliverance in American Politics* (New York: Alfred A. Knopf, 1986).

15. See David W. Noble, *The Progressive Mind* (Chicago: Rand McNally, 1970), for a discussion of the similarity among the visions of Theodore Roosevelt, Woodrow Wilson, Charles Beard, John Dewey, and Thorstein Veblen. See also Bernstein, *A Perilous Progress,* 15–73; and Richard T. Ely, *Outline of Economics* (New York: Macmillan, 1983).

16. Yonay, *The Struggle over the Soul of Economics*; Morgan and Rutherford, *From Interwar Pluralism to Postwar Neoclassicism*; Davis, *The New Economics and the Old Economists.*

17. A number of scholars have described the vision of neoclassical economists as a commitment to a utopia that transcends the human experience with space and time. See, for example, Robert Nelson, *Heaven on Earth: The Theological*

Meaning of Economics (Lanham, Md.: Rowman & Littlefield, 1991); Jane Kelsey, *Economic Fundamentalism* (London: Pluto Press, 1995); Paul Smith, *Millennial Dreams: Contemporary Culture and Capital in the North* (London: Verso, 1997); and Lanny Ebenstein, *Milton Friedman* (New York: Palgrave Macmillan, 2007).

18. Peter Clarke, *The Keynesian Revolution in the Making* (Oxford: Clarendon Press, 1988); W. Carl Biven, *Who Killed John Maynard Keynes? Conflicts in the Evolution of Economic Policy* (Homewood, Ill.: Dow Jones–Irwin, 1989); Robert Lekachman, *The Age of Keynes* (New York: Random House, 1966).

19. Nils Gilman, *Mandarins of the Future: Modernization Theory in Cold War America* (Baltimore: Johns Hopkins University Press, 2003), 156–98.

20. Daniel Lerner, *The Passing of Traditional Society* (New York: Free Press, 1958); W. W. Rostow, *The Stages of Economic Growth* (Cambridge: Cambridge University Press, 1960).

21. See Gilman, *Mandarins of the Future,* 161–94.

22. Ibid., 196–99.

23. See the discussion of Dewey, Beard, and Veblen and of their expectations that World War I would redeem the world in Noble, *The Progressive Mind.*

24. Arturo Escobar, *Encountering Development: The Making and Unmaking of the Third World* (Princeton, N.J.: Princeton University Press, 1994).

25. Ngaire Woods, *The Globalizers: The IMF, the World Bank, and Their Borrowers* (Ithaca, N.Y.: Cornell University Press, 2006); John Brenner, *The Economics of Global Turbulence* (New York: Verso, 2006).

26. Barry Bluestone and Bennett Harrison, *The Deindustrialization of America* (New York: Basic Books, 1982); Jefferson Cowie and Joseph Heathcott, eds., *Beyond Ruins: The Meaning of Deindustrialization* (Ithaca, N.Y.: Cornell University Press, 2003); Joel Blau, *Illusions of Prosperity: America's Working Families in an Age of Economic Insecurity* (New York: Oxford University Press, 1999); Doug Henwood, *After the New Economy* (New York: New Press, 2003); Tamara Draut, *Strapped: Why America's 20- and 30-Somethings Can't Get Ahead* (New York: Avalon Books, 2007); Gar Alperovitz and Lew Daly, *Unjust Deserts: How the Rich Are Taking Our Common Inheritance* (New York: New Press, 2008); Michael Perelman, *The Confiscation of American Prosperity: From Right-Wing Extremism and Economic Ideology to the Next Great Depression* (New York: Palgrave Macmillan, 2007).

27. Martin J. Burke, *The Conundrum of Class: Public Discourse on the Social Order in America* (Chicago: University of Chicago Press, 1995).

28. Bryan Caplan, *The Myth of the Rational Voter: Why Democracies Choose Bad Policies* (Princeton, N.J.: Princeton University Press, 2007). The neoliberal context of Caplan's book is discussed in Alfredo Saad-Filho and Deborah Johnston, eds., *Neoliberalism: A Critical Reader* (New York: Pluto Press, 2005); Gérard Duménil and Dominique Lévy, *Capital Resurgent: Roots of the Neoliberal Revolution* (Cambridge, Mass.: Harvard University Press, 2004); David Harvey,

A Brief History of Neoliberalism (New York: Oxford University Press, 2005); and Jodi Dean, *Democracy and Other Neoliberal Fantasies: Communicative Capitalism and Left Politics* (Durham, N.C.: Duke University Press, 2009).

29. Edward S. Herman, *Triumph of the Market: Essays on Economics, Politics, and the Media* (Boston: South End Press, 1995); Joseph Stigler, ed., *Chicago Studies in Political Economy* (Chicago: University of Chicago Press, 1988); Daniel Yergin and Joseph Stanislaw, *The Commanding Heights: The Battle between Government and the Marketplace That Is Remaking the Modern World* (New York: Simon & Schuster, 1998).

30. Michel Albert, *Capitalism against Capitalism* (London: Whurr, 1993); Suzanne Berger and Ronald Dore, eds., *National Diversity and Global Capitalism* (Ithaca, N.Y.: Cornell University Press, 1996); Peter A. Hall and David Soskice, eds., *Varieties of Capitalism: The Institutional Foundations of Comparative Advantage* (Oxford: Oxford University Press, 2001).

31. Robert Skidelsky, *Keynes: The Return of the Master* (London: Penguin, 2009).

32. Antonio R. Damasio, *Descartes' Error: Emotion, Reason, and the Human Brain* (New York: Putnam, 1994).

33. Thomas Metzinger, *The Ego Tunnel: The Science of the Mind and the Myth of the Self* (New York: Perseus, 2009), 6.

34. Richard Bronk, *The Romantic Economist: Imagination in Economics* (Cambridge: Cambridge University Press, 2009).

35. George A. Akerlof and Robert J. Shiller, *Animal Spirits: How Human Psychology Drives the Economy, and Why It Matters for Global Capitalism* (Princeton, N.J.: Princeton University Press, 2009).

36. Steven Pinker, *The Blank Slate: The Modern Denial of Human Nature* (New York: Viking, 2002).

37. Carmen M. Reinhart and Kenneth S. Rogoff, *This Time Is Different: Eight Centuries of Financial Folly* (Princeton, N.J.: Princeton University Press, 2010).

38. John Quiggin, *Zombie Economics: How Dead Ideas Still Walk among Us* (Princeton, N.J.: Princeton University Press, 2010).

39. Viviana A. Zelizer, *Economic Lives: How Culture Shapes the Economy* (Princeton, N.J.: Princeton University Press, 2011).

40. Kenneth Sayre, *Unearthed: The Economic Roots of Our Environmental Crisis* (Notre Dame, Ind.: University of Notre Dame Press, 2010).

41. Krugman, *The Return of Depression Economics.*

42. Robert J. Samuelson, *The Great Inflation and Its Aftermath: The Past and Future of American Affluence* (New York: Random House, 2008).

43. Thomas Kuhn, *The Copernican Revolution* (Cambridge, Mass.: Harvard University Press, 1957).

44. Elinor Ostrom, *Governing the Commons: The Evolution of Institutions for Collective Action* (Cambridge: Cambridge University Press, 1990).

45. Benjamin M. Friedman, *The Moral Consequences of Economic Growth* (New York: Alfred A. Knopf, 2005).

46. Robert H. Frank, *The Darwin Economy: Liberty, Competition, and the Common Good* (Princeton, N.J.: Princeton University Press, 2011).

4. Literary Critics Become Cultural Critics

1. See the discussion of Parrington in my *Death of a Nation,* 79–88; and Hofstadter, *The Progressive Historians.*

2. See the discussion of the metaphor of two worlds, Europe and America, in my *The Eternal Adam,* 1–39.

3. See the discussion of the post–World War II revolution in the literary canon in my *Death of a Nation,* chap. 7.

4. See the discussion of Matthiessen, Smith, and Marx in ibid., chap. 4.

5. Ibid.

6. Ibid.

7. See the discussion in my *The Eternal Adam,* 1–48.

8. Ibid., 24–34.

9. Ibid., 34–47.

10. This revolution is discussed in Jonathan Freedman, *The Temple of Culture: Assimilation and Anti-Semitism in Literary Anglo-America* (New York: Oxford University Press, 2000); Annette Kolodny, *The Lay of the Land: Metaphor as Experience and History in American Life and Letters* (Chapel Hill: University of North Carolina Press, 1975); Houston A. Baker Jr., *Blues, Ideology, and Afro-American Literature: A Vernacular Theory* (Chicago: University of Chicago Press, 1984); Paul Jay, *Contingency Blues: The Search for Foundations in American Criticism* (Madison: University of Wisconsin Press, 1997); and John Carlos Rowe, *At Emerson's Tomb: The Politics of Classic American Literature* (New York: Columbia University Press, 1997).

11. Bill Readings, *The University in Ruins* (Cambridge, Mass.: Harvard University Press, 1996); Noble, *Death of a Nation,* introduction and chap. 1.

12. See H. Stuart Hughes, *Sophisticated Rebels: The Political Culture of European Dissent, 1968–1987* (Cambridge, Mass.: Harvard University Press, 1988); Tony Judt, *Marxism and the French Left: Studies on Labour and Politics in France, 1830–1981* (Oxford: Oxford University Press, 1986); Bryan D. Palmer, *Descent into Discourse: The Reification of Language and the Writing of Social History* (Philadelphia: Temple University Press, 1990).

13. Jean-François Lyotard, *The Postmodern Condition: A Report on Knowledge* (Minneapolis: University of Minnesota Press, 1984).

14. See Steven Connor, *Postmodernist Culture: An Introduction to Theories of the Contemporary* (Oxford: Basil Blackwell, 1989), chap. 2.

15. Michel Foucault, *Madness and Civilization: A History of Insanity in the Age of Reason* (New York: Pantheon, 1965); *The Birth of the Clinic: An*

Archaeology of Medical Perception (New York: Vintage, 1973); *The Order of Things: An Archaeology of the Human Sciences* (New York: Vintage, 1973); and *The Archaeology of Knowledge* (New York: Harper & Row, 1976).

16. Michel Foucault, *Discipline and Punish: The Birth of the Prison* (New York: Vintage, 1979).

17. Michel Foucault, *The History of Sexuality,* vol. 1 (New York: Vintage, 1980); *The Use of Pleasure* (New York: Vintage, 1988); and *The Care of the Self* (New York: Pantheon, 1986).

18. Allan Megill, *Prophets of Extremity: Nietzsche, Heidegger, Foucault, Derrida* (Berkeley: University of California Press, 1985); Connor, *Postmodernist Culture.*

19. Jean Baudrillard, *The System of Objects* (London: Verso, 1968); *The Society of Consumption* (Paris: Gallimard, 1970); *For a Critique of a Political Economy of the Sign* (St. Louis, Mo.: Telos Press, 1973); *The Mirror of Production* (St. Louis, Mo.: Telos Press, 1973); *Symbolic Exchange and Death* (London: Sage, 1993); "The Ecstasy of Communication," in *The Anti-Aesthetic: Essays on Postmodern Culture,* ed. Hal Foster (Port Townsend, Wash.: Bay Press, 1983); *America* (London: Verso, 1988); and *Seduction* (New York: Palgrave, 1974).

20. Baudrillard, *America.*

21. Fredric Jameson, *Sartre: The Origins of a Style* (New Haven, Conn.: Yale University Press, 1961); Daniel Bell, *The End of Ideology* (New York: Free Press, 1960); Fredric Jameson, *Marxism and Form* (Princeton, N.J.: Princeton University Press, 1971).

22. Fredric Jameson, *The Prison-House of Language: A Critical Account of Structuralism and Russian Formalism* (Princeton, N.J.: Princeton University Press, 1972).

23. Fredric Jameson, *The Political Unconscious: Narrative as a Socially Symbolic Act* (Ithaca, N.Y.: Cornell University Press, 1981); and *The Syntax of History* (Minneapolis: University of Minnesota Press, 1988).

24. Fredric Jameson, *The Political Unconscious*; and *Postmodernism, Or, The Cultural Logic of Late Capitalism* (Durham, N.C.: Duke University Press, 1991); Ernest Mandel, *Late Capitalism* (London: Verso, 1975).

25. Quoted in Connor, *Postmodernist Culture,* 50. See Kenneth Frampton, *Modern Architecture: A Critical History* (New York: Oxford University Press, 1980).

26. Fredric Jameson, *Late Marxism: Adorno, or, The Persistence of the Dialectic* (New York: Verso, 1990).

27. See Noble, *Death of a Nation,* chap. 6.

28. Quoted in Connor, *Postmodernist Culture,* 67.

29. Charles Jencks, *The Language of Post-modern Architecture* (London: Academy Editions, 1984); Jane Jacobs, *The Death and Life of Great American Cities* (New York: Random House, 1961); Robert Venturi, *Complexity and Contradiction in Architecture* (New York: Museum of Modern Art, 1966); Magali

Sarfatti Larson, *Behind the Postmodern Facade: Architectural Change in Late Twentieth-Century America* (Berkeley: University of California Press, 1993).

30. Kate Millett, *Sexual Politics* (New York: Doubleday, 1970); Shulamith Firestone, *The Dialectic of Sex: The Case for Feminist Revolution* (London: Women's Press, 1970).

31. Judith Butler, *Gender Trouble: Feminism and the Subversion of Identity* (New York: Routledge, 1990).

32. Alice Jardine, *Gynesis: Configurations of Woman and Modernity* (Ithaca, N.Y.: Cornell University Press, 1985).

33. Allan Bloom, *The Closing of the American Mind* (New York: Simon & Schuster, 1987); Roger Kimball, *Tenured Radicals: How Politics Has Corrupted Our Higher Education* (New York: Harper & Row, 1990).

34. Lawrence W. Levine, *Highbrow/Lowbrow: The Emergence of Cultural Hierarchy in America* (Cambridge, Mass.: Harvard University Press, 1988); and *The Opening of the American Mind* (Boston: Beacon Press, 1996); Andrew Ross, *No Respect: Intellectuals and Popular Culture* (New York: Routledge, 1989).

35. Patrick Brantlinger, *Crusoe's Footprints: Cultural Studies in Britain and America* (New York: Routledge, 1990); Laurence Grossberg, *We Gotta Get Out of This Place: Popular Conservatism and Postmodern Culture* (New York: Routledge, 1992); Stanley Aronowitz, *Roll over Beethoven: The Return of Cultural Strife* (Hanover, N.H.: University Press of New England, 1993); John Fiske, *Power Plays, Power Works* (London: Verso, 1993); Angela McRobbie, *Postmodernism and Popular Culture* (London: Routledge, 1994); Simon During, ed., *The Cultural Studies Reader* (London: Routledge, 1993); Jeffrey Williams, ed., *PC Wars: Politics and Theory in the Academy* (New York: Routledge, 1995).

36. Quoted in Thomas Frank, *One Market under God: Extreme Capitalism, Market Populism, and the End of Economic Democracy* (New York: Doubleday, 2000), 296. Frank is very critical of a number of academic cultural critics who, in the 1980s and 1990s, denied the existence of class hierarchy and corporate power.

37. Arran E. Gare, *Postmodernism and the Environmental Crisis* (London: Routledge, 1995). Some of the many overviews of postmodernism that ignore ecological issues are Alex Callinicos, *Against Postmodernism: A Marxist Critique* (New York: St. Martin's Press, 1990); John McGowan, *Postmodernism and Its Critics* (Ithaca, N.Y.: Cornell University Press, 1991); Jodi Dean, ed., *Culture Studies and Political Theory* (New York: Routledge, 1989); David Harvey, *The Condition of Postmodernity* (Oxford: Basil Blackwell, 1989); and Simon During, *Cultural Studies: A Critical Introduction* (New York: Routledge, 2005).

38. Michael Bérubé, *The Left at War* (New York: New York University Press, 2009); Mike Davis, *Planet of Slums* (New York: Verso, 2006).

39. Andrew Ross, *The Failure of Modernism: Symptoms of American Poetry* (New York: Columbia University Press, 1986); Andrew Ross, ed., *Universal Abandon: The Politics of Postmodernism* (Minneapolis: University of Minnesota Press, 1988); and Ross, *No Respect*.

40. Andrew Ross, *The Celebration Chronicles: Life, Liberty, and the Pursuit of Property Value in Disney's New Town* (New York: Ballantine, 1999); Andrew Ross, ed., *No Sweat: Fashion, Free Trade, and the Rights of Garment Workers* (London: Verso, 1997); Andrew Ross, *No-Collar: The Humane Workplace and Its Hidden Costs* (New York: Basic Books, 2002); *Low Pay, High Profile: The Global Push for Fair Labor* (New York: New York University Press, 2004); *Fast Boat to China: Corporate Flight and the Consequences of Free Trade* (New York: Pantheon, 2006); and *Nice Work If You Can Get It: Life and Labor in Precarious Times* (New York: New York University Press, 2009).

41. Walter Benjamin, "The Work of Art in Our Age of Mechanical Reproduction," in *Selected Writings*, vol. 3, 1935–38 (Cambridge, Mass.: Harvard University Press, 2002).

5. Ecologists on Why History Will Never End

1. Henri Paul Eydoux, *The Buried Past: A Survey of Great Archaeological Discoveries* (New York: Praeger, 1966).

2. Roger Newton, *From Clockwork to Crapshoot: A History of Physics* (Cambridge, Mass.: Harvard University Press, 2007); Robert Westfall, *The Life of Isaac Newton* (Cambridge: Cambridge University Press, 1993).

3. Peter J. Bowler, *The Non-Darwinian Revolution: Reinterpreting a Historical Myth* (Baltimore: Johns Hopkins University Press, 1988); Mary Midgley, *Evolution as a Religion: Strange Hopes and Stranger Fears* (London: Methuen, 1985); Akerlof and Shiller, *Animal Spirits*.

4. Peter Gay, *Freud: A Life for Our Time* (New York: W. W. Norton, 1988); Jonathan Lear, Freud (New York: Routledge, 2005); Donald Levy, *Freud among the Philosophers: The Psychoanalytic Unconscious and Its Philosophical Critics* (New Haven, Conn.: Yale University Press, 1996).

5. Albert Einstein, *The Meaning of Relativity* (Princeton, N.J.: Princeton University Press, 1945).

6. I. Bernard Cohen, *The Birth of a New Physics* (New York: W. W. Norton, 1985); Brian Greene, *The Fabric of the Cosmos: Space, Time, and the Texture of Reality* (New York: Alfred A. Knopf, 2004).

7. Loren C. Eiseley, *The Unexpected Universe* (1964; repr., San Diego, Calif.: Harcourt Brace, 1994), 32, 46; Newton, *From Clockwork to Crapshoot*.

8. Fritjof Capra, *The Tao of Physics: An Exploration of the Parallels between Modern Physics and Eastern Mysticism* (Berkeley, Calif.: Shambhala Press, 1975); Roger S. Jones, *Physics as Metaphor* (Minneapolis: University of Minnesota Press, 1982); Richard Olson, ed., *Science as Metaphor: The Historical Role of Scientific Theories in Forming Western Culture* (New York: Wadsworth, 1971).

9. Stephen M. Barr, *Modern Physics and Ancient Faith* (Notre Dame, Ind.: University of Notre Dame Press, 2003); Frank J. Tipler, *The Physics of Christianity* (New York: Doubleday, 2007); John Polkinghorne, *Quantum Physics*

and Theology: An Unexpected Kinship (New Haven, Conn.: Yale University Press, 2007).

10. Snow, *The Two Cultures.*

11. William Vogt, *Road to Survival* (New York: William Sloan, 1948); Fairfield Osborn, *Our Plundered Planet* (New York: Little, Brown, 1948).

12. Frieda Knobloch, *The Culture of Wilderness: Agriculture as Colonization in the American West* (Chapel Hill: University of North Carolina Press, 1996).

13. Chris Mooney and Sheril Kirshenbaum, *Unscientific America: How Scientific Illiteracy Threatens Our Future* (New York: Basic Books, 2009).

14. Carroll W. Pursell, ed., *From Conservation to Ecology: The Development of Environmental Concern* (New York: Crowell, 1973).

15. Barry Commoner, *The Closing Circle: Nature, Man, and Technology* (New York: Alfred A. Knopf, 1971); and *The Poverty of Power: Energy and the Economic Crisis* (New York: Alfred A. Knopf, 1976); Nicholas Georgescu-Roegen, *The Entropy Law and the Economic Process* (Cambridge, Mass.: Harvard University Press, 1971); Herman Daly, ed., *Toward a Steady-State Economy* (San Francisco: W. H. Freeman, 1973).

16. Jeremy Rifkin, *Entropy: A New World View* (New York: Bantam Books, 1980).

17. Steinberg, *Down to Earth*; Rachel Carson, *Silent Spring* (Boston: Houghton Mifflin, 1962).

18. Frederick Buell, *From Apocalypse to Way of Life: Environmental Crisis in the American Century* (New York: Routledge, 2003); Chris Mooney, *The Republican War on Science* (New York: Perseus, 2005). See also Seth Shulman, *Undermining Science: Suppression and Distortion in the Bush Administration* (Berkeley: University of California Press, 2006).

19. Mark Dowie, *Losing Ground: American Environmentalism at the Close of the Twentieth Century* (Cambridge: MIT Press, 1995).

20. Mike Hulme, *Why We Disagree about Climate Change: Understanding Controversy, Inaction, and Opportunity* (Cambridge: Cambridge University Press, 2009); Paul Ehrlich and Anne Ehrlich, *One with Nineveh: Politics, Consumption, and the Human Future* (Washington, D.C.: Island Press, 2005).

21. Paul R. Ehrlich, *The Population Bomb* (New York: Ballantine, 1968).

22. E. F. Schumacher, *Small Is Beautiful: Economics As If People Mattered* (New York: Harper & Row, 1973); Raj Patel, *The Value of Nothing: How to Reshape Market Society and Redefine Democracy* (New York: Picador, 2009); Brennan R. Hill, *Christian Faith and the Environment: Making Vital Connections* (Maryknoll, N.Y.: Orbis Books, 1998); David M. Lodge and Christopher Hamlin, eds., *Religion and the New Ecology: Environmental Responsibility in a World in Flux* (Notre Dame, Ind.: University of Notre Dame Press, 2006).

23. Francis Fukuyama, *The End of History and the Last Man* (New York: Free Press, 1992).

24. Andrew Szasz, *Shopping Our Way to Safety: How We Changed from*

Protecting the Environment to Protecting Ourselves (Minneapolis: University of Minnesota Press, 2007).

25. William L. O'Neill, *A Bubble in Time: America during the Interwar Years, 1989–2001* (Chicago: Ivan R. Dee, 2009).

26. Tim Flannery, *Now or Never: Why We Must Act Now To End Climate Change and Create a Sustainable Future* (New York: Atlanta Monthly Press, 2009).

27. McKibben, *Eaarth*.

28. Paul Gilding, *The Great Disruption: Why the Climate Crisis Will Bring on the End of Shopping and the Birth of a New World* (New York: Bloomsbury Press, 2011); Richard Heinberg, *The End of Growth: Adapting to Our New Economic Reality* (Gabriola, B.C.: New Society, 2011); Chris Mortenson, *The Crash Course: The Unsustainable Future of Our Economy, Energy, and Environment* (Hoboken, N.J.: John Wiley & Sons, 2011).

29. Thomas Friedman, "Something's Happening Here," *New York Times*, October 11, 2011.

30. Gilding, *The Great Disruption*, 5.

31. James Lawrence Powell, *The Inquisition of Climate Science* (New York: Columbia University Press, 2011).

32. Merchant, *The Death of Nature*.

6. When Prophecy Fails

1. Robert Shiller, *Irrational Exuberance* (Princeton, N.J.: Princeton University Press, 2000).

2. Anthony F. C. Wallace employed his revitalization paradigm in several of his books. One example is *The Death and Rebirth of the Seneca* (New York: Random House, 1970).

3. Thomas Friedman, *The Lexus and the Olive Tree: Understanding Globalization* (New York: Farrar, Straus and Giroux, 1999).

4. Catherine Besteman and Hugh Gusterson, eds., *Why America's Top Pundits Are Wrong: Anthropologists Talk Back* (Berkeley: University of California Press, 2005).

5. Thomas Friedman, *The World Is Flat: A Brief History of the Twenty-First Century* (New York: Farrar, Straus and Giroux, 2005).

6. Roberto Patricio Korzeniewicz and Timothy Patrick Moran, *Unveiling Inequality: A World-Historical Perspective* (New York: Russell Sage Foundation, 2009).

7. John Kampfner, *Freedom for Sale: Why the World Is Trading Democracy for Security* (New York: Basic Books, 2010).

8. Douglas S. Massey, *Categorically Unequal: The American Stratification System* (New York: Russell Sage Foundation, 2007). See also Michael J. Thompson,

The Politics of Inequality: A Political History of the Idea of Economic Inequality in America (New York: Columbia University Press, 2007).

9. Ha-Joon Chang, *Bad Samaritans: The Myth of Free Trade and the Secret History of Capitalism* (New York: Bloomsbury Press, 2008).

10. Thomas Friedman, *Hot, Flat, and Crowded: Why We Need a Green Revolution—and How It Can Renew America* (New York: Farrar, Straus and Giroux, 2008).

11. See William C. Berman, *America's Right Turn: From Nixon to Clinton,* 2nd ed. (Baltimore: Johns Hopkins University Press, 1998); David Harvey, *A Brief History of Neoliberalism* (New York: Oxford University Press, 2005); John Micklethwait and Adrian Wooldridge, *The Right Nation: Conservative Power in America* (New York: Penguin, 2004); Jacob S. Hacker and Paul Pierson, *Off Center: The Republican Revolution and the Erosion of American Democracy* (New Haven, Conn.: Yale University Press, 2005); Thomas Frank, *The Wrecking Crew: How Conservatives Ruined Government, Enriched Themselves, and Beggared the Nation* (New York: Henry Holt, 2008); and Max Blumenthal, *Republican Gomorrah: Inside the Movement That Shattered the Party* (New York: Perseus, 2009).

12. Mark Smith, *The Right Talk: How Conservatives Transformed the Great Society into the Economic Society* (Princeton, N.J.: Princeton University Press, 2007).

13. Mason, *The End of the American Century,* 1.

14. Steven Weber and Bruce W. Jentleson, *The End of Arrogance: America in the Global Competition of Ideas* (Cambridge, Mass.: Harvard University Press, 2010).

15. C. J. Campbell, *The Coming Oil Crisis* (1988; repr., Essex, England: Multi-Science, 1997); John Mitchell, with Koji Morita, Norman Selley, and Jonathan Stern, *The New Economy of Oil* (London: RIIA/Earthscan, 2001); Vaclav Smil, *Energy at the Crossroads: Global Perspectives and Uncertainties* (Cambridge: MIT Press, 2003); Richard Heinberg, *The Party's Over: Oil, War, and the Fate of Industrial Societies* (Gabriola Island, B.C.: New Society, 2003); Paul Roberts, *The End of Oil: On the Edge of a Perilous New World* (Boston: Houghton Mifflin, 2004).

16. James Howard Kunstler, *The Long Emergency: Surviving the End of Oil, Climate Change, and Other Converging Catastrophes of the Twenty-First Century* (New York: Grove Press, 2005); Thom Hartmann, *Threshold: The Crisis of Western Culture* (New York: Viking, 2009).

17. David Brooks, "The Return of History," *New York Times,* March 25, 2010.

18. Joseph A. Tainter, *The Collapse of Complex Societies* (Cambridge: Cambridge University Press, 1988): Jared Diamond, *Collapse: How Societies Choose To Fail or Succeed* (New York: Penguin, 2005).

19. *Time,* 174, no. 22, December 7, 2009.

20. Niall Ferguson, "An Empire at Risk," *Newsweek,* November 30, 2009; and

The Ascent of Money: A Financial History of the World (New York: Penguin, 2008).

21. Scott Rasmussen and Douglas Schoen, *Mad as Hell: How the Tea Party Movement Is Fundamentally Remaking Our Two-Party System* (New York: Harper, 2009). See also Mark Stephens Jendrysik, *Modern Jeremiads: Contemporary Visions of American Decline* (New York: Rowman & Littlefield, 2008).

22. James C. McKinley Jr., "Texas Conservatives Win Curriculum Change," *New York Times,* March 12, 2010; Barrett Sheridan, "Texas Cooks the Textbooks," *Newsweek,* May 21, 2010.

23. Jill Lepore, *The Whites of Their Eyes: The Tea Party Revolution and the Battle over American History* (Princeton, N.J.: Princeton University Press, 2010); Ilya Prigogine, *The End of Certainty: Time, Chaos, and the New Laws of Nature* (New York: Free Press, 1996).

24. Robert Reich, *Supercapitalism: The Transformation of Business, Democracy, and Everyday Life* (New York: Vintage, 2007).

25. Tony Judt, *Ill Fares the Land* (New York: Penguin, 2010); Richard Wilkinson and Kate Pickett, *The Spirit Level: Why Greater Equality Makes Societies Stronger* (New York: Bloomsbury Press, 2009); Robert D. Putnam, *Bowling Alone: The Collapse and Revival of American Community* (New York: Simon & Schuster, 2000); Robert H. Frank and Philip J. Cook, *The Winner-Take-All Society: Why the Few at the Top Get So Much More Than the Rest of Us* (New York: Free Press, 1995).

INDEX

DAVID W. NOBLE is professor emeritus of American studies at the University of Minnesota. He is the author of several books, including *Death of a Nation: American Culture and the End of Exceptionalism* (Minnesota, 2002) and *The End of American History: Democracy, Capitalism, and the Metaphor of Two Worlds in Anglo-American Historical Writing, 1880–1980* (Minnesota, 1985).

DAVID R. ROEDIGER is professor of history at the University of Illinois at Urbana–Champaign. He is the author of *How Race Survived U.S. History: From Settlement and Slavery to the Obama Phenomenon*; *Colored White: Transcending the Racial Past*; and *Toward the Abolition of Whiteness: Essays on Race, Politics, and Working Class History.*